Crossing the Gender Divide

by Rachael Evelyn Booth

Reviews for "Crossing the Gender Divide"

4 STARS – "As Powerful as Beth F. Coye's "My Navy Too" and Jennifer Finney Boylan's "She's Not There: A Life in Two Genders" - This memoir takes me, a cis-gender reader, into the author's lived experience, first as a child whose body let wrong, then experiencing multiple travails before reaching an authentic self – AND the right person to share it with. Written with directness, clarity, and humor.

4 STARS – "If you want to laugh, cry and become informed about a real life, this book is the one to read." - Even though the author has been through so much heartbreak in her life, she tells her story with great humor. I have learned so much about transgenderism through her book and glad to have been enlightened on the subject through her real-life experience.

4 STARS – "Great book!" - I laughed, I cried. I am sorry for how difficult and sad her life was, and I am so happy that she found her way and made her dreams come true. This book is a real inspiration to any to follow their dreams no matter how difficult it may seem to attain them.

4 STARS – "Written with directness, clarity, and humor. - Cis-gender people like myself should read this book!"** - I read this memoir straight through. It's a powerful account of feeling from childhood that you're in the wrong body, using joking to cover up as a teen and adult. Rachael Booth goes through so much before she can be her authentic self and find the right person to share her life with.

4 STARS – "Funny! Poignant!" - There was so much in this book I could identify with. Rachael's experiences are heartbreaking, funny, poignant and very personal as she shares them here without reservation.

4 STARS – "What a good writer! I couldn't put it down!"- It reads as a memoir, an adventure tale, a mystery (what is going to happen next?). It took me a while and lots of reading to understand that transgender people aren't playing at being the opposite sex, but truly struggling with their identity. Rachael's book should cut down the learning curve for anyone who wishes to move from ignorance to compassion on this topic.

This book is dedicated to all those who suffer the silent, lonely hell of transsexualism and to their families who suffer simply because they don't understand.

It is also dedicated to all the people that my life has touched with pain during the years when I was searching for myself. I have no greater regret.

For Marilyn, who is my life.

Author's note for the new edition of this book.

When this book was originally written and first published in 2007 the terms "transsexual" and "transsexualism" were widely used. Since that date, the accepted terminology is now "transgender". Transsexualism as a definition is still used, but not by the transgender community itself.

Also used at that time was the term "Sexual Reassignment Surgery" or SRS for the surgery that brings a person's body into conformity with their gender identity. Today the surgery is more widely and much more correctly known as "Gender Confirmation Surgery" or GCS.

Rather than perform a tedious and potentially disruptive cut-and-paste to the text to update this terminology, the original terms have been left as originally written.

Rachael Booth
2022

Other books by Rachael Evelyn Booth

The Little Port in the Corn Fields:
A History of Evansport, Ohio

Time Slip
When Yesterday Ends

For more information on upcoming books and to see more of
Rachael's poetry, go to her website at

http://rachaelbooth.wix.com/books

Cover Design by SelfPubBookCovers.com/Island
Cover photography by G M Fotography & Framing, Littleton, NH

Table of Contents

Prologue

It was just another warm, comfortable evening in the summer of 1957. The air was heavy with the memory of the afternoon's usual brief but violent thunderstorm. The sun was just ending its daily journey across the sky, signaling the crickets to emerge from their daytime hiding places and start their evening serenade. From somewhere in the distance a solitary lawnmower droned away at its weekly chores as a dog barked happily at some imaginary danger. A light, cooling breeze wafted gently out of the west carrying with it the bouquet of a nearby early harvest and, more importantly, the hope that this just might be **THE** night.

In the center of an open patch of ground surrounded by soft waves of golden wheat sat a young boy, motionless, peering intently at the cloudless evening sky. As he had all summer long on nights just like this one whenever there were no clouds to obscure his view, he sat alone, holding his breath, waiting for the right moment to recite the magical phrase he knew so well. As his eyes scanned the darkening heavens, his thoughts drifted back to previous nights when he had performed the ritual so he could try to understand what he had done wrong that had kept the magic from working. With five-year old eyes, the boy searched the amber sky, oblivious to the world around him, with only one goal in mind: tonight, he would get it right.

Suddenly his breath caught in his throat as if afraid to scare the moment away. There it was! Shining brightly through the summer haze...the **First Star**! Time seemed to stop as he stared at the tiny shining spot in the sky. The boy knew he shared a secret kinship with this little star. Like him, it was totally alone, sharing its vast and empty *world with no one and with no others like it in sight. For one brief moment the boy felt that the star and he were one, crying out against the emptiness surrounding them both.*

But this moment was precious and would not last long. The boy's breaths were coming faster now, and his heart thumped loudly in his chest with a quickened, worried beat. With sweaty hands clasped rigidly in his lap and eyes closed tightly in fervent prayer, the boy spoke in his imperfect, young voice the magic words that he had uttered countless times before – and that he would repeat for many years to come:

"Star Light, Star bright,
First Star I see tonight,
I wish I may,
I wish I might,
Have the wish I wish tonight:

I wish I was a girl."

*Shaking with both excitement of possible success and fear of repeating past failures, the boy slowly opened his eyes and peered cautiously up at the sky. There didn't seem to be any other stars visible yet. Maybe tonight he really **had** seen the very First Star after all. Maybe tonight would be the last night he would have to spend as a little boy. But there – just over there – was that a star? Had he missed it before, or had it just now appeared? Was **that** one the First Star and not the one he had just wished upon so intensely? He hoped with all his heart that it was not. Fearing the worst and knowing that he couldn't perform the ritual again this night, the boy rose from his magical place and started back to the small house in the woods that was his home. There was nothing more to be done. It was now* in the hands of the star and the magic that only it could perform.

* * *

The rest of the evening was like all the others, sitting in front of the black and white TV with his family in their rural Ohio home, waiting for bedtime and the magical transformation that somehow he knew would only come in his sleep. As always, the family knew nothing of the young boy's anxiousness or of his constant war within himself for peace. To them, just as to all others in his life, he was a perfectly well adjusted and happy little boy without a care in the world. That he loved to help his mother cook, clean and do the laundry and ironing was of no great concern. And since no one had objected much to his delight in these tasks, he thought that he was justified in the nightly quest for his dream. After all, didn't **all** girls do the exact same things that he liked to do? Didn't his stepfather on occasion even remark that he was doing girls' work? It was all very strange. He couldn't quite understand why he was forced to dress like a boy. He knew from changing diapers that his baby sister didn't have the little thing that he had between his legs and thought that somehow this must be important. He wondered if hers hadn't grown yet or if his might fall off soon. Maybe that's what caused his family to think he wasn't a girl. Whatever it was, it just wasn't fair. Little girls got to wear pretty dresses and bows in their long, silky hair. He had to wear pants and his mother cut his hair so short that all he was left with was a mere shadow on his scalp and a little tuft of hair above his forehead she called a "pineapple". Realizing that there must be some unspoken **Adult Reason** why he was forced to live this way, and afraid of incurring the wrath of his step-father who didn't seem very happy about the chores he liked to do with his

3

mother, he never said a word about his feelings to anyone. He figured that, when the time came, they would all realize their mistake and he'd be allowed to be what he was: a girl. But until then, he just had to continue with the Rituals.

Of course, there was more than one Ritual. There was, for instance, the Water Fountain Rituals where, each day at school, the boy would watch carefully for any female classmate who seemed to be heading for the water fountain. As soon as he was sure she was going to take a drink, he would rush to be directly behind her in order to get the first drink after her and increase his chances of swallowing the "germs" that made her a girl. It just could be that, for some unknown reason, he didn't have the right germs in him and needed them to help the Star do its work. After a drink from the fountain that was slow enough to ensure that any germs that may have been left behind had time enough to get to him, he would scan the water fountain to see if the girl had inadvertently left behind any strands of hair. If she did, he would snatch it up quickly and walk away, trying to place it unnoticed onto his own head so that it, too, could help the germs (and the Star).

These little Rituals, and many others like them, were designed to help as much as they could to show the Star that he was serious and would do anything to help it do its magic. All other things were unimportant. The Star must know of his sincerity. Otherwise the magic wouldn't work.

The boy went to bed that night after having recited his automatic prayers to an uncaring god to keep him safe until the morning. After a goodnight kiss from his mother, he uttered a silent, personal prayer to this god to please talk to the Star and help to fix him so that he wasn't so unhappy.

He went to sleep in eager anticipation of his new life.

When he awoke the next morning, a quick but nervous check below the sheets proved again that nothing had changed. He ran his fingers through the long hair that still wasn't there and felt a little more of himself die. He hadn't seen the First Star after all. And his parents' god still wasn't listening. He wondered through his silent tears why this invisible god hated him so much. Now the Rituals would have to start all over. He didn't know how much longer he could continue. Bitterly disappointed once again, the boy got out of bed and began yet another of a lifetime of long and endless days.

That young boy was me.

* * *

This is the story of a life of struggle - of hiding, of fear, and of triumph. It is the story of a person born with a condition known as transsexualism, a birth defect that most people learn about through television talk shows where shock is the main goal and facts are few and far between. I intend with this book to shed some light on the human element of this condition, without the shock, without the sensationalism and without boring the reader to death with mountains of clinical terms and statistics. I've tried here to describe my life as it has been – heartbreaking and hilarious, cruel and enlightening. It is of the utmost importance to me to show people that this condition is real; that it is neither imaginary nor a matter of choice; that people who must go through this suffer a living hell. Some do not survive. They end their agony through the only means they know – suicide.

This is also the story of one person who somehow found the courage deep inside to face down society and do what she had to

5

do to keep herself alive regardless of the very real possibility of losing everything and everyone she held dear in life – even life itself. I hope with this book to help the reader to understand this condition from a personal and emotional viewpoint in the short time it takes him or her to read it. For the sake of those who are struggling with this affliction, and their families and friends who are struggling to understand it, I hope I succeed.

Believe me, wishes *CAN* come true.

Chapter 1
And God chuckled...

I was born at approximately 11:30 on the night of November 28, 1951 in a small hospital in the quiet little northwestern Ohio town of Bryan. My mother, Doris Evelyn Ball, was a 19-year-old woman who came from a desperately poor family of 11 children. My father, Ernest Eugene Thompson, was a 24-year-old ex-Army Sergeant and current truck driver. My parents gave me my middle name from my father and named me Ricky Eugene. Where they came up with my first name is a bit more obscure. My mother told me in later years that they had wanted a girl and my name was to be Ricky either way. I never knew if she had been serious about that or not, but I latched onto it as further proof that I should have been born differently. But she has also said that my father didn't want me to have a nickname, so he gave me one to keep me from having one (?). My brother, a year younger than me who is also Ernie's son, was named Danny for the same reason. It is a bit strange but then again, I was to find out later that my father was far from normal. In retrospect, I can't imagine being called "Dick" so I guess not being called Richard wasn't such a bad thing after all. Actually, the name Ricky is fine if you either stay a little kid for life or end up with a 23-inch neck playing linebacker for a professional football team where no one would dare to make fun of you. I didn't fit either category, so I simply had to put up with the name. Except for problems getting teachers to believe that my given name was actually Ricky and not Richard, I had few problems with it while I was very young. The real problems started when I hit the magical social age in junior high school when "cute" things become "dorky" things. And the word "dorky" hadn't even been invented yet. It was waiting for me.

Other than the name, there was nothing particularly remarkable about my birth. Well, almost. I was born with the prerequisite number of fingers and toes. I had lots of thick black hair and a complexion so dark that my parents weren't totally sure I actually belonged to them. Since the only minorities that Bryan and the entire region had were a few Catholics (we never actually *saw* any), they had to trust the name tag identifying me as theirs. Actually, the dark hair and complexion came from my mother's family's Native American heritage. No one else in my family got it. They all had light skin and hair. I was already a pariah in my own family.

Our family lore has always revolved around the story of my maternal grandfather, Harvey Ball, and the beginning of his family line. For all the years of my young life, my grandfather told us stories of how his great grandmother had been the daughter of Chief Sitting Bull of the Hunkpapa Lakota. It is common knowledge that Sitting Bull fled in the mid-1800s with his family and other members of his tribe to Canada to keep from being put on a reservation by the US Army. Canada had offered the tribe sanctuary but nothing else; the tribe would have to fend for itself. My grandfather told us that while Sitting Bull was there, one of his daughters eloped with a Canadian and left the tribe. When the tribe eventually returned to the United States because they could no longer feed themselves in Canada, they were immediately put on the reservation in the Dakotas where Sitting Bull's daughter eventually rejoined them years later.

My adult life has been dedicated to trying to find some sort of proof of this story and, for years, I failed miserably. I read every book on Sitting Bull that I could find and, while all of them recount his days trying to survive in Canada, not one of them ever mentioned anything about his daughter eloping while they were there; that is until 1993 when I read the newly released book "The Lance and The Shield. – The Life and Times of Sitting Bull" by noted western historian Robert M. Utley (published by Henry Holt and Company of New York). On page 226 of Mr. Utley's book, the very story that I had been told all my life was there in black and white.

My grandfather was not a learned man; he was born into poverty, fought in World War 1 where he suffered through a mustard gas attack which caused him permanent health problems, and then worked for the railroad in rural Ohio for the rest of his life. I seriously doubt that he ever entered a library in his life and even if he had gone into a library, if I couldn't find any books in major city libraries or on the internet that contained the story of Sitting Bull's daughter eloping, there is no way he could have found such a book or article in a small town Ohio library. My only conclusion is what he always told us: that he passed this story down to me from word of mouth from his mother who got it from her mother who got it from her mother, the daughter of Sitting Bull. I'm still trying to find proof of this story.[1]

Overall, I was a 100% normal baby with all the right parts. Or so it seemed. Just like all hospitals did then and still do today, they looked between my little legs and proclaimed to the world that I was *A Boy* (insert trumpet fanfare here). I was immediately wrapped in a blue towel so there would be no mistaking which pronoun to use when referring to me when people stopped by and looking in the nursery window. Of course, with a name like "Ricky" on the bassinet, I guess they needed to display all the clues they could. My strict and

---

[1] Since initially writing this I've discovered that my Grandfather's story of our relationship to Sitting Bull was pretty much "bull". Although my mother's family did come from Native Americans, it was almost certainly Ojibwa from Michigan and Ontario. Oh well, it was fun thinking that I had royal blood.

unwavering indoctrination into the world of sexual identity had begun.

All this declaring and tagging is all well and good; and it is usually quite correct. As a matter of fact, around 4,999 times out of 5,000, it's absolutely flawless. But it seems that, during my life, it has been my dumb luck to always find out that I'm the special *one* who is always chosen to be the "first of the new policy" or the guinea pig for the new rules. I seem to have started out losing some cosmic lottery right off the bat. Even though all the signs of my body told everyone all they thought they needed to know about who I was or what I was supposed to be, there was no way to look inside my head to see what was in there. No one knew then (and they're only beginning to study it seriously now) that sometime during gestation, it was possible for hormones to send a signal to the body to tell it to be male and forget to tell the brain the same thing. So, the little female fetus, as we all start out, gets a few wires crossed in the mail and ends up with a few things she didn't order. Of course, she doesn't know that she's got someone else's *things* and starts out life totally unaware of the problem. And it takes years for her to realize that something is wrong. Unfortunately, since researchers have only just begun to explore this hormonal line of thought in the last few years, countless children, girls as well as boys, have been cheerfully and faithfully queued into the given gender stereotypes simply by how they pee. It's amazing how such a tiny bit of skin can mean so much.

So, to the casual observer, I was considered just another normal, healthy baby boy. But someone at the hospital that night had some insight that he or she probably didn't even realize. I was to find out about it later in life when I applied for my first passport. Let's jump ahead a little here.

* * *

10

I was stationed overseas in the Navy and had to get a passport for the international travel that was part of my job, so I sent home to the Bryan records department for a notarized copy of my official birth certificate. When I received it, there didn't seem to be anything outwardly amiss. It had my name on the top with the all-important raised seal on the bottom that made it official. That's pretty much all I looked at. When I took the document in to the Passport office, the clerk glanced at it and then looked at me. He looked at the birth certificate again, asking me if I was sure this was mine. I told him I was sure. Unexpectedly, he started laughing and passed the document around the office. Always on my toes to notice that something was not quite right, I quickly deduced that there was some sort of problem that I probably should know about. When the office staff was finally able to compose themselves, they handed my document back to me and pointed at something I had overlooked. It seems that, according to my official birth certificate, Ricky Eugene Thompson was a *Female*. It was not a "typo" or a smudge or somebody writing over something already there as their sick little idea of a joke. Right there on the Xeroxed piece of paper where the box was reserved for *Sex* were the letters "*Fe*". Someone on that night in November knew something that no one else knew. Either that or they thought I had a lot of iron in me.

I preferred to think of it as prophecy. Of course, this only served to further justify to me at the time who I really felt I was. We latch onto what we can when we're drowning. Maybe God thought it was pretty funny. I've always felt that She had a rotten sense of humor.

Now let's return to our original time line.

* * *

My early family life was one of great turmoil. Most of what I know about it has been trickled down to me over time by relatives willing or able to discuss it with me, but I have been able to piece together most of the story of what happened to my father during my early days.

My father, Ernie, was a very moody and violent man. He evidently had a history of mental problems, even during a time when those kinds of things weren't really diagnosed, let alone understood. One report I got from a relative was that he was discharged from the Army because of "psychological instability" although I've never seen any documentation that proves it. He wasn't in the Army very long at all. I do know from my mother that he beat her often, most times for the slightest of "infractions". (I am sure that I must have witnessed much of it but, since he died when I was only two years old, I thankfully don't remember any of it.) He was also evidently a racial bigot with a cruel sense of humor. For years as a child I would go outside looking for the black Cocker Spaniel that my father had named, calling for him all over the rural neighborhood in which we lived. One day at school I heard someone who had also never encountered a minority person in his life (except for the occasional Catholic) refer to a black person as a "nigger". I simply beamed and said, "That's my dog's name!" I was a laughing stock at school for a long time afterwards. When I came home that day crying, my mother had to explain to me why they were laughing at me. All I knew was that someone was making fun of me and my dog. And to me that's all it was. To my father it must have been pretty funny. To this day I've never been able to understand why my mother didn't change that dog's name after Ernie died. She never raised me to be a racist and I certainly am not one now.

My mother put up with my father's violent temper and constant beatings for a long time even though her siblings and friends constantly urged her to leave. During the early '50s the general rule of thumb was that if your husband was hitting you, you must be doing something to deserve it – like not having his dinner on time or having the nerve to disagree with him on something. Your place was obediently at his side no matter how badly he treated you. One night the beatings got so bad that my mother ended up in the hospital with a broken nose. Whether it was fueled by fear for herself or fear for my one-year-old brother and me, she finally found the courage to file a complaint against him with the police. In response to this almost unprecedented action, he was temporarily put in jail for abuse. This was an unbelievably gutsy thing for a battered woman to do at the time and remains so, unfortunately, today. Needless to say, this did not sit well with Ernie at all. The police came to the house and removed all of the guns that Ernie had just in case he decided that he would take the abuse to another level when he returned home. When he got out of jail the next day, a friend of my mother's came over and said, "My God, Doris, Ernie's out of jail and he's on his way coming home. I think he has a gun. Get out of the house." For some reason, perhaps like a deer paralyzed in a speeding car's headlights, she stayed. Ernie came home that afternoon with a shotgun that he had retrieved from a caboose that the local railroad let him use from time to time when he wanted to be alone. The police didn't know about that one. He stormed into the house and raped my mother at gunpoint.

After he was finished, he left the room for a short while, maybe to contemplate what he had done or to stew in his rage about what my ungrateful mother had done to him. When he returned to the bedroom, he was still carrying the gun. My mother was lying in the bed crying and clinging to my baby brother and me. I had evidently heard her crying and crawled in bed with her to see what was wrong. She grabbed my brother as well to hold onto with me. With his face still twisted with pain and rage of the humiliation to which he felt she had subjected him, he held the shotgun up and aimed it at my mother's head. As his finger tightened on the trigger, my mother held us closer and closed her eyes, waiting for the explosion that would end her life and her pain. But the explosion didn't come. As the seconds crept by, Ernie's finger wavered on the trigger. He slowly lowered the gun and told my mother in a voice shaking with rage, "If I die, I going to come back and haunt you every second of every day". Then he turned and slowly walked out of the room. My mother said she could only guess that he didn't shoot because he didn't want to hit Danny or me. Maybe something clicked in his head telling him that what he was about to do was wrong. We'll never know.

Not understanding what was happening and wondering where my father was going; I wriggled from my mother's grasp and jumped out of the bed to follow him. I found him sitting alone in the living room still holding the gun…only this time the barrel was in his mouth. As I stood and watched curiously with my two-year old eyes, my father pulled the trigger and, in a horrible thunder of noise and blood, ended his life in front of me. He was only 26 years old. It took relatives days to clean the room. It took me two weeks to stop screaming at night. My mother took what she called "nerve pills" for almost 35 years and suffered from frequent nightmares. She hardly ever talks about him, and she never talks about that night.

Fortunately for me, I remember none of this. As I tell the story to you, it is just that to me: a story. I have managed to get bits and pieces here and there about it but not nearly what I would like to have. My father's family severed all ties with my mother after his death, so they've been no help. They actually blamed her for his death. I suppose in their minds they figure that she drove him to suicide by not being a "good wife" to him and treating him so badly. After all, the beatings that she had received were just administration of Ernie's "husbandly duties". Even my mother's lawyer could barely contain his contempt for her for causing all of this mess. But although I have no conscious memory of it, I imagine that somewhere in the recesses of my mind I still remember that man and that night. Somewhere inside it's possible that I can still hear the roar of the gun and see my father's life sprayed on the living room walls. Somewhere inside of me that young child may still be screaming. But with any luck those memories will never be released from the safety of the walls that were built to protect me from that gruesome night ever hurting me again.

My mother had told my brother and me for years that our father had died in "the war". I never knew or questioned what war it was, but I felt pride that my father had died fighting for his country, even though I wondered who he was and what he had been like. It wasn't until I was in my teens that my Grandma Ball, my mother's mother, decided for some unknown reason to tell my brother Danny the truth about what happened. He told me what she had said and I didn't believe him. We went to our mother and asked her. That's when we learned the truth even though we could tell how hard it was for my mother to talk about it. She was so angry at her mother for telling us this that she didn't speak to her for years afterward. She had always thought that she would tell us when we were "ready". I think it was more when *she* was ready, which might have been never.

I have spent a lot of time and money (to the delight of a lot of therapists) wondering about what that night could have done to me. I have wondered what kind of an effect the type of man my father was had on my image of myself. I've wondered what kind of person I would have turned out to be had he lived and raised me with his ideals. My mother says that if she'd stayed married to him much longer, she'd be dead now. Many people would just look at the situation and think that it's no wonder I turned out like I did. Why would I want to be a man when all I ever saw a man do was hurt my mother and then go away forever in such an awful manner? It seemed pretty obvious to me for a very long time that my father had caused all of this. But then I started wondering why my brother Danny wasn't affected in the same way. After all, he grew up in the same house and witnessed pretty much the same things I did. Although my brother has enough problems to fill his own book, he has never even hinted at any sort of sexual identity problem.

Time for another time-line switch.

* * *

In September of 1989 I went with two transsexual girlfriends to an international symposium on Gender Studies in Cleveland, Ohio. It was there that I learned of studies that had been done on transsexual children in trying to determine patterns that caused their affliction. Like homosexuality, transsexualism has long been thought to be an aberration brought about by circumstances that, once uncovered, could be "cured". Doctors would look for such things as a domineering mother or father, lack of either parent or child abuse. If they found one of these things, they would focus on "fixing" that problem and the person would mercifully be able to lead a normal life. But doctors have long been baffled by their general inability to come up with an effective "cure" for transsexualism (or Gender Dysphoria as it is more clinically known). They could never seem to find an outstanding reason for the disorder and, most of the time, all efforts at treating it with psychotherapy were unsuccessful. The only thing that seemed to help in a lot of the cases was Sex Reassignment surgery, or SRS, which they deemed as a failure on their part. One of the studies discussed at the symposium was conducted by a mental health specialist who was a member of the Harry Benjamin Foundation, a group devoted to the study and treatment of Gender Dysphoria. This specialist, whose name I have unfortunately never been able to find again, had studied the lives of young boys and girls who claimed to be transsexual to see if there was some indication of a social problem that could have caused their disorder. What she found was that in most of the cases she studied, the children who were the most determined to assert that they were really of the opposite gender were those who had experienced some sort of major family trauma between the ages of two and three. Her report stated that these children were usually unable to come to terms in any way with the body in which they had been born and were adamant about their feelings of what gender they really were. Others that had not had the trauma but still felt like they were in the wrong body seemed more likely to be able to compromise with their situations and were more apt to find ways to live as one gender while feeling like the other. A child's self-image and sexuality, along with perceived gender role, is pretty well set in stone by the time the child is around two years of age. She concluded that this trauma, coupled with a purported biological propensity towards transsexualism, could very well have "shut the door" on any future treatment of the disorder short of SRS.

I was stunned. I had never heard of a study like this one and was eager to learn more. I spoke with the specialist after her lecture and told her the story of my father. She suspected that even if I had received psychological help after the suicide of my father that it probably would not have made much of a difference. Keep in mind that all of this happened in 1953 when most adults would never have thought of going for psychological treatment, let alone sending their children for it. Most patients in psychiatric hospitals at that time were condemned to prolonged isolation, electro-shock therapy or lobotomies. So even in the extremely remote chance that anyone would have thought to get me any help at the time, there was little hope that it would have been of any benefit at all.

But the key factor that I came to realize here is that my father's suicide was not to blame for how I felt inside. It might have been a deciding factor in just how deeply ingrained my self-image was, but, in and of itself, it was not the root cause. In this light, I cannot blame my father for my problems. Although I am quite certain that I would never want to be anything like the person that has been described to me over the years, he did not cause me to feel the way I did about myself. I knew I had to keep searching for my answers elsewhere.

Chapter 2
Early Life at Home

Rural Ohio was a really nice place to grow up. For the first few years of my life after Ernie died, we lived in the small town where I was born. Bryan was a quiet little farming town that has hardly changed in the years since I lived there. Situated in the corner of Ohio with Michigan and Indiana only ten or so miles away to the north and west, Bryan has thrived through the years from the business of the surrounding farming community. The town's only real claim to fame is one that everyone knows but few realize: it's the only place in the world where they make the famous Etch-A-Sketch. Almost every child has owned an Etch-A-Sketch at one time or another and almost every mother in the Bryan area has worked at the Ohio Art Company where they're made[2].

The center of town is designed as a square lined with little stores. When I was growing up, there was a G. C. Murphy's "five and dime store" where each Christmas my siblings and I would be given a few dollars each to go and buy Christmas presents for each other. I would always buy my mother her little special bottle of "Evening in Paris" perfume. She always accepted it graciously and probably threw it away at the first chance. God that was wretched stuff!

There was the little restaurant on one corner simply known in my family as "The Newsstand" where we would go to get the treat of all treats: the fountain Cherry Coke or, if you were *really* daring, the Chocolate Coke. There was Newberry's department store and a pizza shop on another corner that always smelled like heaven. There was the movie theater that I spent an entire afternoon in once watching Walt Disney's "In Search of the

---

[2] They're actually made in China now but still say "Ohio Art Company, Bryan, Ohio.

Castaways" three times for fifty cents. It has now become a duplex. It's not any bigger; it's just two screens with seats crammed closer together. Big time in the little city. And there was the fancy store, Gorney-Winzeler's that had beautiful things only the rich people could buy and we could only just stare at.

Nestled in the center of the town square was the real jewel. Surrounded by its sea of parking spaces was a green shady park replete with benches, water fountains, and even a bandstand that at some time long ago had actually hosted bands. Long before I was born that was the place where the townspeople, decked out in their summer finery, could sit on the benches under the trees and listen to the bands on a warm summer afternoon.

In the middle of this oasis stood the most magnificent structure of all: the Court House. An old towering brick building with a single spire atop it adorned with a clock face on each of its four sides, the Court House was truly a place of wonder for us. For there, inside that official building with its official halls and courtrooms that we didn't care one hoot about, was *The Elevator*. It was the only one in town. As a matter of fact, it was the only one for 50 miles in any direction. To find another one, you had to go to either Toledo (no one I knew actually ever *went* to Toledo) or to Fort Wayne, Indiana, the burial place of Johnny Appleseed. When we went into town, this elevator was all ours. And we rode it up and down every chance we got until someone inside the building would spot us and tell us to go play somewhere else.

Outside of town to the west was Moore Park with its artesian wells for which Bryan was originally settled, a public swimming pool, and a playground that contained an actual World War II fighter plane that kids could play in and either cut themselves badly or fall out of and break a limb or two. It was great fun. The plane is gone now. I wonder why?

On the other side of town was the Bryan Drive-In where my family spent many nights in our old station wagon watching old Biblical movies with sound piped through tinny speakers that clipped onto the car window and never quite worked properly except to very effectively let in mosquitoes large enough to carry one of us away. But going to the Drive-In was always a treat because my mother would make a huge bag of popcorn for us (sometimes we even got to buy some *real* popcorn from the concession stand) and bring along a bottle of pop (that's *soda* for those of you non-mid-westerners) for each of us as well. We would always wear our pajamas because none of us would ever quite make it to the end of the second movie.

Our lives centered around this little town. My mother remarried a few years after my father's death and her new husband, Lisle, worked for the Ohio Gas company, from which he eventually retired. My step father was a very private man. He and my mother had known each other before my mom had married Ernie. Strangely, as I grew, my resemblance to Lisle became uncanny. People would even remark upon his introducing me as his son that they could tell right away. My Mother swears that I was started on an Army cot on an Army base hundreds of miles from where Lisle lived but I've never been totally convinced of it – and that was a *bit* more information than I actually needed. My brother Danny looks like our birthfather[3]. Actually, I've always hoped that I could prove that Lisle really was my father because I would much rather have known that I was from him than from Ernie.

---

[3] Weeks after Ernie's suicide my mother looked in her rear-view mirror and saw Ernie sitting in the back seat glaring at her. It scared her to death because he had promised to haunt her forever. As Danny grew older he resembled Ernie so much in visage and personality that, along with Ernie showing up in her car, she was convinced Ernie **had** come back. Danny wasn't treated very well for years because of this.

Lisle came from a strict German family with very intense, demanding and rather intimidating parents. The only people I ever saw Lisle defer to were his Mom and Dad. I think he was always aware of that, and it made him uncomfortable, so we didn't visit them as much as we would have liked. I remember idyllic days watching my Grandpa Hageman milk cows with a very attentive entourage of kittens standing behind him following his every move. Every once in a while, he would reach back and squirt milk on one of the kittens and the others would descend in a horde to lick the fresh milk off whoever had been the target. I remember, too, sitting under their giant weeping willow tree in the summer breeze, listening to the hissing of the leaves as they slid across the grass. The weeping willow tree is still my very favorite.

My stepfather's strict German upbringing, combined with his relatively short physical stature made him a bit on the brooding, volatile side – but not abusive in any way. In his younger days he was evidently quite the scrapper. An incident in which he hurled a heavy typewriter at a co-worker while he was in the service earned him the name "Herkie", short for Hercules. It was a joke that he never appreciated but couldn't shake for years. My brother and I called him that for quite some time until we either felt more comfortable calling him Daddy or he just outright told us to stop. No one seems to remember when or why we stopped calling him Herkie. He never liked the nickname and I've only heard one other person call him that in recent years. And that was someone even he hadn't seen for a long time. I have called Lisle "Dad" for years with no misgivings at all. In fact, it seems strange to me to be writing this and referring to him as my stepfather when I've really never known anyone else as my father. So, to make things simpler and more comfortable for me, I'll just refer to him as Dad from now on. It seems more proper somehow. My brother Danny, on the other hand, used the fact that Lisle wasn't his real father as justification for rebellion in his teenage years. I know that this really hurt Dad a lot. Danny knew that, too.

Dad was always an intense, focused person. My mother and he had two children, my sister Debbie and my brother Tim (just nicknames – their real names are Deborah and Timothy – they got off easy). Life was not easy for my parents. And because Dad was also a very stubborn man with old-fashioned ideas, he wouldn't let my mother work for quite a few years. So, they struggled to maintain a house with four growing children on my father's small salary alone. We didn't have much, but we were always well cared for. I remember times when the only breakfast cereal we had was shredded toast with sugar and milk. Sometimes we even had suppers of pancakes with homemade syrup made from boiling sugar water and adding a dash of maple extract.

Perhaps because of all the stress and problems of raising a family on a small income, my dad seemed generally on edge most of the time. He was very demanding of us but even more demanding of himself, a trait he passed on to me. I knew he wanted to do better for us and was upset that he couldn't. So, we generally heard lots of criticism from him and precious little praise. He seemed to always be tired and cranky. Suppertime at our house was always something to be dreaded. At the supper table Mom would pass on to him all of our daily nefarious exploits. After hearing these, if he looked at you over the top of his glasses without raising his head, you knew were in big trouble. The results were normally spankings or grounding, depending on your age.

We only lived in Bryan for a few years. I attended kindergarten there and got in trouble one afternoon for deciding to walk home from school with the mailman on his rounds.

When I came home a couple of hours late the babysitter and my parents were understandably frantic. And that was before all the stuff you hear nowadays about disappearing kids. I didn't sit down for a while after that, and the mailman got a piece of my mother's mind. I don't remember much from that time other than that. I was only about 4 years old. When I was five, we moved to the suburbs.

Of course, the suburbs of a sleepy, rural town like Bryan – population at the time probably around five or six thousand – aren't really anything to talk about. The suburbs we moved to was a small town about four miles away called Williams Center, population a whopping 150. We lived in a newly built 3-bedroom ranch house at the end of a long driveway. Our little community was nestled inside a small forest along with four other homes just down the road from the teeming metropolis of Williams Center. We're *really* talking country here. But this is where my life really began. This was the site of my little field where I spent so much time searching for that special Star.

Chapter 3
Grade School, Nancy Drew and Gym Class

Growing up is arguably one of the most difficult things a person will ever do. No one is ever immune to the pressures and the pain of becoming socially aware and independent whether they're the class clown, the school jock, or even the town bully. All children feel the intense pressure and horrible fear of failure that comes with learning to be accepted by their peers. Some are able to handle this fear fairly successfully; others are not so lucky. While some children affect a façade of arrogance to hide their fear of humiliation and rejection by becoming bullies (later to become used car salesmen or politicians), others become punching bags and carry terrible scars from the experience well into their adult lives. Some, in fact, are never able to forget and carry their scars with them to their graves. Others, like me, simply erect walls around themselves and try hard to let no one past.

There are all manners of tests that must be passed by children in their day to day lives outside the protection of their safe homes with Mom and Dad. These tests range from the subtle to the sublime, like weighing the pressure from your parents to do well in school against the pressure from your classmates not to be a bookworm. Or being polite to others and running the risk of being run roughshod over by those more assertive. These pressures are enormous for any "normal" child. For a child who is different they can be devastating.

I did very well in grade school. I liked learning new things, a habit I've thankfully never outgrown. But because I was a rather small child, I never excelled at anything physical. I had a thin, small frame and eyesight so bad that I wore corrective glasses at the age of four. After I'd been wearing them for a while, my brother and I had a fight and they were broken. I didn't get a replacement pair because it was assumed that my eyesight had returned to normal. And besides, my parents had no money to buy me new glasses anyway. By the time I reached third grade my eyesight had deteriorated so badly that the only way I could tell what was on the classroom blackboard was to sit in the front row, squint hard and then finally ask the child next to me what had been written. After several visits to the school nurse and lots of notes home I finally had to get a pair of glasses. I got the most inexpensive glasses you could get – big black plastic horn rims – the kind with the invisible "HIT ME" sign taped to the front. When I stepped out of the optometrist's office in Fort Wayne that day with my new glasses, I was amazed that I could actually see clearly to end of the block and beyond! My mother had to tell me to shut my mouth because I was gaping like a tourist. But the fascination with my new world was short lived. I found out soon enough that for a kid who got good grades to begin with, glasses like mine were the kiss of death. What few physical sports activities I had participated in before were now curtailed completely because of the risk to my glasses and the accompanying fear of what my parents would do should they get broken. And the worst thing you can do as a young boy growing up is not to participate in sports. The second worst thing is to get good grades. The *absolute* worst thing is to do both. I was always a person of absolutes.

As a child who knew that I was somehow different from the rest, I spent a lot of my time alone. At recess I would usually go out and play with the younger children instead of those my own age. I got more pleasure out of helping the smaller children with the swings and the monkey bars than I did out of the arguing and fighting that always accompanied the competitiveness of games with my peers. Because of my size and because, perhaps, my classmates somehow sensed a difference in me, I was always the last to be chosen for any sadistic class games like Red Rover when I did choose to participate. And each time I was the very last one left standing for someone to be stuck with, it was just one more little push towards the swings and the younger children who were glad to have my company.

As a result of my not participating in a lot in games in which I knew I wasn't wanted, I generally lacked the ability to play team sports well. So, when I *was* eventually picked to play, I would invariably not know how to properly play the game and would usually do something stupid that would bring the wrath of my teammates down on me. Of course, they would blame any loss on me. For a while I would be humiliated and would not even consider playing with them anymore. But the pressure to prove myself and end the constant taunting would soon become too much and I would be right back trying again. I knew that if I was to be accepted by the boys that I had to play and act like the boys. I thought that if I could do that, then maybe they wouldn't pick on me as much. I spent much of my early childhood trying to redeem myself in others' eyes. That would end in later years. But even now, years later, I still prefer to play sports in which I compete only against myself rather than take the chance of playing on a team where I could make a mistake and lose the game for everyone. There are some things, it seems, that we never grow out of.

* * *

Students were not my only problems in the early years of school. I also had my share of humiliating experiences at the hands of teachers. In the second grade we had to bring in our afternoon milk money to the teachers every month. One time my mother gave me my money in a check sealed in a long plain envelope. Out of curiosity I wanted to see what the check looked like, so I tore off one end of the envelope and looked inside. I didn't see anything, so I turned the envelope around and tore off the other end. To my horror I discovered that I had inadvertently torn off both ends of the check along with the envelope! I put the torn ends together in the envelope and fearfully turned them into the teacher, Miss Onderveck, who was collecting money from all of the students in the class. When she got around to my money, she held up the torn check and asked me what had happened. I told her it was an accident, but she didn't want to hear that. She said that what I had done was terribly irresponsible and made me sit on the floor in front of my classmates and go through the wastepaper basket, pencil shavings and all, until I found the missing check ends. Thoroughly humiliated and with the entire class laughing at me, I sifted through the garbage for what seemed to be an eternity. When I couldn't find them, she made me start over. By this time, I was crying which made the whole class, especially the boys, laugh even harder. When I still couldn't find the check ends, the teacher looked once again inside the envelope and surprisingly found them inside. With no apology, she ordered me to clean up my mess and sit back down. I couldn't even look at the rest of my classmates for the rest of the day.

One day in the third grade I was trying to hear what the teacher was saying in class but couldn't because the student behind me kept trying to talk to me. We were not supposed to talk in class. Exasperated, I turned and asked him to be quiet. Of course, the teacher heard *me* talking and not him. Even though I had never been admonished for anything like this before, she came over to my desk and put a large piece of duct tape over my mouth. I had to sit like that for the rest of the class. And if that wasn't bad enough, when class was over and it was recess time, the teacher made me keep the tape on my mouth until the start of the next class and ordered me to go outside and play with the rest of the children like that. I was mortified. I spent the entire recess curled up under the stairwell that led up to the outside doors and the playground.

These episodes, and others like them, served to help break down my self-confidence just a little more and drive yet another spike deeper into the heart of the problems that I was already having with my classmates for being different. Aided by the actions of the teachers, the haranguing only intensified. I found myself retreating further and further into my own little world and pushing myself even more into schoolwork to fill the void. Of course, I got smarter than most of the kids but that only served to make me more disliked than before.

* * *

During this time, life at home was also a challenge. My relationship with my siblings was always a trial. My brother Tim was still an infant so my only dealings with him were in rinsing out his dirty diapers. I would, on occasion, play with my sister Debbie but only to the point where I knew no one would be concerned by my interest with her toys. We loved playing with her Easy Bake Oven until she would cry that I wasn't letting *her* use it. My relationship with my full brother Danny was tumultuous at best. Danny would often tell all of us how much he hated us. He was never very quick to learn things, so I easily became frustrated with him. This would anger him, and he would begin calling me names and becoming physically abusive. And if I didn't react negatively to his name-calling (I laughed at him when he started calling me "slimy-snake" – he thought that was a terrible insult – I thought that was hilarious in itself) he would get just that much more furious. Danny also had a

29

fascination with fire from a young age. Once when we were both very young, he placed all of our mother's underwear in a furnace register in the floor of our house and set them on fire. He also set his mattress on fire once while under the covers in his bed. We had bunk beds at the time, and I awoke that morning to the smell of smoke. When we discovered what the source of the smoke was, Dad and I dragged the smoldering mattress outside where it immediately burst into flames upon contact with the fresh air. He swore to Dad that he hadn't been playing with matches. It finally came out that he had been playing with a *lighter*. Yet another time he set a teepee that our mom had made for us out of old blankets on fire with my sister in it and then ran away when she started screaming. If it hadn't been for a quick-thinking neighbor, she would have burned to death. Danny was always the sort to do things without ever thinking about the consequences of his actions. We didn't get along at all. It took years before we became warmer toward each other.

I spent a lot of time reading. I read every Nancy Drew and Trixie Belden mystery I could get my hands on. But I didn't tell anyone what I was reading. Other boys were reading the Hardy Boys (if they were reading anything at all) and would have had a field day with me had they known that I was reading "girls" books. I tried the Hardy Boys once but didn't like them much so for safety's sake I only read my books at home. I also set a personal goal for myself to read every book of our encyclopedia collection and every word in the dictionary. I used to shuffle through the pages of the dictionary each day and stop at a random page, pointing my finger somewhere on one of the open pages. Whatever word my finger was pointing to was one that I would try to use at least once in a sentence that day. I took the term "bookworm" to a whole new dimension.

By the time I reached the seventh grade it started to become more and more evident to me that not only was there something horribly wrong but that it wasn't going to change. I was spending far too much time with the younger children and far too little with kids my own age. What time I did spend with my peers was spent with the girls. I was accepted by them, but only up to a point. We could talk and be friends, but we couldn't really hang out together. I was, as far as they knew, a boy. There was a limit. The boys didn't want much to do with me unless they were looking for someone to "de-pants" and shove into the girls' bathroom. I spent almost as much time in the girls' bathroom at school as I did in the boys' room during school. To compensate for all this, I threw myself more into school work and music. I had found out early that I liked to play musical instruments and sing. My first public vocal performance was when I was around nine years old singing "The Old Rugged Cross" in church one Sunday. I was nervous but did well. The applause was infectious. I had found something that people didn't make fun of me for. And since I had taken piano lessons from an early age, I was no stranger to audiences. With piano lessons always came the dreaded public Recital. And on top of that my mother always made me play Christmas songs at a VFW party for children of deceased Veterans each year. I always hated that. I liked performing but was always terrified of making a mistake and looking stupid. There is nothing I hated worse than being laughed at. In school I turned my musical skills toward learning the baritone horn in the band and singing first tenor in the choir. I wanted to sing alto with the girls, but the teacher wouldn't let me (not that I would have ever asked) even though our voice ranges were very similar.[4]

---

[4] I'm singing Alto in a local chorale group now. So there!

31

Most important of all, I found myself identifying more and more each day with girls and less and less with the boys. The early childhood rituals had been put aside but the thought still remained: I was not who or what I was supposed to be. I knew it but nobody else seemed to – at least I never heard anyone say it out loud. I was about to find out just how serious this problem was becoming for me.

* * *

Seventh grade ushered in my most feared class yet: **Gym Class**. Up to this point there had been no gym class for us – just recess periods. But now we were expected to play team sports, do gymnastics and generally anything that would tend to make a person sweat profusely. Of course, that meant that we all had to take showers after class. *Together.* I had never taken a shower with anyone else before. I suppose that could be difficult thing for any kid to do for the first time. But for me it was pure terror. Even though I knew that my body was that of a boy's, my mind wasn't. And my mind fought tooth and nail to keep me from stripping and getting into the shower with a bunch of boys. I was so ashamed of my body and so convinced that I didn't belong there that I just knew that they would all point and laugh at me. For the longest time I made excuses whenever I could not to have to take a shower. Sometimes I would just wet my hair when no one was looking to make it seem that I had showered. If I could, I would simply sneak out without doing anything at all. But none of those ruses lasted very long. One day as I was trying to clandestinely leave, one of my many fellow student "benefactors" kindly pointed out to the gym teacher that I hadn't taken a shower. I was turned around and marched into the shower stalls while the teacher watched to make sure I took the shower. I couldn't possibly have been more embarrassed. I kept

32

my back to him and had my towel handy to cover myself upon leaving. I eventually learned to take quick showers either before anyone got into the locker rooms or to wait until after everyone had left. There was no rational reason for me to do this. I knew it but I couldn't help myself. I didn't want the boys looking at my body. It just wasn't right. I was a girl.

To make matters worse, this was also the start of the dreaded hormonal changes that everyone goes through. My voice was going up and down like the elevator in the Bryan Court House. One week I could sing soprano with the best of the girls. The next week I was singing baritone. My voice finally settled on a tenor tone in adulthood. This was a very confusing time for me. I was watching all the other girls around me start to blossom into womanhood. I waited in eager anticipation for the same to happen to me and put an end to all of this silliness. People would finally know who I really was once and for all and they would just leave me alone. But on the other hand, I was horribly frightened of the changes because I knew that they would be gradual and not overnight. That could only result in more teasing and bullying than I'd ever known. Part of me wanted the changes and part of me didn't. But one thing was for certain: no part of me thought that the changes would do anything to me but make me female. I was in for a big surprise.

Chapter 4
Tampons and Other Confusing Things

With hormones going haywire, I stepped timidly into my teen years. Boys' voices were getting deeper and their hands were beginning to search the high school halls for unsuspecting training bra straps to snap from behind. They were making their first steps on their journeys from belligerent little bullies to belligerent little male chauvinist pigs. Their talk began to turn from Saturday morning cartoons, riding bicycles and beating up sissies to hunting with Dad, working on cars and beating up sissies (some things never change). The little girls that before had been my only real friends were developing into young women and, for reasons I couldn't fathom, were taking interest in the boys. I was caught somewhere in between.

As my body began to change, I watched for the signs that would tell me that my womanhood was impending. I checked my chest every day to see if there was any growth. And just to help out, I had turned from wishing on The Star to taking one of my mother's birth control pills from her night stand once a week. Somehow, she never seemed to miss them. (I wonder where she thought they were going.) Anyway, I figured somehow that if she was taking something that was only meant for females, then it just might help me be female, too. Little did I know that the pills were full of estrogen, the very hormone that could actually help affect my change. One day I was doing my morning chest inspection when I noticed swelling around my nipples. I was absolutely ecstatic! It was happening at last! And as the days went on, so did the swelling. It wasn't long until I had nipples that were quite obviously enlarged and standing out proudly on their own. Then my stomach sank as one small reality sunk in. How was I going to be able to go to gym class

34

like this? I had to somehow find a way to be even more secretive than ever now and make sure that no one ever saw me in the showers. It was a serious problem but not one that I felt I couldn't overcome somehow. It was worth it.

At this point, my life was full of discoveries. One day while looking around the bathroom at home for something I came across a two-piece contraption with a spring in the middle that I finally deduced was a chest exerciser to increase your bust. All the women in my mother's family are small busted and my Mother was evidently trying to do what she could to rectify the condition. I now officially adopted the exerciser as my own and used it whenever no one was at home. I knew that I didn't want to get caught using it because everyone still thought I was a boy. Boys don't use things like that. It eventually did me no more good than it did my Mother.

Also, in my searching I came across my mother's feminine protection items – sanitary napkins and belts (this was before the sticky pads that didn't need the belts). I wasn't quite sure what these were for but knew that they went together. I thought that maybe because girls didn't have penises that they leaked a lot of urine and needed the pads to protect their clothes and keep from smelling too bad. (Youth is wasted on the young, isn't it?) I figured out how to hook the pads to the belt and wore many a pad without anyone being the wiser.

Then my mother switched to tampons when they became available. I found them one day looking for a new pad to use. This was something entirely different. At this point, even though I was in my teens, no one had ever talked to me about sex at all. I knew that girls didn't have penises and had to sit down to pee, but I didn't know that there was any other plumbing involved. I also had discovered from listening closely to my girlfriends at school that some of them had started what they called their *periods* and it was somehow painful and messy. I heard them talking about tampons and pads for this purpose. My first thought was to feel silly that I had thought all along that the pads were used for stray urine. But once I saw what a tampon looked like, I wasn't exactly sure what they did with it. But it was fairly obvious that they were meant to be inserted somewhere. Some place in the back of my mind the *Rituals* started again. I decided that since my breasts were starting to grow, they needed all the help they could get, so, in addition to taking the birth control pills and using the breast exerciser, I started using my mother's tampons. And since I was totally ignorant of female anatomy, there was only one place that I knew of *down there* where they could possibly be inserted. Let me tell you, they were *very* uncomfortable. I just couldn't imagine how girls could wear these things inside all day and not be fidgeting just waiting to take them out when they got home. But I figured that since it was only for a few days each month, they just got used to them somehow. And if they could do it, so could I.

Other changes were starting to occur by now; changes that I had no control over and scared me to death. The main one, and the worst of them all, was the dreaded **Penis with a Mind of Its Own**. I woke up one morning feeling like I had to go to the bathroom so bad I wasn't sure I was going to make it downstairs. When I reached down to try to squeeze the thing in an effort to keep from peeing, I discovered that my penis had swelled up and turned hard as a rock, pointing straight up. How was I going to pee out of THIS? What in the hell was happening to me? This wasn't supposed to be happening. The damn thing was supposed to be shrinking and falling off, not getting bigger! I didn't know what to do. No one ever told me about this. I thought it was some sort of horrible unforeseen side effect of the birth control pills, so I swore to stop taking them right away. It finally did eventually shrink back to where it had been but stopping taking the pills didn't seem to help. It would get that way from time to time all by itself whether I was taking the pills or not. The worst of it was when it happened while I was sitting in my seat in school. All of a sudden without a thought from me the thing would start to grow. I just knew that I'd be called on at that moment to stand up and say something or go to the front of the class to do something on the blackboard. If I was lucky, the bell would go off and I could just sit in my seat until the moment passed and I could get up without embarrassment. I carried a lot of notebooks in strategic places in those days.

By now my breasts were getting to be fairly prominent. So prominent, in fact, that my mother noticed. I was extremely pleased that this was happening to me but still scared that I would be teased mercilessly at school for it if anyone found out. I was wearing loose fitting shirts with a t-shirt underneath to hide it from everyone. But when Mom found out about it, she took me to the doctor to have me examined. The doctor poked and prodded at me with my mother looking on (and me wanting to die of embarrassment) and finally told her not to worry. He said that my hormones were just going a little crazy and that it wasn't so unusual for this sort of thing to happen. They'd go away in a few months all by themselves. All my hopes fell with a silent thud to the floor of the examination room. I was more dejected than ever and obviously I couldn't tell my mother why. Of course, the swelling did eventually go away, and I unfortunately went back to developing physically as a boy. I remember a few years later sitting in the living room reading a book when my sister came in to complain to Mom that her chest itched and hurt. My Mother hugged her and proclaimed proudly that her little girl was growing **Boobs**! I angrily but silently left the room with my forever flat chest, hurting inside as my sister giggled in delight. It wasn't fair. It just wasn't fair.

The teen years are, more than anything else, the time when children become socially aware. They start becoming more interested in dressing and acting just right. They begin to be more acutely aware of who they are and how they are to react in society. For me it was no different. I was still a loner. I had no girlfriends, just friends who were girls. I wasn't interested in boys because I generally thought of them as uncouth pigs, an opinion that I still hold with a fair amount of certainty. I did have a few close friends who were boys, though. I always hung around with the class clowns because no matter how I felt, I always liked to laugh and to make other people laugh. That ability saved me from countless beatings at the hands of the school tough guys that kept notches on their belts with my picture on them. But all in all, I was becoming more aware that I was different.

One thing that wasn't different about me, though, was that, immediately upon hitting my teen years, my face erupted with a severe case of acne. I didn't just have a pizza-face. I had pizza-face with the works! One week I'd have a third eye in the center of my forehead and the next I'd have a second nose trying to grow on the end of my original one. I tried every over-the-counter medication there was but all I ever managed to do was put a glob of light color over my dark skin and make things look even worse (as if the kids at school needed something else to help them make fun of me). My complexion eventually cleared up – somewhere around the age of 30. My face looked so bad in school that when they airbrushed my skin for the color version of my high school graduation photo, even *I* didn't recognize myself. The also gave me red hair.

* * *

My Mother and I were basically the same height and build. We even sounded alike. People were forever mistaking me for my mother on the phone. When no one was home, especially in the summer months with both my parents working and my brothers and sister out playing somewhere, I would go into the closet in my parents' bedroom. It was a huge closet that had two doors, one on each side of the room. It extended all the way around the back of the room behind the wall and came out the door on the other side. There I would find my mother's dresses, skirts, blouses and shoes, all of which fit me almost perfectly. These times were some of the happiest of my childhood. I can still remember the musty, hot smell of that closet on those summer afternoons. I would carefully go into my mother's lingerie drawer and pick out something nice. Then I'd go into the closet (physically and metaphorically) and pick out a pretty outfit to wear. I felt perfectly normal in her clothes. That they fit me so well further served to convince me that I should be wearing these kinds of clothes all the time. I never stayed in their closet too long, though. I could never be sure when someone might come home. My greatest fear was being found like that; a fear that would eventually be horribly realized.

One day while I was picking out the latest outfit from my mother's wardrobe, I came across something I hadn't seen before – a bag of women's night gowns and undergarments. I knew they weren't my mother's things because all of cup sizes of the bras were too large. I later found out that she had been given the bag of clothing by a long-time friend of the family named Suzie who asked her to give them to charity. But I decided then and there that they were mine. I needed some charity, after all. So, I took a few of the items to my bedroom and hid them. Since I had a room of my own, I had some privacy with the door closed. But in the old house where we lived, mine was the only room that didn't have any kind of central heating at all. To get heat in my room meant leaving the bedroom door open which meant either giving up my privacy or shivering all night. And to make things worse, my parents' room was right across from mine and my dad would come into my room first thing every morning bright and early to wake me up for school. Privacy? What privacy? But at least for a while I could close my bedroom door, put on some nice underwear and a pretty nightgown and snuggle into bed to read for a little while. Then before I got too tired, I would reluctantly take everything off; put them back into their hiding places, open my bedroom door and then climb back into my warm bed to sleep. That's how it was supposed to work.

One night sometime around Christmas I had performed my little nightly mini ritual with one small exception: I was so comfortable and warm that I fell asleep before I took off my teddy and bra and panties. Although she had never done this before, my mother chose this particular night to come upstairs to wake me so I could play the piano for their guests, including her friend Suzie. At first, I didn't realize what was happening and sat up in bed, exposing my pretty nightgown for her to see. When I saw the look on my mother's face, I was instantly awake and trying frantically to come up with something believable to tell her. She just looked at me, startled, and said, "What the hell are you doing?" The only thing I could get out was a sheepish grin and the lame excuse, "I knew you were coming up. I was just trying to play a joke on you." She stopped for a moment, probably wanting to believe my nonsense, shook her head and told me to take those clothes off and come downstairs. So, with my stomach-turning flip-flops and having been more embarrassed than I'd ever been in my life, I did just that. When I was done, I went quietly back up to my room and lay down to die.

The next morning when I came downstairs for breakfast, I discovered that Suzie had stayed the night. And to my horror, my mother had told her about my little "joke" the night before. Suzie was sitting at the breakfast table laughing about it. When she saw me walk in, she asked if the little red bra fit me well. Everyone had a good laugh. I laughed along with everyone else but inside I was ready to have someone take a dull knife, cut my heart out of my chest, throw it on the floor and stomp on it to put me out my misery. But the best I could do was not to show my embarrassment and just go along with the joke. I never wore those things again. And the bag disappeared from my parents' closet.

* * *

I gave my mother several hints during those years that things were not quite right with me but somehow, she never saw them. One overly blatant hint came during a summer vacation. Each year our family would go to a little lake in nearby Indiana during the summer months and go camping. It was always our favorite thing to look forward to and our only real family vacation together. One time after my brother and I had put up our huge unwieldy canvas tent in the summer heat at the start of our vacation, she told me we were all going down to the lake, so I should go get into a bathing suit. So, I did. I got into hers. It was a nice blue-patterned one piece. Hey, she just said put one on. She didn't say *which* one. I came out of the tent and told her I was ready to go. She took one look at me, laughed, called me a "round head" (her favorite playful insult) and told me to get my own suit on. She didn't even notice that I had my penis and testicles tucked between my legs so there was no bulge in the front. But everyone laughed, and I knew I was going to get away

41

with it because I was obviously just being my practical-joking self and it was nothing serious. Right. No one thought anything more of it. So, I went back into the tent and put my own bathing suit on, exposing my flat, bare chest for all to see – but not before borrowing one of my mother's tampons. (When it was my mother's time of the month, it was mine as well.) Properly dressed, we all headed down to the beach. Just as I was getting ready to go into the water, my mother called from behind to tell me that I had blood running down my leg.[5] I immediately ran into the water to wash off the blood. Then I went into the bathroom on the beach and removed the tampon. She never questioned where the blood had come from. It's just as well. What was I going to tell her – that I cut myself shaving?

It was also around this time of my life that I learned about sex – or at least something about sex. I overheard some of the boys at school talking about something called "whacking off". I had never heard of such a thing, so I asked them what it was. They looked at me like I was an alien from Mars. How could I possibly not know what "whacking off" was? After they got through laughing at me (again), one of them finally decided to take pity on me and took me aside to explain it to me. He told me it was easy. You just grab your penis and pump it like a jack handle. When I asked why anyone would want to do that, he stifled yet another laugh and said, "Because it feels really good". He promised that I'd know what he meant when I tried it.

So, I went home and tried it. I stood in front of the bathroom mirror and, feeling pretty foolish, grabbed my penis and began pumping it up and down – not back and forth as is commonly done, but literally up and down like a jack handle. Nothing happened. I figured that the guys were just pulling my leg again and gave up. This was stupid. I was really getting tired of them making fun of me all the time.

---

[5] I *told* you those things were uncomfortable!

I was so incredibly naïve in those days that even today I'm surprised I survived. But I really had no interest in my own body or what was happening to it. I was more interested in what I thought should be happening to it and wasn't. And since my body was not doing what it should be doing, my only recourse was to try to be as close to a female body as I could so I could see what it was supposed to be like. That was when I decided to start looking for a girlfriend.

Chapter 5
High School, Love and Similar Catastrophes

Life was becoming more difficult. As I grew more socially aware, it became increasingly evident that I couldn't discuss my inner feelings with anyone, even my best friends. I was learning that my classmates thought I was something called a "queer" which was a term I really didn't understand other than it was probably not a good thing to be called. I looked up the word in the dictionary at school one day while I was working as a volunteer librarian (a job that was yet *another* nail in my social coffin). When I discovered that it was a derogatory word for a homosexual, I had to look *that* word up. That one threw me. Why would they call me that? Did I like boys? Hell, no! I hated boys! But then again, girls liked boys and maybe I didn't like them because I wasn't allowed to be a girl. Maybe if I really was a girl, I'd like boys. I just couldn't see that ever happening. This was all very confusing.

After thinking about it for a while, I decided that I couldn't be a homosexual. Boys in my mind were one step on the evolutionary ladder below swine. There's no way I could ever like a boy in *that* way. I did have a few friends who were boys that I liked but they were different. They were all funny and intelligent, definitely an anomaly in the area where I lived. I sometimes played chess with one of my male friends instead of eating lunch. Actually, he played chess. I just sat there and watched him slaughter me. There's even a picture of one of my many horrible defeats in our High School Yearbook. We were also all class clowns who loved nothing more than to make each other laugh. But I felt nothing for them but friendship and couldn't conceive of ever feeling anything more. I just didn't find boys physically attractive. But then why did I find girls physically attractive? The more I thought about things like this, the more confused I became. I didn't know it at the time, but I was not only struggling with my gender identity, but with my sexual orientation as well, both totally separate issues about which I knew nothing.

I had never really considered any romantic interest in girls until one year when some of us from the Music Department at school went to the Ohio State Music Contests in Bowling Green, a small university town near Toledo. I had been playing the tuba in the high school band for quite some time and decided to enter the contest with a tuba solo. Didn't know there was such a thing, did you? It's not exactly something you would listen to at night with a glass of wine and a roaring fire, but it was surprisingly pleasant and more than a little difficult. During one of the lulls in the competition, I happened upon a girl from my school named Charlotte who was entered in the competition with a piano solo. I had seen her before but really didn't know her. Neither of us knew anyone else so we just ended up sharing lunch together. We hit it off right away. She was smart and funny, and we could make each other laugh. Her smile and demure nature were infectious, and I thought she was one of the prettiest girls I had ever seen. I offered to sit in on her performance of Brahms' Rhapsody in G Minor as moral support. She gratefully accepted. What I heard was unbelievable. I had never heard anyone play such a difficult piece of music before, especially by heart, and I was very impressed. Over the years I have tried to play that piece myself and have never come close to being able to play it anywhere near as well as she did that day. I was so impressed with her that I decided to put my shyness aside and try to get to know her better. We became fast friends and started seeing each other often at school.

It wasn't long before our friendship blossomed into something more. I was totally intrigued by her. This was the closest I had ever been to a female body before and I wanted to know all about it. We really enjoyed each other's company and my parents as well as hers approved of our dating. We went everywhere together and became quite an item. It did wonders for my image at school and even more for my self-image. I had found someone who was genuinely interested in me and didn't think of me as a total dweeb (and the word hadn't even been invented yet).

Up until that time I was somewhat of a human punching bag for all of the school bullies. Being small and usually reserved in manner, I was a prime target for all sorts of public humiliation and torture. I was constantly harassed, punched and generally terrorized. But somehow my relationship with Charlotte (I actually had a *girlfriend*!) gave me a new inner strength to fight back. One day while on the way home in the school bus, two of the more notorious town bullies sat themselves right behind me. I dreaded what was to come. They like to play a little game they called "Rap Ricky Really Hard on the Top of His Head with Our Knuckles" and settled in for another fun episode. As the rapping began, I did what I usually did – nothing. I just sat there with my eyes watering from the pain and kept quiet. They always quit after they got bored. In one way I guess you could say I won by not reacting. There wasn't anything else I could do. One of the guys was twice my size. What was I going to do, turn around and hit him back? As miserable as my life generally was, I was still rather fond of keeping my bones intact. And not only would I get creamed by them, I'd get in trouble at school for fighting on the bus. This time none of that mattered (except the getting in trouble at school part). I sat there, letting them take turns on my head, each blow harder than the last trying to elicit some kind of response from me. This time I was getting mad. The more they hit the madder I got. I didn't say anything, but I got off the bus one stop ahead of where I usually did and ran home, knowing that these two goons were going to pass right by my house on their way home when they got off the bus at their stop. I stood on the sidewalk and waited for them, my anger growing into boiling rage.

The main instigator of this abuse was an extremely large boy named Wayne. For some odd reason, it didn't matter to me then that he outweighed me by at least one hundred pounds. I'd had enough, and he was going to answer for this once and for all. I was so angry that it didn't matter that this could be my last day alive on earth. When Wayne and his buddy approached my house as I knew they would, I took off my glasses and stood in the middle of the sidewalk to block their way. I stepped straight up to Wayne, looked him in the eyes and heard myself say, "Okay, you fat pig. Take off your glasses or I'll break them on your face." Needless to say, he was surprised. This meek little mouse that only minutes before had been sitting in tearful silence on the bus was now roaring in outrage – ok, squeaking – but it was still with outrage. Wayne looked at me, smiled, and reached up to take off his glasses. As he handed them to his friend my right fist doubled up and the color of red, I had been seeing darkened into a suicidal crimson. He had no sooner started to turn his head back to me when something inside me (I think it was my sense of self-preservation) snapped. With all my might I threw my fist up and across and punched him in the nose so hard that I hurt my knuckles. In that instant my inner mind saw Wayne topple to the ground like a Goliath with me as the diminutive David standing triumphantly over his crumpled and bleeding body. Unfortunately for me, Wayne had never read that story in Sunday school – if he ever went – and had no idea that the story line required him to fall down in defeat. Instead, his head merely moved a few inches to the side and looked at me in total disbelief. "This little shit actually hit me!" he must have been thinking. He touched his fingers to his nose and drew back a little blood. His eyes grew wide and he muttered, "You little son of a bitch", between his clenched teeth. He reached forward, grabbed me and lifted me off the ground effortlessly. It was then that my entire life passed before my eyes. (I was only 14 at the time so there wasn't much to pass so I had to call for a couple of replays of a few particularly nice things.) I was fairly certain that my life as an ambulatory person was about to end, and I braced myself for the inevitable flash of pain that would darken my world. Instead, Wayne threw me to the ground in the yard in front of my house – and sat on me, pinning my arms and legs. I was totally helpless. I was not, however, totally rational. I thrashed and struggled under him trying to free myself, all the while screaming every epithet at him I could muster along with the insane promise that if I got free I was going to kill him. Now *that's* incentive to let me up, isn't it?

It was then that my dad drove up and parked in the driveway right beside us. I was at once afraid that he would come out and stop this, which would be totally humiliating to me, or that would *not* come out and stop this, thereby allowing me to die a useless and tragic, yet somehow stupidly heroic, death by asphyxiation and exasperation. He did worse than either of those. As I glanced up at him from my somewhat embarrassing position, I saw him sitting in the car trying hard not to laugh. Now, in retrospect I guess it probably did look a little funny, what with a 90-pound kid screaming death threats while lying helplessly pinned under a 250-pound behemoth. At the time, however, I didn't quite see the humor in the situation. Wayne saw my dad drive up, finally got off of me and simply walked away. Still angry and deeply hurt at seeing my dad's reaction, I got up and ran into the house. I didn't talk to him for weeks after the incident; about the same time it took for my knuckles and ribs to stop hurting. Magically, however, my stature at school had grown. Word had gotten around that I had actually stood up to Wayne – well, sort of. It didn't matter that he won the "fight"; it mattered that I finally fought back. The bullying at school stopped. I was looked at in a whole new light. Instead of being regarded as a 90-pound sissy, I was regarded as a 90-pound lunatic, especially by Charlotte. But she thought I was a brave lunatic. Our romance blossomed.

* * *

Charlotte and I spent as much time as we could together. She lived on a farm near the school where they had a barn with a hayloft. Her brothers had created an intricate system of tunnels under the bales of hay that we used to our advantage. We could enter the tunnels and crawl to where there was a space large enough for us to lay side by side. We could move some of the hay on the floor aside to expose cracks in the floor that would let in light and fresh air from below. Then we would kiss and fondle for what seemed like hours. I was fascinated with her breasts. Part of me was excited by the feel of them and part of me was jealous that she had them and I didn't. But no matter how much we fondled and kissed and professed our love, I couldn't bring myself to go any further. I was horribly afraid that if I tried to touch her "elsewhere" that she would think of me as no better than the other boys who I considered to be walking pig hormones. Even in the heat of the moment my interest in exploring her body further was purely based on curiosity and not sexual in nature. I think that this is what eventually destroyed our relationship and lead to the first of several devastating breakups in my life.

These hayloft sessions went on for months with no escalation. Our relationship ultimately began to cool. I began to think that maybe she, like my other classmates, was starting to think I was "queer", too, so I decided to do something about it. One night when we were sitting together at her house, she invited me out for a walk. We only went as far as the barn but didn't go up into the hayloft. Instead, we simply stood by the door kissing, a little at first and then passionately. My hands started to explore as my courage built. Before I knew it I had touched her in a place I had never touched any girl before. It was very warm and wet. She was shivering. Then, as we started to sink toward the floor of the barn, I did something that I'll never forget. I stopped. I had been raised to know that doing this sort of thing was wrong somehow if you weren't married. It sure didn't feel wrong, but I just couldn't bring myself to go any further. She looked at me in disbelief for a moment, fixed her clothes and then walked out. I was left alone knowing that I had done something wrong but not quite sure what it was. Was she angry for me taking liberties like that or for stopping? I didn't know what to think. I went home in confused silence.

After that night Charlotte because increasingly distant from me. When I would try to talk to her, she would make excuses about why she had to be somewhere in a hurry and that she'd see me later. She rarely did. Then, around Christmas time, an even stranger thing started to happen. Our mutual friends at school started looking at me with puppy-dog sad eyes and shaking heads. The more distant Charlotte became the more sad looks I got. Being totally naïve, I had no idea what was going on until Christmas Eve when I went to church services with Charlotte and her parents. I had spent all of my money from my assistant janitor's job at school to get her a nice watch for Christmas and was looking forward to giving it to her to show how much I still loved her. I just knew that would bring her back to me. But when they came to pick me up at home for the service at their church, I immediately sensed that something was terribly wrong. Her parents were usually very happy to see me and very talkative. This time, however, we drove to the church in almost complete silence. When we arrived, her parents got out of the car and tersely told us that they would be inside when we came in. I was grateful that they had left us alone so I could give Charlotte my gift and get the passionate kiss that I was sure would be my reward.

We were alone at last. Charlotte started to give me my gift, but I stopped her and insisted that she receive my gift first. I held my breath as she opened it. I was deathly afraid that she wouldn't like it. As she held the watch in her hand my heart swelled. Surely, she would know how I felt now. She smiled, gave me a perfunctory kiss on the cheek and handed me my gift. I opened it with trembling hands. It was a watch, too. And this one was engraved on the back with "From Char with Love". I could hear a choir singing her love for me in the distance. I was happier at that moment that I had been for a long time. Then she looked at me with sad eyes and said, "We can't see each other anymore. I'm seeing someone else."

The choir stopped singing. In its place was a hollow, empty silence. My world fell apart under my feet. I was stunned and didn't know what to say. I couldn't speak. All I could do was stare at her in disbelief. Now I knew why all our friends had been looking at me so sadly. Everyone knew about her seeing someone else – everyone but me. From somewhere in my state of shock I finally found my tongue and asked her, "Why"?

She said that it was just something that happened and that was all there was to it. There was a coldness in her voice that I'd never heard before. Of course, she wanted us to remain friends because she enjoyed my company. By now I was beginning to lose my fight to hold back a torrent of tears. So instead of breaking down, I steeled myself and told her that we should go inside and join her parents. We walked in silence to the church.

When we sat down, her parents asked me if I was all right. They didn't even look at Charlotte. It was clear that they didn't approve at all of what she had done. Perhaps they had even ordered her to tell me the truth instead of stringing me along. I didn't hear anything that happened in the Christmas Eve service; I just sat in silence replaying her words over and over in my head, feeling a jabbing pain in my eyes each time. My mind raced to find a reason why she would do this to me, but I could find no answers. When the service was done, I was driven home in an even greater silence than before. As I left the car, not a word was spoken. They drove away as I walked dejectedly into my house. As I passed my mother sitting in a chair in the living room, she immediately saw that something was wrong and asked me what had happened. The dam finally broke. With tears streaming down my face, I managed to utter something to the effect that life was just not fair. I ran up to my bedroom and, locking the door, I cried for what seemed like hours.

The next week at school was a hard one. It was a small country school (my graduating class had a little over 90 students in it) and it was difficult if not outright impossible not to run into everyone you knew at some point in the day. My friends were all asking me how I was. I must have been walking around like a zombie. I was angry at all of them for not telling me earlier what they knew. I didn't want to talk to any of them. Even the bullies left me alone that day. I made up my mind to confront Charlotte one last time and return the watch with the false claim of her love on the back that I couldn't bring myself to wear. I had been lied to and humiliated and I couldn't bear being reminded of it or her every time I looked at my wrist. I'd never hurt so badly in my life. I met her at her locker between classes and, as several of our classmates anxiously watched while trying to look like they weren't watching; I gave her the watch back without a word. I turned and walked away. Later a mutual friend showed me a picture of the boy that she had dumped me for. He was from another school. The picture showed the two of them happy together at some school function. He was very tall with short, cropped hair and big ears. He was not what I considered very good looking at all. I had never had much of a positive image of myself before, but I did think that I was at least a little on the pleasant-looking side. Charlotte herself had made me feel that way for the first time in my life. Seeing this guy who reminded me of a cross between Goofy and Bullwinkle shattered what little ego I had managed to hold on to. I was crushed. All I could think was that I must be really bad for her to dump me for someone who looked like *that*. I angrily confronted her one last time and told her that she had better keep her boyfriend away from me because if I ever saw him, I'd beat him up. I couldn't believe those words were coming out of my mouth, but I really didn't know what to say. I just needed to lash back somehow and not just sit and take this hurt quietly. I didn't speak to Charlene again for at least a year.

I know that most of us have gone through something like this at some time or another in our lives. But this event was pivotal for me in that I was just starting to get some kind of positive image of myself as a male for the first time in my life and it had been summarily and coldly dashed to pieces in my face. Of course, Charlotte had no idea of what turmoil was going on inside of me so she had no way of knowing just how devastating this breakup was for me. I began to crawl back inside myself, back to the walls that protected me from the outside world. My feelings about whom and what I was became even more confused and I my cross-dressing became more frequent. Over the next two years of high school, I had only two other very casual girlfriends but nothing that I pursued with any vigor. All

I wanted was to get out of high school and get out of the area so I might be able to find myself in the outside world.

I decided to join the Navy.

Chapter 6
Realization and Boot Camp

Lest you think that high school for me was all drudgery and pain, I should let you know that, although the happy moments were few and far between, there were actually some good times. The fondest memory I have is of my sophomore year when our Music and Drama Department staged a production of the musical "Oliver!" My relationship with Charlotte was over and I had started a bit to come back out of my self-imposed internal prison, I did something that was totally unlike me – I tried out for the lead part of Oliver Twist in the musical. There were two of us who auditioned for the part. The other boy was older and shorter than me with short, longish blonde hair. I was taller than him with short, dark hair. Oliver Twist was supposed to be a small, helpless boy. I didn't really fit that bill too well. At one time I had been one of the smallest kids in the class, but I did what a lot of boys in my family did – I started growing like a weed in my early teens. However, there was one thing I could do that the other boy couldn't – I could sing. Even though the butterflies in my stomach might disagree, I enjoyed even then performing in front of people. Because I always had a talent for music, performing was the only way I had of getting positive feedback to help me feel at least a little good about myself. So even though I felt I had little hope of getting the part, I auditioned for it with my fingers crossed. Unbelievably, I got it. My classmates were amazed that mousey little Ricky would even think about trying out for the lead in a musical, let alone get it. I was surprised, too, but grateful. Of course, I had to make sure I didn't fall on my face and confirm my classmates' beliefs, but I felt fairly confident that I could handle the part. And it was just the thing I needed to take my mind off how much I still hurt inside.

Opening night of the musical caused all of the butterflies in my stomach to go into a panic. And to add to my nervousness, my Dad had actually showed up to watch something at school in which I was involved – for the very first time. Although I was ecstatic that he was there as this was probably the most important moment in my life so far, it put even more pressure on me because I wanted so badly to impress him. As it turned out, everything went pretty well. At one point in the musical, I was sitting on a coffin in an undertaker's basement singing *"Where Is Love?"* My Mother told me afterwards that there wasn't a dry eye in the house. I was so into the part that I was even crying while I was singing it. It didn't take much acting to feel that particular song. Still, it was definitely one of the most memorable events in my life.

After *"Oliver!"* my confidence started to gain strength. I was already working as the Art Editor for our school newspaper and yearbook and eventually asked for the position of Editor in Chief of the newspaper when the position became available. It turned out not to be the nice job I thought it would be. One of the girls on the staff wrote a gossip column that was sometimes a little tasteless and very often cruel – but highly popular. One time I let something be printed about a couple against my better judgment and it resulted in their extreme embarrassment in front of the whole school. I decided then and there that there would be no more gossip column in the paper. My reporters disagreed. They saw it as being something that was an integral and expected part of the newspaper regardless of the devastating effect it could have on others. They threatened to quit if I pulled the column. I could not in good conscience allow something I was doing to humiliate others. I knew all too well what that felt like. So, I called the reporters' bluffs and pulled the column anyway. They all quit. For the rest of that year, I produced the school newspaper entirely by myself. I quit the next year. It was just too much work. The gossip column returned quickly upon my resignation and people went back to dreading that their social lives would be harpooned by some unfeeling gossipmonger. It was my first lesson in management. It was certainly not to be my last.

Also, during that time, I organized charity events to raise money for different things at school. One of them was a "car bash". A local junk yard supplied an old car that we moved to the school parking lot and charged 25 cents a shot to hit with a sledge hammer. All of the glass had been removed, of course. But the school bullies who still didn't like me showed up in a gang, took the sledge hammer from one of the students who had paid and started beating on the car. It's kind of hard to mount a sufficient threat to someone who's facing you with a sledgehammer and you have nothing. So, I did the only thing I could – I went back inside the school to get a teacher. By the time I got back with reinforcements, the boys had pushed what was left of the car out into a field and overturned it. My feelings for men in general were not uplifted by this macho display of cheap bravado. And once again I was publicly humiliated.

By this time, I had had just about enough of life in general. The things that had been going so well for me at school were taking turns for the worst. My confidence was failing, and my cross-dressing was continuing unabated. Realizing this, I started to think of ways that I could get out and "find myself". My favorite uncle in the world was my mother's only brother Jim who was an electrician in the Navy. When he would come home on leave, I'd marvel at his uniform and dreamt of someday emulating him and joining the Navy. I even had my hair cut short in a flat-top like his one summer. My head broke out terribly from the Butch Wax that was needed to make my hair stand up until it was trained. And I was mortified that I had actually had my hair cut so short. My Dad had always insisted that we boys have short hair, but this was ridiculous. And I had become accustomed to having my hair longer because of my need for it in the musical[6]. So, I let my hair grow out so my scalp could heal for the rest of the summer.

* * *

I'd always wanted to see the ocean and I felt that if I stayed in northwestern Ohio, my chances of ever seeing it or any other part of the world would be just about zero. I could go to college, but my parents couldn't afford to send me, and I was very tired of fellow students and abuse anyway. For some reason I had received an offer of a scholarship to a local mortuary college. Somehow, I just couldn't see myself as a mortician. It seemed so morbid, and I don't think I could deal well with grieving people all the time. Since I was so enthralled by my uncle's tales of sailing the seas and visiting foreign ports, I decided to join the military and get out of Small Town, USA. The year was 1969 and the country was deep into the Vietnam War. As I was in danger of being drafted anyway if I didn't go to college, I decided to enlist and choose the service I wanted to enter rather than let Uncle Sam choose for me. Because of what happened to my father, my Mother never allowed guns in the house. I had never hunted or shot a gun in my life, so I just couldn't see myself slogging around in some steamy jungle shooting at people. I wasn't too fond of the idea of being shot at, either. I wanted to get out and see the world, but I wanted to eventually go to school and continue my education, too. The military offered the GI Bill which would help put me through college after I got out. Another factor was what I was going through internally. I knew

---

[6] I milked that one for all I could get out of it.

by now that my body wasn't going to change the way I wanted it to, so I'd have to find a way to live in it. I figured, like so many male-to-female transsexuals of my era, that if I immersed myself in the world of men that I would be able to find my place in it. So, it was decided. I would join the Navy for four years, see the world, stay out of the jungles of Vietnam, go to school on Uncle Sam's dime when I got out and become a music teacher. My music teacher in school, Mr. Kroeckel, who was my only real adult friend, was thrilled by my choice of vocations but warned me that I'd have to start saving my money now so I could afford to eat on a teacher's salary later. I was surprised at this because I believed, as I still do, that there is no other profession in the world more important than teaching. I just assumed that salaries were commensurate with job importance. Then I found out how much professional sports figures make. It still galls me that some high school drop-out who can hit and catch a ball can make millions of dollars a year for playing a child's game and our teachers, who are shaping the lives of the leaders of the future, must work two jobs to make ends meet. Don't get me started.

* * *

I actually joined the Navy early in 1969, long before I graduated from High School. A Navy representative came to the school to talk to people and signed a few of us up on inactive reserve duty. Two weeks after I graduated in May of 1969, I left my home in Ohio for boot camp at the Great Lakes Naval Training Center outside of Chicago, Illinois. I first had to take a bus to Cleveland where we were given complete physicals to make sure we could be in the military. I actually saw a guy standing in line who, when they said, "Drop your shorts, bend over and spread your cheeks", dropped his shorts, bent over and grabbed his face and pulled. He probably became an officer. I

59

passed all of the tests with flying colors and was put on a plane for Chicago. This is where we learned the unofficial Navy motto "Hurry up and wait." We arrived at O'Hare airport sometime around 7 pm and were told to sit quietly and wait for the bus that would take us to the base. The bus arrived around midnight. I'm sure that this was all pre-arranged.

We stepped off the bus, tired and apprehensive, to a scene out of a World War II prisoner camp movie. The camp was dimly lit with buildings that looked like they were built specifically to maintain some carefully conceived sub-human limit for comfort and cheeriness. As our numbed senses were being bombarded by people screaming at us, we were herded from one building to another where we had to wait for long periods of time for ill-fitting clothing and substandard sheets and blankets to be thrown at us. Finally, and gratefully, we were marched (we *never* walked from that time on) into the barracks where we were each assigned bunks to get a good night's sleep before our official indoctrination into Hell the next day. It was now about two o'clock in the morning.

We were awakened at 0500 hours[7] after a refreshing three full hours of thrashing around on uncomfortable beds under scratchy blankets. Then we were marched quickly to breakfast where we had to stand quietly for about an hour in line to be able to eat. It was then that I discovered why they called the dining facility the "Mess Hall". One of the first things they teach you in the military is that whatever fancy food you were used to in civilian life was not adequate for *Real Men*. Only pansies ate that stuff. Real men ate food that provided them nourishment without all that extra "taste" stuff thrown in. There were even persistent rumors that someone working in the kitchen had gone over the edge and had been caught urinating in the powdered

---

[7] Five a.m. for all of you non-military types. "Stupid o'clock" for everyone else.

egg mixture. They had no idea how long he'd been doing that before they caught him. It turned out that the story was all made up just to unnerve the new recruits. It's used all the time. The real lesson I was starting to learn, however, was just what kind of mistake I had made in deciding to join the Navy. I had actually hoped that I would find that men were different outside of high school; that I could actually find something in others that would make me feel good about myself, who I was and who I was supposed to be. Instead, I found people screaming in my ears in the chow line, "All right, you faggots! Nuts to butts! Make the girl in front of you happy!" Some of the guys in line were taking those suggestions quite literally. More than once I had to elbow the guy behind me who was grinding away. It was very distressing to be sandwiched in between two men, especially when what you felt from behind was definitely not a roll of Life Savers. Didn't they throw people out of the service for doing these sorts of things? Why were they telling everyone to do it? I was beginning to get the distinct impression that I had made a terrible mistake. I was ready right then and there after the first day to tell someone that I had changed my mind. But we were too busy being terrorized and hurried from one place to another to complain – not that you could actually complain, of course.

After a few days of this kind of abuse I discovered that because of my background in music, I was being assigned to something called the "Band and Choir Company". I didn't know there was such a thing. It seems they needed a backup tuba player for the band that performed in the official camp ceremonies like graduations, local civic propaganda parades and public executions of recruits who told them they had changed their minds about being in the Navy and wanted out. The bad news was that there weren't enough musicians yet for a full company, so I had to wait in what they called a "Holding Company" until more unfortunates were brought in.

The people who were placed in holding companies generally consisted of three types:

1) Raging Lunatic Homicidal Psychopaths who were under special scrutiny to see if they should be kicked out of the Navy on the spot or sent to Vietnam as field officers,

2) Criminals With Records who, if their crimes in the outside world had not been serious enough, would instantly be kicked out of the Navy, and

3) Those Who Clearly Needed A Few More Weeks Of Abject Terror To Toughen Them Up Or Kill Them Outright.

Since I had never killed anyone and had never so much as stolen a piece of candy[8], they put me in Group Three with the rest of what they called the "New Meat". Unfortunately for us, there was no distinction based on any of three groups concerning where we were all housed. All three groups were harmoniously thrown together into one barracks to either learn how to become one big happy family or kill each other trying. Either way the Navy didn't care just as long as no one made a mess. Late one night I was awakened by the sound of a young man clearly from Group One who was making love with much gusto to the radiator at the far end of the barracks. The radiator was turned on at the time which probably explained much of the screaming. Another man, who constantly complained of being followed, watched and threatened was finally given a party by members of Groups One and Two intent on showing him that

---

[8] Ok, so I did *try* once to steal a piece of candy once when I was kid but the Boot Camp people never found out about it.

his fears were misplaced. Actually, the party turned out to be a traditional Navy "Blanket Party" where, in the wee hours of the morning, a few fun-loving souls surround your bunk, throw a blanket over your head and beat you senseless with socks filled with bars of soap until you're convinced that no one is out to get you. But hey, a party's a party, right? We never saw either the guy with the really hot date or the one with Zest imprinted across his forehead again. I assume they were made Lieutenants and immediately put in charge of razing peasant villages in Vietnam.

One day after a couple of weeks of sleeping under my mattress in hopes that no one would discover I was there, I was told that my company was finally forming. At last, the *real* boot camp was going to start. I was WAY bored doing nothing but pleading for my life and attending Working Parties[9]. I was marched along was the other part of the camp where the rest of my company was assembled. As it turned out, a lot of my new company turned out to be clever Group One and Two liars who managed to talk their way into what was considered *cream puff* duty in boot camp – namely Band and Choir Company. For instance, there was one guy who was immediately assigned as our Recruit Master At Arms (RMAA), a sort of policeman, because he was the biggest and strongest of us all with a low IQ to balance out his great strength. Just to show who was boss, this guy used to pick up the smallest guy in the company and do clean and jerks with him. I never saw the RMAA play and instrument or sing. But I never saw him show any special interest in radiators, either.

---

[9]Again with the word party! A "Working Party" was something you were volunteered to join so that you could enjoy the world of mopping, scrubbing, sweeping and polishing – all the things that are most often instantly recognized as being *fun* things to do.

As it turned out, the rest of boot camp was not at all what I expected it to be. I thought we would all be out running in the fields for hours with a rifle and pack, doing calisthenics and running through obstacle courses until our eyes bled. In actuality, we were not allowed to do *any* of those things. They were afraid that we would hurt ourselves and not be available on a moment's notice to play or sing at the official camp functions or executions. So, most of our exercise was limited to marching to and from classes and meals while singing "Anchors Aweigh" in full harmony whenever passing by another company running or marching in the other direction. And when we weren't in classes or eating, we were in band or choir rehearsal. Since I was only the backup tuba player, and the first-string tuba player (whom I never met) never seemed to graduate, I was not able to practice with the band even once during my entire stay in booth camp. Instead, I was always held back to clean the band room when everyone went off to practice. I never once laid my hands on a musical instrument except to lean it for someone else to play. But I got damned good at handling a mop and broom and a polishing rag, let me tell you.

Somewhere around mid-point of our thrilling boot camp experience, we were all marched off (singing all the way, of course) to take a battery of tests that were designed to tell the Navy in what fields our individual talents lay so they could assign us to do the exact opposite when we left boot camp. The tests took two full days to complete and covered everything from Mechanics (I didn't know a carburetor from a pipe wrench) to Quantum Physics – which no one in the Navy understood so the page was blank. One of the tests was called the FLAT, or Foreign Language Aptitude Test. They actually had someone make up a language for the test. For each section, you were given a few rules of this fake language and then told to use those rules to fill in a blank in a gibberish sentence with the correct form of a given word.[10] A few weeks after the tests were given we were all called in to talk to a Detailer whose job it was to assign you to your official job in the Navy based on the results from the tests. When asked what I wanted to do in the Navy, I told the Counselor that I wanted to be Hospital Corpsman (more commonly known in the Navy as a *Pecker Checker*). He laughed and informed me that, while there was, in fact, a great need for Hospital Corpsmen in the Navy what with Vietnam still going strong, three out of four went to Vietnam and three out of four of *them* didn't come back. I screwed up my nerve and told him in no uncertain terms that I wanted to change my mind and pick something else. I had previously also put down submarine Radio Operator or Torpedo-man on my "wish list". I was told that with my eyesight (I wore glasses), there was no way in hell that I would ever get on a submarine. Of course, my Recruiter assured me that with my grades in school, I would be a shoo-in for submarine school.[11] When I asked him what they needed, he told me that I had a perfect score in the FLAT test and that they recommended I be a foreign language interpreter. I had wondered what that test had been for. In High School I had taken two really exciting years of Latin, taught by a woman old enough to have been around when the language was spoken fluently. I really didn't do all that well in the class, mostly because I was bored to tears, but I did score second highest in the school in the Latin SAT test. Go figure. I had also taken a year of French after dropping out of a Physics class that I was flunking. I'd never flunked anything, and my parents would

---

[10]These were probably the same guys who decided that all things nautical should have their own names like *scuttlebutt* for drinking fountain, *head* for bathroom and *sheet* for ropes.

[11] Recruiters: you just can't shoot 'em.

have had a whole herd of cows if that had happened. I scored a perfect 'A' in French class. It was easy for me.

The Detailer proceeded to tell me that interpreter duty included overseas assignments in embassies where I would get to wear civilian clothes (for which I would receive a special clothing allowance) and work with foreign dignitaries in posh offices. Everyone raise your hand if you think he was telling me the truth. Now all of you who raised your hands go stand in a corner until you can come up with enough money to buy this nice bridge I own in Brooklyn.

I told the Detailer that sounded interesting and that I would consider it. He wrote it down as my fourth choice for duty. Then, with me sitting right in front of him and without any more discussion, he wrote at the bottom of the page that I was recommended for foreign language interpreter duty. So much for choices. Three weeks later I learned that I was to be sent to the Defense Language Institute West Coast (DLIWC) in Monterey, California for a period of 47 weeks to learn Mandarin Chinese. I was expecting "normal" languages like Spanish and French but Mandarin Chinese? I didn't even know that was more than one *kind* of Chinese! And just to show that the Navy really knew what they were doing, one of my friends in my company, Richard from Maine, had spoken fluent French before he could speak English. He, too, did well on the FLAT and he, too, was assigned foreign language interpreter duty. But not in French, which would have been logical. He went to Monterey with me to learn Mandarin Chinese. It cost the government tens of thousands of dollars to train someone for a year in a foreign language and here they had someone who could just walk into the job without any other training or cost. A Marine Lieutenant in our class had been born and raised in Korea and then, after being adopted by an American family, came to the U.S. and learned to speak English. He took the final exam to qualify him to be a Korean linguist and passed, but they wouldn't give him a "native speaker" status because, as they explained to him, they "didn't give those out". And instead of just making him a Korean linguist, they paid all that money to train him in Chinese and totally ignore his other fluency. Our tax dollars hard at work, huh? It's no wonder I didn't stay in long enough to retire.

I survived boot camp fairly well with few incidents other than severe boredom. I did find out later, however, that it was generally thought that my friend Richard and I were homosexual lovers because we spent so much time together. Here we go with the "queer" stuff again (the term "gay" had not yet been invented). It might have had something to do with our having volunteered to clean the showers all the time. We would strip down and take showers while we were cleaning them. It seemed the logical thing to do and it kept me from having to be naked in front of all the other guys in the usual group shower sessions. For some reason I never felt uncomfortable around Richard. But we were not to discuss my inner feelings until much later, though. There were still some things I didn't want anyone to know about, especially since I had learned early on to equate my condition as somehow being synonymous with "gay" which would immediately get you beaten to a pulp if not outright killed and then thrown out of the Navy in disgrace. I didn't need any more help with my image, thank you very much. One time we were allowed to go on "liberty" (we had a day off) and go into Chicago to do whatever we wanted as long as we were back on base by a certain time. Most of the guys went to bars and returned staggeringly drunk recounting how many times they'd gotten laid. I went to the Science and Industry Museum, The Sears Tower and the Natural History Museum. When we were all back in the barracks and talking about what we had done, Richard suggested that I not spread what I did on my liberty around. I valued his opinion, so I took his advice.

* * *

Thus began my nine-year career in the Navy. Even though I really hated most of this time, I did make a friend that I would remain close to for many years and who would become my closest confidante. Richard ended up getting married less than a year after we got out of language school when we were both stationed at the National Security Agency in Fort Meade, MD. Since the Navy to this point had not showed me any role models to help me understand who and what I was, and it seemed unlikely that it ever would, I started to think about marriage as a way to find my place in the world. He seemed comfortable enough with it. After all, how could I possibly feel like a woman if I had a wife and children? I was to learn a whole lot about myself in the coming years, sometimes painfully so.

But for now, I was off to Chinese Language School, Radiotelephone School and my first sexual encounter with a woman.

Chapter 7
First Times for Everything

I started Chinese Language School in the late summer of 1969. While on leave during the time between boot camp and language school I went camping with my parents at the same lake in Indiana that we had always gone to when I was growing up. It was only about 50 miles from Fort Wayne where I was supposed to catch my plane out to the West Coast. After an enjoyable respite from the idiocy of boot camp, I was excited to go to my very first duty station and my very first experience with the great outside world.

The morning I was to leave for California I went into the tent and changed into my brand-new Navy "Crackerjack" uniform. I was very proud of that uniform and my parents took great pleasure seeing me in it. We left the campground with what we all thought was plenty of time to spare. For some reason the traffic wasn't what we had expected, and we ended up driving into the airport as my plane was taxiing down the runway. Luckily for me another plane was leaving later that day that would get me into Monterey well before midnight. Midnight was important because, in the Navy, you have to report in to your duty station before midnight of the date on your orders. After that I guess you turn into a sea cucumber or something (pumpkins are for landlubbers). So, I changed my ticket for the later flight, and we returned to the campground for a leisurely early afternoon swim.

Later in the afternoon we left again for the airport with even more time to spare. This time the traffic was even worse. When we got to the airport, my plane wasn't taxiing down the runway this time. It had already taken off. I was officially starting to get worried. There was one more flight leaving for San Francisco

69

that evening that would allow me just enough time to get to the last flight from there to Monterey, getting me in before the magical hour of midnight. I changed my ticket again. This time I elected to just stay at the airport and wait for my plane so I could do something novel like getting on it before it left this time. My parents sat with me for a little while and then, with a few hugs, kisses and handshakes, left to go back to the lake. I managed to get on the plane this time and headed for my first duty station away from home and the beginning of my Navy "adventure" (it wasn't just a job).

The flight to San Francisco went, thankfully, without a hitch and I arrived with time to spare to get to my Monterey flight. I hurried to the gate where I was informed that…are you ready for this?…my plane was canceled because of heavy fog in Monterey. There were no more flights on any airline going into or out of Monterey for the rest of the night. Now I knew I was *definitely* in trouble. There was no way I was going to be able to get to Monterey before midnight now unless I drove. I didn't have money to rent a car and had no idea how far Monterey was from San Francisco, anyway (only a couple of hours' drive, as it turns out). My only recourse was to take the bus. I had called them to see what was available and found one leaving soon. Now I wasn't overly worried about this because they had told us in boot camp that if you ever had trouble and weren't going to be able to get to your duty station on time, all you had to do was call them and explain the situation. If it was out of your hands, you couldn't be blamed for anything. This situation seemed to fall into that category. This was the Navy! Surely, they wouldn't lie to me.

I called and explained the situation to them, informing them that the next bus into Monterey wouldn't get me there until the next morning. They assured me that there was no problem and that all I had to do was to check into the Quarterdeck (that's

Navy talk for the Main Office) as soon as I got in. Feeling better, I headed for the exits to find the bus station.

A man who said he was a taxi driver told me I had to go to the Oakland bus station to catch the bus for Monterey and that he could take me there. I got into his cab with another sailor who was going to Treasure Island for duty so we could drop him on the way. The trip to the Oakland bus station took over an hour. When we pulled up to the station and I paid the man, I noticed for the first time that there was no "Taxi" sign on top of his car. That struck me as kind of odd. When I went to get my ticket for Monterey, the man at the counter said I had to take a bus first to the San Francisco bus station and change buses there. It turns out that the San Francisco bus station was only a few minutes from the airport. My first time away from home and I'd already been fleeced. Welcome to the real world. I wasn't in Ohio any more. I got on the bus to San Francisco, where I changed over to my new bus for my final destination. This bus stopped at every dinky little town it encountered, no matter if there were people living there or not. It was a very long night.

By the time I got to Monterey, it was eight o'clock the next morning. Sailors were just getting ready to raise the flag in the courtyard at the Naval Postgraduate School as I walked into the Quarterdeck Office (I had to stop and salute first as the flag raising ritual took place). I announced myself to the Petty Officer of the Deck (POOD) and handed him my orders, explaining to him that I had called in like a good little sailor to tell them I'd be late. I was very proud of myself for handling my first Navy problem in "the real world" like such a professional. I figured that they would be very glad that I had done such a good job of following all the instructions that I had been taught. After checking to see that my story was true, the POOD immediately informed me that I was on restriction to the barracks until I was summoned for an XO's Mast. My Navy scorebook had just been officially started: Navy 1, Ricky 0. XO's Mast meant I had to stand at attention in front of the Executive Officer (the XO) of the Command and explain myself while getting chewed out royally. Restriction meant I couldn't leave the base. As I was just fresh out of boot camp, I still thought of Chief Petty Officers as one step removed from God (so did they). Having to face the wrath of a real live officer was unthinkable. They might as well have told me that they were going to rip out my fingernails with a rusty pair of Ebola-laced- pliers. They let me sweat in fear of this encounter for a full two weeks before they figured I'd learned my lesson. I was finally paraded in front of the XO who did his solemn duty in instilling the fear of the Navy in me, as if I didn't have enough already. It worked. I was never again late for any duty assignment; ever.

While I was waiting for my class to form at the nearby Defense Language Institute, I was assigned to *real* Navy work. I got to swab decks, chip paint and repaint the Hydrographic Research vessel that the Naval Postgraduate School had down at the docks. And as another first in my Naval career, I go to take my first trip to sea – on that 39-foot boat. Before this time, I had been out on Lake Erie once on a huge ferry boat. I hadn't gotten the slightest bit seasick at the time and, after all, Lake Erie was *huge* so this couldn't be so different, could it? Not only did I get seasick, I got seasick to the point where I was:

1) afraid I was going to die, and
2) afraid I *wasn't* going to die.

Somehow, I survived, albeit several pounds lighter upon returning to dock than when we left. I didn't volunteer to go out to sea on that boat again. After a few weeks, my Chinese class was ready to start. I packed my bags and moved to the top of the mountain overlooking the beautiful Monterey Bay.

* * *

The DLIWC was located on an Army base atop a large hill on the outskirts of Monterey. I said "mountain" before because I was from Northwestern Ohio. Where I came from, we had only *heard* of hills (and Catholics, remember) and this was much bigger than I thought a hill should be. The view of the bay was astounding and one that I never got tired of. The buildings all looked old and everything we did involved walking either up the hill or down the hill. We never had to worry about not getting enough exercise.

The barracks were really two-person rooms, complete with separate desks and lamps for studying. Every morning we had to assemble in the courtyard in front of the barracks for inspection where we stood at attention while an alcoholic Army Master Sergeant would stagger by, reeking of his liquid breakfast, and tell us our shoes were too long or that our hair needed polishing. We eventually came to pass the time trying to guess what he had been drinking this morning by the odor when he passed by.

Classes were different than anything I had ever encountered before or anything I expected. All of the teachers were native-born Chinese people who tried not to speak English in class unless there was no other way to explain themselves clearly. For forty-seven weeks, five days a week and six hours every day, we studied in an endless cycle of repetition and drills. We even took tapes with us to study in the lab after classes were over. By midway through the course, those of us who hadn't gotten kicked out for inability or insanity were speaking Chinese in our sleep (much to the annoyance of any roommate in the barracks who was taking a different language).

I had one odd thing happen to me while I was stationed in Monterey, though, that I didn't understand at first. One of my favorite things to do there during my time off was to go down to the beach and squat down to look at the little tidal pools to see the amazing life in them. I could (and did) sit there for hours just staring. I was from Ohio, and this was the first time I had ever seen the ocean, after all.

Once when I was spending time there, a complete stranger came up to me and struck up a conversation. He was a very nice, neat looking young man, impeccably dressed and seemed very friendly. We talked about the ocean and how much he loved it, too; about where I came from and what I was doing in Monterey. He said he lived up in San Francisco and liked to come to Monterey for the beautiful scenery. We talked for quite some while and finally started to walk up to Fisherman's Wharf for a little lunch. We stopped in the men's room, and he continued to talk to me at the urinal next to me, which I found odd. Then we went to wash our hands and he commented me on how great it was that I did that. It showed him that I was very concerned about being clean. That particular comment, along with his non-stop talking to me as I urinated, started to make a few alarm bells go off in my head. Something didn't seem quite right here. As we walked out of the men's room, he asked me if I'd be interested in coming up to San Francisco to stay a few nights with him and his roommate. Believe it or not, at this point in my life, I really didn't know anything about gay men or gay sex, or gay anything (remember where I came from). But this *really* didn't sound right to me. I told him I couldn't because of school and thanked him for the invitation and made my excuses that I had to get back up to the base. He said it was nice to meet me, shook my hand, and I walked away. When I discussed this odd conversation and behavior to my best friend who was much more worldly than I, he laughed and told me what this guy had been up to. He thought I might be gay and wanted me to join him and his "roommate" up in San Francisco for "a little fun". When he described to me what "a little fun" meant, I blanched. It was the first time, but certainly not the last time, that someone had thought I might be gay and had solicited me for something I wasn't interested in.

During that time, I had another first – I got rip roaring drunk on my eighteenth birthday. My friends found out that I had never drunk any hard liquor in my life, so they decided to make a man out of me (just what I wanted) and bought me a pint bottle of Old Crow bourbon. I thought it was a bit strong at first but after a few drinks it wasn't so bad after all. When they discovered half-way through the bottle (I was drinking it all myself) that I still didn't seem to be the slightest bit drunk, they dared me to chug the rest of it. Of course, I believed it wasn't going to have any effect on me at all, so I obliged and downed what was left. I still can't believe I drank the whole thing. I was sitting on the floor against a locker in a room in the barracks building where my friends were watching me expectantly. Suddenly someone shut off my equilibrium switch. My friend Richard from boot camp was sitting across from me watching carefully for signs of the inevitable with his feet braced against mine. All of a sudden, I couldn't sit up straight. I just fell over. I started to laugh and sat back up. This was definitely a strange feeling. I fell over in the other direction. I started howling with laughter, trying to sit up and not fall over the other way. Since we weren't supposed to be drinking in the barracks, my friends thought that it would be more prudent if we went outside to a small park in the woods where I could be as noisy as I wanted without getting us all in trouble.

I only remember bits and pieces of that night. They were having great fun with me, convincing me that I was back in boot camp and would be "AZMOed" (put back to my first day) if I didn't do 100 chin-ups. I could barely stand. Actually, after a few minutes I couldn't even do that. I remember pleading with them not to AZMO me and crying hysterically. Most clearly, though, I remember at one point falling down. Ordinarily this wouldn't be a big deal, but I distinctly remember falling and hitting my head very hard on a rock. I lay there staring at the rock with my brain trying to convince me that it hadn't been a good thing to do that. But I was amazed that it hadn't hurt. So, I stood up and fell down on it again. Luckily someone saw what I was doing and stopped me before I gave myself a concussion. As they carried me out of the park, I finally passed out. The last thing I remember was coming to in the shower where one of my friends was holding me and trying to get me cleaned up (and keep me from drowning) so they could throw me into bed.

The next morning, I experienced another first: I didn't have a hangover. My friends were amazed. They thought I was not going to able to function for another week at least, I had been so drunk. But aside from a slight upset stomach late in the afternoon, I had no ill effects from my first night spent in a drunken stupor. Nevertheless, I didn't like the feeling of not being in control of myself. When I had started laughing loudly, I had alternated it with crying. My "problem" with the way I felt inside was getting worse and was only exacerbated by my unfamiliar surroundings and loneliness. No one understood what the crying was about. They just thought I'd gone off the deep end. It was lucky for me that I hadn't said anything while I

76

was going through that emotional roller coaster. I never got drunk like that again.

Also during that time, I met a 15-year old boy named John who delivered newspapers to the barracks. We became close friends and would go bicycle riding often on the famous Seventeen Mile Drive in Carmel-By-The-Sea. He and his little brother and sister lived with their parents just a short walk down the hill from the school. John's father, Elmer, was a local school teacher. His mother, Lovey, was a British citizen who would tell me tales of when she had been a nurse in England during World War II where she met her husband. They became my family away from home. But something was horribly wrong with John's mother. She started spending more and more time in bed. I would visit her every day after school, and we would talk and laugh until the kids came home from school. Then in December of 1969, my school closed for Christmas break. Most of the students went home on leave and I was no exception. Before I left, though, I went down to John's house to say goodbye. No one but Lovey was home, but she welcomed me in and asked me to come into her bedroom. The room was unusually dark, but she asked me not to turn the lights on; they hurt her eyes. It was then that she told me what I had already come to fear. She was dying of cancer. The children didn't know – or at least she hadn't told them just how sick she really was. She told me that she didn't think she'd see me again after I left and that she just wanted to say goodbye. I tried to reassure her that I would see her when I got back but she was adamant. Then Lovey asked something of me that I hadn't expected. She asked me to take care of her family for her after she was gone. I didn't know what to say to this.

"There's something about you that you're not sharing", she said quietly. "I think it's something that you don't want people to know about you, but I think I've always known. You're not at all like any man I've ever known. That's why I like you so much. I'm grateful for having had you as a friend. I know that my husband and family will be in good hands with you to take care of them when I'm gone".

This was the first time in my life that anyone had seen through me so completely. I didn't know whether to be embarrassed or grateful. By this time, we were both crying. I thought of protesting what she was saying but I knew it wouldn't make any difference. She was dying, and she wanted to speak her mind. Even through all of this, I was still so ashamed of myself that I couldn't even bring myself to tell this wonderful woman the truth, even though she somehow already knew.

She was very tired and politely asked if I would go so she could sleep. She made me promise that I would look in on her family for her. We hugged and said our goodbyes. I told her that I loved her and that I'd see her when I got back from leave.

She was gone when I returned. There had been a nice funeral for her while I was away. The family was still reeling from the loss, the children especially. As I had suspected, they'd really had no idea how serious their mother's illness was. Elmer was trying hard to be stoic and keep the family from falling apart but he was suffering as much as if not more than the children. For the rest of the time I was in Monterey, I went down to John's every day after school, fixed dinner for the family and made sure the chores around the house were done by the kids. Elmer was very grateful for the help, and I was happy and honored to give it. Although it was a terribly sad time, it was also a very uplifting time for me. This was my first time actually playing a stereotypical role of the mother and wife in a household and I found that I enjoyed it immensely. Someone had seen me as I truly was for the first time in my life and had entrusted me with this important task. When I left Monterey in the summer of 1970, John and I wrote to each other for a while but somehow we eventually lost track of each other. I haven't been able to locate him or the rest of his family since. I miss them all.[12]

I graduated from Chinese Language School with a three-two rating. The rating system was set up on a scale of 1 to 4 with four being the equivalent of native-born speaker and 1 meaning "stick to English". The dual number system was used to differentiate between the ability to understand the spoken language and the ability to read the written language. All DLIWC language courses were designed to give the graduating student a three-two proficiency level, so I lived up to their expectations and exceeded my own. I had struggled with the language for the first few months and, when the rest of the class went to San Francisco for the Chinese New Year celebration, I took the opportunity to stay behind and have the teachers to myself for the entire day. That one day turned me around and was integral to my successful completion of the course.

Because of my ability in the language, along with my standing in the class and a small voluntary extension of my service obligation to the Navy, I was awarded the rank of 3rd Class Petty Officer upon my graduation from the next school I had to endure, radiotelephone school at Goodfellow Air Force Base in San Angelo, Texas.

* * *

San Angelo is a sleepy little town in the middle of Absolutely Nowhere, along the Concho River in west central Texas[13]. The

---

[12] My son helped me to find John but unfortunately what he found was John's obituary. He died in his early 50s. I spent two days crying when I heard this.

only reason the town exists is because of the military school (that is now long gone) and Angelo State University. I remember a sign along the road as you left the San Angelo airport that read, "Welcome to San Angelo, Texas, Home of Miss Wool of America", a tribute to the international tourist attraction contest held each year in honor of the local sheep industry. San Angelo actually was a nice little town, though. Everyone was friendly, and the atmosphere was always laid-back. You could walk from one end of town to the other in fairly short time.

Radiotelephone school was interesting but unexciting. I can't really say a lot about what I learned there because of security issues to which I am still held this day. But I did have some fun and some life-changing experiences there. While I was at Goodfellow I had a chance to visit Carlsbad Caverns in nearby New Mexico several times. It remains one of the most awesome places I've ever seen, and I highly recommend it to anyone who is enthralled by the wonders of nature. I also learned one day, upon observing a large weather balloon being released into the sky on the base, what the payload was that was hanging beneath it. A young Navy seaman in one of the classes pointed up in wonder during a break one day and wondered aloud what it was. An old Air Force Staff Sergeant looked at him and then looked back up at the balloon. With a perfectly straight face, he looked back at the seaman and asked, "You know how the Navy has burials at sea?" "Sure", replied the sailor. "Well, that's the Air Force's version". The sailor just continued to look up and uttered an awe-struck, "Oh!" The rest of us were trying hard not to fall apart laughing.

The biggest draw for the military boys at the base was to go to a little town in Mexico across the border from Del Rio, Texas,

---

[13] Turn right in Texarkana and drive for 3 days until you almost reach the other side of Texas.

called Ciudad Acuña, only a couple of hours' drive away. My friends at the base had heard of the town and thought it would be fun to go. They invited me along without telling me the real reason they were going. The main attraction was not the nice little shops that I was interested in where they sold hand-tooled leather goods or onyx chess sets; it was a little section of the back streets called "Boys' Town". Boys' Town was the only place in Acuña that had neon lights. Almost every building was either a bar or a brothel or both. I had never been to such a place in my life and I was very uncomfortable being there. Of course, the guys that I was with thought it was a hoot and made it a point to take me there. They thought it would be fun.

My friends took me into a little bar where we sat at a table and drank beer for a while. As we sat down, scantily clad women would come over and sit on my friends' laps, nibbling on their ears and asking for drinks. I didn't really know quite what to think about this but I tried to look disinterested so no one would come over and sit in my lap. It didn't work. A tall, cadaverously pale woman that reminded me of something out of a vampire movie came over and silently sat down in my lap. She wrapped her arms around my neck, quickly whispering something in my ear and then turned away. I didn't understand her at first. All I could say was, "What?" She looked at me like I was crazy and then bent down again and said, "Fuckie, fuckie?" The color drained out of my face. I was totally embarrassed and horribly uncomfortable. I'd never been in this kind of place or this kind of situation my entire life and I didn't like it at all. I couldn't think of anything to say that wouldn't offend this woman, so I didn't say anything at all. I just sat there sipping on my beer. Eventually, she gave up and walked away, looking for some other prospect. My friends had been paying as much attention as they could while keeping their own lap-mates happy with stimulating conversation. They asked me what was wrong. I told them that I didn't like this place very much and that I'd like to leave. They had other plans. One had already gone in the back with his first partner of the evening. Someone finally started putting one and one together and asked me if I'd ever had sex before. When I said no, they all roared. They'd never met an actual virgin before and found it hysterical that I was so uncomfortable in the bar. They also decided that it was their God-given purpose in life to get me laid that very night. I have to admit that part of me was curious at the idea but most of me was aghast at the notion that I might have my first sexual encounter with a woman in a place like this. I politely declined their invitation. And besides, I didn't have any money. That was all they needed to hear. They all reached into their pockets and put enough money on the table in front of me to pay for whatever I wanted to do. They said it was a gift. Again, I declined. They discussed this for a few moments and decided to take a different tack – they'd get me drinking until I was so drunk I couldn't say no. I thought they had given up. Instead, after a couple of hours and several pitchers of beer, the girls in the bar started to look pretty nice to me. I was feeling no pain. It was about that time when another woman came over and sat down in my lap, uttering the same elegantly phrased offer as the corpse before her. This time the guys put the money directly in my hands and all yelled together, "Try it! You'll like it!" Right then I discovered an ability that I didn't know I had. Somehow, I found that I could actually detach myself from what was going on around me. I literally felt as if I were watching myself from somewhere else as I let the woman take me by the hand into a little back room behind the bar. It was if it was someone else going through the motions. What a strange sensation. It turns out that I was to use this previously unknown ability in the future to get me through some very uncomfortable times.

The woman closed the door to the small room, took my money and started to get undressed. Fascinated and embarrassed at the same time, I stood there and watched as she became the first naked female I had ever seen in my entire life. I stared at her pendulous breasts, her wide hips, the small patch of hair between her thighs; all those things that I had so longed for myself. She was not a pretty or slim woman, but to me she was the most beautiful thing I'd ever seen. I didn't know what to do. She looked at me for a moment, standing fully clothed in the room and staring. She took my hand and said softly in broken English, "First time do this?" I swallowed hard and told her, "Yes". She smiled and started removing my clothes. My nakedness in front of her was thoroughly embarrassing and I tried to hide my rising maleness with crossed hands. She slowly pulled my hands away and, murmuring to me softly in Spanish, pulled me next to her on the bed. She began to stroke and kiss my body, trying to make me feel more at ease. The sensations of her caresses were thrilling to me but not as exciting as my actually being able to touch her. My hands moved timidly toward her body; toward her naked breasts. The hardened point of her nipples stood out in stark contrast to the surrounding velvet softness. I touched one breast, and then the other, reveling in the softness that was denied me. My exploring hands traced the rounded curves of her hips and, somehow finding courage, dipped hesitantly into the soft thatch of hair between them. She moaned slightly and lay back on the bed, pulling me with her. My mouth kissed her neck and then dipped to find the silky smoothness of her breasts. As I watched from somewhere in the corners of my mind, I saw my tongue exploring the musky dampness between her thighs. The smell and taste of her was almost overwhelming. I had no preconceived ideas at all about what female genitalia actually felt like and was surprised at the heady smell and wetness that I found. I lost myself totally in the

83

experience. Then I felt the strongest urge I'd ever felt in my life make my body rise and position itself between her opening thighs. Using her hand, she guided my erect penis into her. The sensation was like nothing I could have imagined. The warmth encompassing me made me feel like it would just melt in there. Somehow my body knew what to do and it began thrusting in and out of her. After only a few seconds, every nerve in my body started to tingle, which quickly grew into a nerve-shattering pulse ending with the most intensive orgasm I had ever experienced. (Up to that point the only ones I had ever experienced were self-induced. I had finally learned how to do it correctly.) My entire body shook with spasms washed over me as I froze above her, teeth clenched and eyes wide in pleasure. With what felt like my very life drained from me, I slumped slowly onto her body. As I lay on her, panting in exhaustion, I started to cry. Even though what I had just experienced was the most physically pleasing thing I'd ever felt, emotionally I was in turmoil. This body under me was what I had longed for all my life – not to have in a sexual sense, but as my own. Up until that time I had only imagined what a real female body would feel like. Now I knew. At that moment I realized just how far away the dream of having that body for my own was. It was hopeless. I had never heard of anyone being able to change their body in this way and, as far as I knew, there was no one else in the world that felt the way I did. I had never felt so trapped in my entire life. The woman below me wrapped her arms around me and held me as I cried softly into her hair. To her, I was overwhelmed by my first experience. To me, I was feeling utter despair.

After a few minutes, I arose and put my clothes back on in silence. I thanked her graciously and, after composing myself, left the room. Before reentering the bar, however, I stopped in the bathroom to urinate. My friends had told me that if you

84

urinated right after having sex, it would keep you from getting diseases. I believed them. What did I know? Luckily, I didn't catch anything. As I walked slowly back into the bar, a great cheer went up from my friends' table and I was greeted with slaps on the back and hearty handshakes. I tried to smile and make everything all right. I had just had my very first sexual experience – with a Mexican prostitute. I was so ashamed of myself. The depression that I felt at that moment and hid from my friends stayed with me for a very long time.

Chapter 8
Marriage and Other Performances

With radiotelephone school (and virginity) behind me, I proceeded to the second Army base I was to visit during my Naval career, Fort George G. Meade outside of Laurel, Maryland. I was to report to the National Security Agency (NSA) for duty. NSA was a very interesting place to work. The building itself is enormous. It boasts (or at least it did) the longest single hallway in any building in the world. You could run marathons in there. There were armed Marine guards everywhere checking packages and personal belongings coming in and going out of the complex. They were also stationed at each elevator to make sure that you had a sufficient clearance before you were allowed to get off at any floor. Curiously enough the base itself was open and unguarded. Anyone who wished could simply drive onto the base and cruise around whenever they want. I doubt that's true today. The only time I ever saw any security on the base was during the trial of Lt. Calley, the fall guy for the Army's massacre at My Lai in Vietnam. He, of course, was found guilty of following orders from his superiors and sentenced to prison. Overall, I can't really talk a lot about what I did at the NSA other than to say that I was helping to keep the bureaucracy of our country going strong behind closely guarded doors.[14]

* * *

There was really nothing very remarkable about Ft. Meade itself. It was just a typical military base where all of the buildings

---

[14] That and if I told you any more, I'd have to hunt you down and kill you.

looked the same. Just off the base on the perimeter roads were the prerequisite bars, fast food restaurants and substandard apartment complexes. But Ft. Meade had one thing that I had not yet encountered that would prove to have a huge impact on my life: the Special Services Division. Special Services was responsible for providing the base personnel with morale-building and wholesome entertainment activities for the troops such as ping pong, billiards and reading rooms – all the things that most of the soldiers never thought about while they were off base drinking themselves into as much of a stupor as their meager paychecks would allow. There was one program that they had that was wildly popular. Every Friday night they held a dance in which young women from nearby Baltimore and Washington D.C. were bused in and thrown to the wolves. A lot of these women, all USO volunteers, were looking for husbands. The soldiers were looking for something a bit different. This dance was known to the men as "The Friday Night Pig Push" because of their perceived lack of women there who looked like the fashion models that they deserved. Any of the women who were even moderately attractive were instantly mobbed by any man there who felt he was *God's Gift to Women*, which is to say most of them. I went to a few of the dances but was much too shy to actually ask any of the women to dance; something I didn't know how to do anyway. I always felt sorry for the poor girls left to decorate the wallpaper because they didn't meet the high standards of drooling soldiers and sailors on the dance floor.

Special Services did offer one thing that I took advantage of as often as I could. They had a piano. As I had been playing piano since I was very young it was something I looked forward to doing almost every day. As a child I hated to practice. As an adult I couldn't practice enough. I still wasn't very good, but I realized how much I missed playing. I still play – better, but nothing to write home (or in here) about.

One day when I went to practice, there was a notice on the bulletin board that caught my eye. They were looking for any interested base personnel to perform in an upcoming talent show. I was intrigued. Once when I was home on leave from language school my father showed me a cheap guitar that he got at a local auction one night. When he said he was going to throw it out I asked him if I could have it. I had become very interested in a new musical trio named Peter, Paul and Mary and thought that maybe I could learn to play guitar and do some of their songs. There was also a new soloist on the music scene by the name of James Taylor whose guitar-playing and songs had also captured my fascination (he's still my favorite). I brought the guitar back to Monterey with me, bought a book on how to play chords along with a book of Peter, Paul and Mary songs, and started to teach myself to play. I quickly found that I really loved playing. Sometimes I would practice so much that my fingers would start bleeding and I wouldn't even notice it until I stopped playing. I actually became quite decent at it. Now, with over a year of playing under my belt, I felt I might have sufficient talent to perform in public, so I decided to try out for the show. I played "Leaving on a Jet Plane" and a Richie Havens version of the Beatles' "Here Comes the Sun". Much to my surprise, I made it. I was now officially an entertainer. A whole new world had opened up for me that was to give me solace and pride for years to come.

We opened the show with a special performance for the officers on the base and were an instant hit. After a few more performances on the base for the regular servicemen and women, we went on the road and played at other bases in the area. There was one place we played other than base, though: the Jessup Men's Correctional Institute just down the road from the base. I'd never been in a prison before let alone going there to entertain criminals. This locale taught me a very important lesson in the world of entertainment – placement is everything. The performer that preceded me on stage was a voluptuous black woman who sang torch songs to canned music while walking through the audience sitting on the frenzied inmates' laps. When she finished, I came onstage; a geeky white sailor with black glasses playing guitar and singing "Leaving on a Jet Plane" to a bunch of guys that couldn't leave on foot. It didn't really matter, though. I don't think too many of them heard the lyrics I was singing. They were too busy yelling, "Bring back the broad!" to notice. I was supposed to play two songs, but I steeled my nerves, finished my first song and rushed off stage, feeling instantly sorry for any of the next performers who weren't "The Broad". But my desire to play was not daunted by this experience. It only served to enhance my drive to expand my repertoire.

* * *

While I was at Ft. Meade, I met a woman. My friend Richard, who had been with me through boot camp, language school and San Angelo, was stationed at the NSA along with me and several of our friends. Richard, who seldom wasted time in getting dates, met a girl at one of the Friday night dances and started to see her regularly. His girlfriend, Marion, decided to set me up with her best friend, Helen, on a blind date. Against my better judgment I went along with it and met Helen at Marion's house one evening. We hit it off right away and before the evening was over, we were kissing passionately on the floor. It turned out that Helen worked at one of the NSA satellite buildings near the Baltimore Airport which was only a few miles up the road from where the main building was. She lived with her mother in the northeastern suburbs of Baltimore.

After that first night Helen and I saw each other as often as possible. Then one day Richard and Marion announced that they were engaged to be married. We were deliriously happy for them, but it put a dangerous thought in our heads. A few short weeks later, after a courtship of barely six months, Helen and I decided to get married ourselves. I was 19. She was 18. Somewhere in the back of my mind I was screaming at myself not to do this. But that voice was overpowered by the other voice in my head that told me to grab the reins while I could. My "problem" had been getting bad before I met Helen and I realized that it had barely crossed my mind at all since we met. Maybe, just maybe, getting married would finally "cure" me. I stopped listening to the dissenting voice and forged ahead. Then we ran into Helen's mother Jocelyn.

Jocelyn was a woman of considerable power, both in her workplace and in her private life. A principal at a nearby elementary school, she had been living without her husband for years. He had just up and left her when Helen and her brother Andrew were not much more than small children. As a result, she had become a bitter and spiteful woman who hated men and kept strong control of her own household. Helen decided to break the news to her mother about us one evening while they were alone. It did not go well. When I was summoned to Helen's house to speak with her mother, I was as yet unaware of how the news had been received. Helen's silence upon meeting me at the front door was my first hint of things to come. Up until that point my relationship with Jo had been one of mostly cool indifference. We got along but rarely talked much. I had become good friends with Helen's brother, also a budding musician. I felt that my rapport with Helen's family was fairly good, although her mother was definitely an imposing and

90

intimidating figure. When Helen, her mother and I sat down at the dining room table, the tension in the room was choking. The worst I had expected was a level-headed conversation about responsibilities and the future. Instead, I was greeted with, "Well, *boy*, what do you have to say for yourself?"

From that moment on, the conversation went straight downhill.

There was no amount of explaining that I could do to make Helen's mother think that our marriage was a good idea. She cut me down at every explanation. I was soon reduced from calm, rational and adult to exasperated, offended and angry. We were told in no uncertain terms that we were *NOT* to get married; she wouldn't allow it. We tried to reason with her but there was just no way to get through. A young man was about to take her daughter away – a man to her who was bound to be just like all the rest. She couldn't and wouldn't accept it. I explained that I had just reenlisted in the Navy for another four years and had received a reenlistment bonus of $10,000 that would help us get started in our new life together. I had a steady job for years to come and, when I got out of the Navy, I was going to become a teacher like she had been. We tried hard to show her that we had thought this whole thing out very carefully before deciding. But she wouldn't listen. Instead of an adult discussion we got juvenile threats. Jo had signed for the loan that Helen got to purchase her car, so Helen made the car payments directly to her mother. Jo told Helen that she had a choice – either she left me or she left the car. Since the car was really in Jo's name, she had every legal right in the world to do whatever she wanted with it. There was no way for Helen to get to work without her car. She also said that not only would she not come to the wedding, she would make sure that none of her family would attend, either, and Helen would be excommunicated from her family forever after. We couldn't believe the things we were hearing. I finally left in a not-so-quiet rage with Helen at the steps crying. By the end of the week Helen had decided to move out of her mother's house and in with her friend Marion. We set the move up for a day in the coming week when we could both take off from work and, more importantly, when her mother was at school and not at home. She hadn't told her mother of her plans.

On the day of the move, we wasted no time in loading boxes and clothes into our two cars. We were down to our last couple of armloads when two of Helen's uncles pulled up and blocked our cars in the driveway. Unknown to us, Andrew had been in the basement of the house when we arrived and, when he saw what we were doing, called his mother who then called her brothers to get there and stop us until she could arrive. Just as quickly, Jo screeched up to the driveway and got out of her car, slamming the door behind her. While I listened to entreaties from her uncles imploring us to "do the right thing", Helen listened to the enraged ramblings of her mother reminding her that if she did this, she would never be welcome at home again. We tried hard to ignore the chaos surrounding us and tried to continue loading the cars. Helen and her mother became engaged in a tug of war with her last armload of clothes. I went up the steps to help, trying desperately to remain calm. Just then Andrew popped up from behind his mother waving a coat hanger at me and telling me to go away. I lost it. I jumped up and grabbed the hanger from Andrew, threw it to the ground and yelled at him to come out on the lawn and face me if he was so tough. This did not sound like me at all, but I was a bit beyond myself at the time.

At that moment, Helen's uncles came up from behind me and pulled me away, trying to get me to calm down. Helen pulled free from her mother and got into her car. I calmly asked her uncles to move their cars and, surprisingly, they did without any argument. I think they realized that this wasn't the emergency that they had been led to believe it was. They must have seen that Helen and I were the only rational people at the house right then. We drove off and left her mother shouting at us from the front porch of her house. We were married a short time later in a chapel on the base. Jo did not show up at the wedding, as she promised, and neither did anyone else from her family. We didn't hear from her again until our son Cal was born almost a year and a half later.

Chapter 9
Impending Fatherhood

As I stated earlier, I had just reenlisted for another four years. The Navy had dangled that $10,000 carrot in front of me along with the promise of another language school. I was going to go back to Monterey! As Helen and I had already been talking about the possibility of marriage, I thought this might just be the thing for us. Up until that point I had really enjoyed my time in the Navy and was seriously considering making it a career. The work was interesting and challenging and I really felt proud of my language ability. The only real problem with this rationale was that I really wasn't doing what the Navy had trained me for yet. I hadn't seen what my career was *really* going to be like.

Just before it was time for me to sign away another four years of my life to Uncle Sam's Bathtub Club, I had to sit down with the Navy Detailer to discuss what language I wanted to reenlist for. It was my choice. I had thought about this long and hard. I had learned one of the most difficult languages in the world and done a pretty good job of it, if I did say so myself. I figured that the Navy, understanding souls that they were, would cut me a break and would have no problem giving me something that wasn't so hard to learn for my second try. I told the Detailer that I had chosen Spanish as my second language. He looked through a long list he had in front of him and, after a few seconds said, "There don't seem to be any openings right now for Spanish linguists. Do you have anything else in mind?"

Of course I did. I had been prepared for just this sort of thing. I had taken French in high school and had received an 'A' after entering the course five weeks into it. I figured French would be a breeze. "French", I said with a smile.

He glanced back down at the list, shook his head and said "Sorry".

Now I was starting to get worried. I was running out of languages on my list. One of my favorite programs on TV while I was in high school was "Combat!" starring Vic Morrow. I had always wished I knew what the German soldiers were saying. I thought German couldn't be all *that* hard to learn. It was based on Latin, after all.

Again, I heard, "Sorry".

Quickly reaching my exasperation level and the end of my carefully planned strategy, I asked the Detailer what exactly there *were* openings for. This time he didn't even glance at the list (which should have told me something). He said, "Well, it seems they have openings for Russian, Hebrew and Arabic linguists right now".

I had to think fast. Russian had always seemed to me to be a strangely beautiful language. And even though they used a different alphabet than the romance languages, it was still phonetic instead of pictures that had to be memorized like in Chinese. What I had seen of Hebrew and Arabic were totally incomprehensible scrawling. And the sound of those languages! Sheesh! I held my breath, crossed my fingers and said, "Ok. I'd like to learn Russian, then".

After one more perfunctory glance at the list, the Detailer looked at me and said, "Russian language classes are full right now for the next couple of years. We might have openings in either Hebrew or Arabic, though."

Dawn was starting to break. I was being manipulated (fancy that!) but at least they were giving me a choice between the two final languages. I thought about it for a moment. If I didn't choose either language, I wouldn't be able to get the bonus check because my reenlistment program depended on my choosing another language. So, I had to pick one. I really knew nothing about either language except that I had heard Jewish friends of mine using Hebrew words from time to time – or was that Yiddish? (Oy vey!) I didn't know from Hebrew. The only thing I had in my mind about Arabic was a picture of either wild-eyed Islamic terrorists or nomads crossing the desert on camels that spat on them. Neither was too appealing. Resigned to my fate, I chose Hebrew.

The Detailer gave me his best sincere look and said, "What the Navy really needs right now is Arabic linguists."

Game, set and match! I gave up. I knew when I was beaten. This guy was a pro. I imagine he became a used car salesman or a televangelist when he got out of the Navy. When I signed the paperwork, I officially became the Navy's first Chinese and Arabic linguist. I figured at least that when I got out of the Navy the demand for my combined language skills would be overwhelming. Right. I didn't have a class start date yet – it would be at least a year. I was only two years into my first enlistment. The four years I had just signed up for were tacked on to the 4 years I was now serving plus the extra year I signed up for to get automatic 3rd Class Petty Officer out of Radiotelephone school (it had only been "awarded" to me on condition of extending my enlistment). I was now committed to nine full years in the Navy. And at least I was going to be sent back to Monterey. There was always that to look forward to – or so I thought.

I got my reenlistment bonus and Helen and I got married. We rented a small garden apartment, our very first real home, in the nearby town of Laurel, Maryland. We used the money to buy furniture and a new car. I paid cash for a brand new, top-of-the-line Toyota which, at the time, was about $2,500. Helen and I settled down to the prospect of a happy life together.

A few months later I got word at work that they were looking for volunteers for the Navy's new "Direct Support" school being started at Goodfellow Air Force Base back in good old San Angelo. If boot camp taught us one thing, it taught us that you NEVER volunteer for anything. When no one stepped up to the offer, the Navy did what it did best – it chose volunteers. I was one of those chosen to volunteer. On top of that I was chosen to volunteer to report directly to the San Miguel Naval Communications Station in the Philippines right after my school was over. Since I was being stationed in the Philippines for a period of three years, my new language school training was postponed. But the Navy had deemed me "command sponsored" which meant that I was going to be able to have my family sent over there at government expense, so it wasn't all that bad. Helen and I made our plans for the move. She was going to accompany me to Texas for my eight-week Direct Support School and then go to Ohio to live with my parents until I could find a place for us to live in the Philippines and send for her. When the time came for the move, we packed up a small U-Haul trailer and the car with our bags and our two cats Jerry and Bart (full name "Bartholomeow") and started the long drive from Maryland to San Angelo, Texas. During this trip we learned a valuable lesson – never feed your cats canned cat food (especially fish) and expect them to use the cat box in an enclosed space where you have to breathe the same air for a thousand miles. The assault to the olfactory senses is horrific. It does tend to keep you from falling asleep behind the wheel, though, because you tend to roll the window down and hang your head out to get air.

* * *

Direct Support School was nothing special. We just learned a few new things about what the Navy expected us to do with our language training to work in "direct support" with the captains of ships to keep the ship safe when sailing into potentially hostile waters. Helen and I had a generally good time there, but it was her first time being far away from where she grew up, so she had trouble adjusting. That, combined with our impending separation when I had to leave for the Philippines and the fringes of my problem starting to surface once again, began to create some tensions between us (she still knew nothing about what I was going through internally). But those tensions were soon laid to rest when we discovered that she was pregnant.

The news hit me like a rock. Me? A father? Was it possible? I was only 19! I hadn't thought about it much before. Could I be a good father with the way I felt about myself inside or would being a father help to push all those feelings aside more successfully than being a husband had? Was it too early for us to have children yet? How would this affect our move overseas? I had no idea how to answer any of those questions, but it didn't really matter because it was out of my hands now. The die was cast, and I was going to be a father whether I was ready for it or not. The more I thought about it the happier I felt. I was going to have a son or daughter that I could raise and show all the fascinating things the world had to offer. I could pass on my love for learning and reading and experiencing new things. I could share a bond the likes that I'd never known. I could make sure he or she would never be a Republican. Yes, maybe this was a good thing after all. The quarreling that had been escalating stopped and we were happy again.

When my school ended, we once again packed our belongings and animals into the car and headed to northwestern Ohio. The trip was uneventful except for a brief time that we got lost in East St. Louis at night. We had no idea that we were in what was considered at the time to be the worst area of St. Louis until we stopped at a diner outside the city later and talked to a waitress who was amazed that we were still alive. We had even stopped and asked for directions. The people there treated us well and gave us good directions to get back on the main road again, although they had a look of incredulity on their faces that we didn't understand at the time.

After a few days' visiting at home, I left for the Philippines with Helen, now showing her pregnancy, settled in with my parents. I sensed that they weren't too happy about the arrangement, but they accepted her without complaint. We said our tearful goodbyes at the airport, and I promised her that I'd get her to the Philippines as soon as possible. We would not be separated for very long. The Navy had promised me.

Right.

The flight to the Philippines was the longest I'd ever taken. I flew from Toledo, Ohio to San Francisco, switched to a military charter plane and then went on to Alaska, a brief stopover in Japan and finally to Clark Airbase in the Philippines. The bus trip from Clark to Subic Bay Naval Base was unbelievable. The road wound around a mountain all the way down into Subic with mountain on one side and cliff (with no guard rail) on the other. The road was barely wide enough for two cars to pass let alone a bus and anything else. The driver somehow managed to keep us from going off the cliff, even though he was driving at what I considered extremely unsafe speeds. I didn't see a lot of the scenery, though, because I spent most of the trip with my eyes closed. The only other time I've been that afraid riding in a car was a taxi ride years later in Rome.

In Subic I had to wait for another bus to take me to the Naval Communications Station about 20 miles to the north. The tropical heat and humidity at sea level were intense. It sometimes felt hard to breathe. No one had air conditioning. All the buses and cars rode with their windows open. The local taxis, one more elaborately decorated than the other, were called "Jeepnies" - sort of a cross between a Jeep and a Jitney - and had benches on both sides in the back for passengers with flaps to pull down over the sides during rainstorms. I was definitely not in Ohio any more.

One of the first things I discovered when I checked into my base was that the Navy had changed my orders. They were cutting my tour of duty at San Miguel from three years to two. That meant I could go to my new language school earlier that I had expected but it also meant that I was no longer command sponsored. I could still bring my family over to be with me for the two years I'd be there, but the Navy now wouldn't pay for it. They had already sent our furniture and other belongings over, but I was going to have to find a way to pay for a plane ticket for Helen to get from Ohio to Manila via commercial airlines. I didn't have that kind of money. And worse yet, since I wasn't command sponsored, we would not be eligible for the nice on-base housing they had and would have to live off base in extremely sub-standard housing with local water and electricity when it was available. I was furious. My wife was back home, pregnant, and expecting to be with me at any time and I was looking at an insurmountable cost for a round trip plane ticket for her. Our household goods were all there in Subic waiting for us, but I couldn't find a decent place for us to live or get her here. I didn't know how I was going to tell her.

I was able to call Helen soon after I got there via a phone system that used short wave radio to contact an operator in the States, who would then connect you with the party you wanted to talk to, only as a collect call. There was always a radio operator listening in who had to throw a switch from "send" to "receive" whenever you stopped talking and said "over". It was very strange. She didn't take the news well. She started crying. I tried to assure her that I would do everything I could to get everything changed back to the way the Navy had promised us, but it didn't console her much. It was no wonder because I didn't believe it myself. From that time on, every time I called her she became more and more hysterical as she became more and more pregnant. We spent hundreds of dollars that we couldn't afford on long distance phone calls, so she could cry plaintively in my ear. I tried several times to get the Navy to reinstate my three-year tour or at least get me command sponsored again so I could get her over there, but it was to no avail. There was nothing I could do. Helen was becoming more despondent every day.

I tried to keep my mind off of this as much as I could so I could do my job. I had traded my need to keep my mind occupied to keep from thinking about my gender identity problem for needing to keep my mind occupied to refrain from thinking about how badly the Navy had screwed me. After work, I spent most of my free hours scuba diving in the crystal clear, warm waters of the South China Sea. It wasn't a bad way to take my mind off of things. Up to that point I had only dived in the frigid, cloudy waters of Monterey Bay. This was like heaven. We could spearfish as much as we wanted and collect the abundant lobsters by hand. There were World War II wrecks to explore and a greater abundance of coral reef wildlife than I had ever believed possible. I got used to the heat and humidity after a while and loved meeting the native people and enjoying this beautiful land. I wanted nothing more than to bring Helen over to share all of this with her.

I was living in the barracks on the base because there was no other place for me to go. Conditions there were abysmal. It was always too hot inside and packed with bunks full of good old boys with pictures of naked women pasted all over their lockers. I hated it. I had met a young couple while I was there, Larry and Cathy, who lived on base in one of the houses that Helen and I were supposed to have gotten. We became very close friends. Larry and I would go scuba diving and bring back fish and lobster that we would catch, put it in their freezer and then have a big party when the freezer was full. We became so close, in fact, that they asked me to move in with them and get out of the barracks. I slept on the couch in their air-conditioned home and took care of their 2-year-old daughter, Lisa, whenever they were out. It was strangely one of the most wonderful times of my life while being one of the worst. Larry and Cathy and I would sit up for all hours of the night just talking about anything and everything. I grew to trust and love them so much that, for the first time in my entire life, I opened up to them about my struggle in life. I had never told another soul about it. Thankfully they were also the first people to show sympathy and caring for me about it.

* * *

Time was becoming critical. I had been in the Philippines for almost six months. With only a little more than a month left before our child was to be born and Helen becoming more hysterical with each phone call, I knew I had to do something. I

101

had discovered that our jobs at San Miguel were being phased out and they were planning on moving everyone to Clark Air Base within a few months. With that in mind, I did two things. First, I put in a request with the Navy Bureau of Personnel (BUPERS) to see if I could get assigned immediately to Arabic Language School. Then I put in for 30 days' leave beginning the first of June. I stated my reasons for leave as wanting to be with my wife when our child was born, adding that her mental condition was deteriorating, and I thought it was very important that I should be there with her. I sent the request through the chain of command feeling certain of being granted the leave. My immediate supervisor, a Lieutenant J.G., approved it and sent it on. It was immediately shot down by his superiors. Comments returned on the officially denied request stated that 1) it would cost me too much money to go back home, 2) I didn't have the leave time on the books to take that much time off, and 3) my job there was too critical for them to allow me to leave then. I was furious. I attached a rebuttal of all of their reasons in preparation to send it back through the chain of command. I had taken a loan out to get the money for the trip home and back so that wasn't a problem. Even though I didn't have 30 days' leave on the books, I had six more years' obligation to the Navy with plenty of time to make that up. I reminded them that our job was so "critical" that we were all working reduced hours in expectation of our move to Clark. I added a note from Helen's doctor back home stating that her mental state was such that my absence could be detrimental to her health and the baby's health. I sent the request through once more. In the meantime, I went to the Base Chaplain to get some advice. He told me, in his infinite wisdom and overflowing concern, that he had been away from home each time one of his children was born and that I should just accept my superiors' decision. Like THAT was going to happen.

Again, my request was refused.

This time I was *really* pissed – so pissed that I did something that most sailors wouldn't ever think of doing. I immediately exercised my rights under the Uniform Code of Military Justice (UCMJ) by requesting a Captain's Mast – a face to face meeting with the commander of the base. There are two reasons for calling a Captain's Mast: when a sailor is about to be busted or jailed (or both) for some serious infraction of Naval rules, or if a sailor needs to meet with the captain to air a grievance after all other avenues up the chain of command have been exhausted. As you can imagine, although every sailor has the right to call a Captain's Mast, officers up the line don't take kindly to a lowly sailor going over their heads. My case was no different. My Captain's Mast was quickly scheduled. I was now officially lower than dirt in the eyes of every officer in the line of command. But, by law, they couldn't do anything about it. I was afraid but determined to have my day "in court".

At the same time, I requested the Captain's Mast, I sent a copy of my leave request and all comments and rebuttals to BUPERS asking them for some relief. I was burning more than a few bridges but I didn't really care. But this particular bridge burning turned out to be worth it.

Just days before my meeting with the Captain was to occur, I received a notification by wire that I was being transferred at the end of June to the Defense Language Institute for Arabic Language School. I was even granted 30 days' leave. Since our baby was due to be born sometime in the middle of June, chances were that I wouldn't be able to be there for his birth but I'd sure be there soon afterward. It was better than nothing.

I quickly cancelled my Captain's Mast request and rushed the BUPERS letter to the base Personnel Office to make sure they knew about it. Within hours I received a call ordering me later that week to report to the office of every officer up the chain of command (except the Captain's). My rear end was now fair game, and they were all going to be certain to get a piece of it.

The very next day I got another wire from BUPERS changing the orders that they had just sent to me the day before. This one ordered them to transfer me to Language School immediately – not at the end of June – and granting me 60 days' leave instead of just 30! I couldn't believe my eyes. Someone in the Navy actually cared. I was actually going to be home for the birth of my child.

The personnel office on the base cut me orders to leave within the week – just two days away. It was hardly enough to time to take care of everything in preparation for leaving. I had to start packing immediately and, at the same time, go all the way to Subic Bay to complete the paperwork that would send our household goods that had been sitting there for months back to the States. I hardly had time to breathe.

The officers on the base made sure I had time enough to breathe in front of them, though. My tight schedule for leaving was not going to interfere with the ass chewing they were looking forward to so much. With each office I visited up the line, the verbal abuse got worse. I was chastised loudly and firmly at each level for not having faith in the judgment of the officer I was facing. I was even further harangued for having withdrawn my request for Captain's Mast and going behind their backs to BUPERS, everything that was perfectly within my rights. In their eyes I was now lower than *whale sperm*, a delightful little naval term used to describe unsavory types like me. But I didn't mind at all. I just kept thinking that I was going to be home for my baby's birth and the officers' rants didn't faze me a bit. And that made them even madder at me. They wanted to see me cower. I wanted to go home. As a result of all of this, my opinion of the Navy, once very positive, had sunk to an all-time low. I realized that I was nothing but a number to them and nothing else. My respect for them and for the Navy had almost vanished. And I still had almost six years left. What had I done?

Before I left, I managed a tearful goodbye to Larry and Cathy and promised to keep in touch. Somehow, though, we managed to lose track of each other through the ensuing years and I wasn't to find them again for another thirty years.

* * *

I made it home in plenty of time for our son, Cal, to be born in the very same hospital in Bryan in which I was born. I wasn't able to be at Helen's side in the delivery room (they didn't let husbands in there at that time) so I spent the time worrying in the waiting room. Cal was born with no complications and no health problems. I was a father. I can hardly describe the feeling of looking at my brand-new son and knowing that he was a part of me. There still was a part of me that was jealous that Helen had been able to carry him and give birth to him and I couldn't but for the time being, I was content to hold this miracle in my arms.

We bought a mobile home just outside of town and began to settle into our new lives as parents. After a month in Ohio resting and getting used to our new family status, we made plans to move to my next duty station. That was the one bad thing about the orders that they had given me for school. I was not going back to Monterey for Arabic. I was going to the Defense Language Institute *East Coast* in Washington, D.C. for school. I didn't even know they had a school there. But it was still better than being stuck in the Philippines with Helen and Cal trapped in Ohio away from me. We were originally told that the Navy would move our mobile home to our new duty station but, after we had bought the home, we found out that was not true. Imagine that! So, we had to put it up for sale and find a place to live in the Washington suburbs. We settled on an apartment complex in nearby Alexandria, Virginia. Unknown to me at the time, this move was going to be the turning point in my life and my quest for inner peace.

Chapter 10
Awareness and Knowledge

My schooling in Washington, D.C. was much different than what I had experienced in Monterey. The beautiful seascape had been replaced by a vast expanse of concrete and buildings; what had been the warm salt air was now reeking with the exhaust of hundreds of thousands of cars stuck in constant traffic jams. The school, which no longer exists, was situated on a small plot of land on the far end of Bolling Air Force Base, just across the Anacostia River from the Washington D.C. Navy Yard. The school was much smaller than its counterpart in California. My Arabic language class consisted of only six people – two Marines, three Army Specialists and me. The class demeanor was totally different as well. In Monterey, the presence of officers kept the classroom orderly and respectful. In Washington, we had no such luck. One of the Marines in the class was constantly disruptive and highly disrespectful of our teachers, all of whom were native Arabic language speakers and all very nice, extremely polite people. I always felt awful for the teachers having to put with the treatment they got in class. The other Marine was just lost all the time and didn't do well in class. He ended up being almost as disruptive as his fellow Marine. One of the Army Specialists in the class was so disgusted by the constant trouble in the class that he eventually just closed himself off and refused to participate in any classroom discussions. Another of the Army Specialists was a man who was having problems at home based on his marrying a self-described witch who was divorced from a self-described warlock, who was now putting evil spells on his ex-wife and her new husband. Other than that, it was a great learning experience. The one Army Specialist left in the group, and I were

107

the only students who were genuinely interested in learning the language.

At the end of the year with the proficiency exams coming up, the classroom tensions had become so unbearable that a few of us went to the director of the school to ask that we be allowed to study separately from our classmates. Thankfully, our request was granted. Those of us who studied in our little group passed the proficiency exams. I passed with a 3-3 level – 3 in both listening and reading comprehension. I did so well, in fact, that I was awarded the rank of Second-Class Petty Officer upon graduation. The others who did not study with us did not do so well. I saw the disruptive Marine months later back in San Angelo. His Arabic was so bad that he had flunked out of radiotelephone school and was mopping floors waiting to be assigned to some other duty for service people with no discernable abilities. There is some justice in the world sometimes.

My home life during this time was becoming more and more strained. Helen and I had rented a small apartment in Alexandria about ten miles as the crow flies from my school but at least a 45-minute drive each way because of the horrible traffic. Our son Cal was basically still a newborn, and we were struggling during his first year with all the problems, restrictions and reality checks that hit all starry-eyed parents during this time. Because of the cost of living in the area and my meager military paycheck, we were quickly developing money problems. I decided to take a part time job after school at a local 7-Eleven store down the street. On the weekends when I had to work, Helen would take Cal and spend the weekend with her mother in Baltimore. Remember how her mother treated us when we were married? The subject of her mother was the first of our many arguments to come.

Because of the way that Jocelyn had treated us I wanted nothing whatsoever to do with her. But with the birth of Cal, her first grandchild, she suddenly decided that she wanted to be part of our lives. Helen and I argued long and hard over whether or not her mother should even be allowed to set foot in our house. Helen eventually won and, without even so much as an attempted apology, her mother started coming to our house to see her grandson. It was all I could do to be polite to her during these visits. Those feelings eventually faded to mutual dislike and feigned civility. She never apologized for her actions. I never expected her to.

It was during my time in Washington that I saw something that would forever alter the course of my life. One night a local TV station news team advertised that they were going to run a week-long news segment during their 11 o'clock program on a little-known phenomenon that was being treated at Johns Hopkins University Medical Center near Baltimore. The condition was called *Transsexualism*. I'd never heard this term before but when they explained that it concerned people who felt that they had been born in the wrong body, every awareness molecule in me went into overdrive. I had to learn more. I tentatively broached the subject with Helen (without saying *why* I was interested) and she dismissed it at once as being a sick condition of a sicker mind. I was disheartened by her reaction but determined to watch the series with or without her. She still knew nothing about how I felt inside.

During the next week I was glued to the television every night watching the 11 o'clock news for their short segments. Of course, since it was a very controversial subject, they always waited until the very end of the half hour to put the segments on but I didn't really care. There were interviews with both doctors and patients in the program at Johns Hopkins and discussions of what Transsexualism was and what it was not. As I listened to the patients talk about their lives as children, my own childhood came crashing back to me. The feelings of something being terribly wrong; of knowing that I was a girl when no one else could see; the loneliness of school; the attempts to do things to find my rightful place in the world as a man – all of these were *my* stories! And these people had lived the same life! The realization that I wasn't alone after all was staggering. Before this time, I had no idea that anyone else in the world shared my problem. Now I not only knew that there were others like me but that were actually people who could help! Every night that week I went to bed on the verge of tears, my mind racing with possibilities and the fear that went with them. What would happen if I looked into this more? Would I lose my wife and child? Would the Navy find out? Would I lose my security clearance and be kicked out of the Navy on a dishonorable discharge? Would I lose my family and friends? The fears began to weigh heavier on me than the problem itself.

Of course, I couldn't keep my emotions hidden from Helen and she soon coaxed the reasons for my depression from me. She did not take the answer well. When I told her that I was considering contacting the hospital in Baltimore to be evaluated and maybe helped, the subject was closed. She wanted nothing to do with this and wanted to hear nothing more about it. I was more alone now than I had ever felt. The woman that I loved had basically told me that I disgusted her and warned me of the consequences of following up on this to any length. But I had no choice. I had to know. I secretly called the reporter at the TV station that had conducted the week-long report and asked her for help. She seemed genuinely sympathetic and gave me phone numbers to call at Johns Hopkins. She asked me to contact her again later to let her know how things were going – a request I was to hear many times during my quest for identity.

I chickened out. Helen's reaction fed my fears so well that I couldn't bring myself to call the hospital. I couldn't do anything that could possibly risk my losing her and Cal. They were my life and my lifeline. I was also convinced that the Navy was watching me and would somehow find out about my calls, kicking me out of the Navy in disgrace. The first real voice of help in twenty years beckoned to me but I couldn't answer. I was more depressed than ever.

After this episode, Helen's trips to Baltimore became more frequent and the stays longer. While she was gone, and I wasn't working at the 7-Eleven, I began cross-dressing again. I became more brazen with time and would wear a bra in front of her as a "joke". She would play that she was mad at me, and I would play that I was hurt. But deep down inside, we both knew that neither of us was playing. I quit my job at the store and took a job as a waiter (waitress to me) at a local restaurant chain where I could make better money. I would come to work wearing a bra (no padding), panties and girdle (I was practicing holding "myself" tucked between my legs) under my waiter's uniform and no one seemed the wiser. I was the only male waiting on tables at the restaurant, so the cross-dressing made me feel more like part of the group. And, of course, being a waitress was such a typically female job that I felt that I fit right in. I don't know how much of this that Helen knew was going on; I don't think she suspected anything. If she did, she didn't let on. But she didn't have to. The distance between us was widening more every day.

* * *

After graduating Arabic Language school in Washington, I was reassigned to my old haunt in Texas, Goodfellow Air Force

111

Base in San Angelo. My further orders were to report to a four-year tour of duty at the Naval Communications Station at Rota, Spain upon completion of training in Texas. Over my objections, Helen finally persuaded me that it would be too disruptive for Cal to have all of us move all the way to Texas for just eight weeks and then move again all the way to Spain. She said she could use the time to spend with her mother until we had to leave the country for so long a period of time. So, I reluctantly left for Texas by myself, leaving my wife and child behind. Something didn't feel right about her insistence that I go alone but I was too blinded by love and need for her to be happy to really feel that anything was amiss.

San Angelo had not changed at all, and the classes remained the same as they had always been – only with a different language. I was lonely and missed my wife and son and called home often. More often than not, though, Helen was not home to receive my calls. I could never get a real answer from her mother on where she was almost every evening that I called, and I slowly began to feel that something was wrong. My feelings were justified when I finally got in touch with her one night near graduation to tell her a plan that I had. I had some extra money saved up along with plenty of leave time on the books. I thought that it would be a great idea for her to come out to Texas for my graduation. Then we could spend a couple of days together seeing Carlsbad Caverns and just enjoying ourselves alone before we had to move to Spain. I figured that would be a difficult change in our young married lives and some time alone would be good for us. It made perfect sense to me. Her mother could watch Cal for us for those few days we'd be gone, something she had always offered anyway.

I was unprepared for the answer I got. Helen felt it would not be a good idea to come down but could not offer any decent reasons for it other than we shouldn't spend the money. I was really hurt. We had been away from each other for almost two months and she didn't want to come spend time alone with me. Marriage wasn't supposed to be like this. She was supposed to want to be with me as much as I wanted to be with her. I began to suspect that something else was going on. The more I thought about all the nights I had called when she wasn't home and never offered reasons why, the more I came to the conclusion that there might be someone else. As much as I tried to tell myself that this could just not be true, I couldn't convince myself. My suspicions mounted, and my anger grew. As I became more despondent over the situation, I found myself thinking that "what's good for the goose is good for the gander" and actually started thinking about having an affair myself. The thought was morally repugnant to me, but I was so hurt that all I wanted to do was to hurt back.

I had met a girl at a party some time before and I found myself contacting her again. We went out on a date, and I actually brought her back to my room in the barracks. As we sat on my bed kissing, I felt more and more ashamed of what I was doing. We stopped and talked about it. She felt that I was justified in my suspicions of Helen and also felt that what we were doing was not right. Just then my roommate walked in and saw us sitting together on my bed. Embarrassed, he excused himself and left hurriedly. I took her home and we never saw each other again. As it turned out, though, this little episode found its way into my life once more from the mouth of my roommate who was to later become a vindictive rival for my wife's affections.

Chapter 11
Divorce and a New Beginning

With school in Texas over, Helen, Cal and I moved to southern Spain. By now, Helen and I were arguing constantly. The situation wasn't helped any by having moved to a new place with totally unfamiliar surroundings and a new culture. Our household goods had gotten delayed in transit, so we had to rely on borrowed items from the base to get by in a strange, empty apartment. Because Helen knew no Spanish (neither did I at the time), she didn't feel comfortable venturing out in the town for quite some while, so she stayed in the apartment with only a small radio and Cal for company while I went to work on the base. By the time I got home in the evening she was ready to climb the walls. There was little I could do to help. The tension and arguments increased, and our marriage continued to crumble.

I soon discovered that my job on the base was primarily to be sent out for what they called T.A.D. (Temporary Additional Duty) on board Fast Frigates, Destroyers or Aircraft Carriers traversing either the Mediterranean Sea for one month or the Indian Ocean for three months. The division in which I worked operated on a revolving schedule where, as one person left to go out to sea, every person below him on the list moved up one place. When the guy who had gone to sea got back, his name went to the bottom of the list where it gradually worked its way back to the top for his next turn to go. It was always a good thing when new people came to the station because that meant more names for the list and less sea duty for everyone. The only exception to that was when the new arrival was a woman. Although women were taught the very same skills as the men at all the same schools, they were not allowed to go to sea. So, they

114

had to stay back at the station and basically do the clerical work that came with the job. A woman's arrival didn't help the sea schedule at all. And because there were more bodies at the station, there was less work to do when the men got back from sea, increasing resentment against the women, along with tension and boredom. One of my best friends at the station was a woman who was in just such a position. She was infuriated that although she was as highly trained as any man there (and more so than many), she was not allowed to do her job simply because she didn't have a penis. I didn't blame her one bit for her anger. It was a lose-lose situation all around for the women.[15]

My turn to go out to go out on TAD came almost immediately upon my arrival. New people were almost always sent out as soon as they arrived. At least they waited to send me until my household goods were finally delivered. I was gone practically the next day to the Indian Ocean, leaving a wife and child alone and frightened for three months in a place where they knew no one. The Navy always expected husbands and wives to be able to handle such situations by themselves, no matter how long they had been married. Our relatively new marriage was not fated to survive this type of life. No matter how much Helen and I argued I still loved her with all my heart. She and Cal were my entire life. Without them I was nothing. I wrote every day while I was out at sea, professing my love and promising that things would be better when I got back. I got sporadic letters from her describing her gradual acceptance of the Navy wife's life in Rota.

---

[15]When describing my Navy experiences to people, I describe my woman friend's story. It wouldn't do to tell people that I went out on board ship constantly during a time when women weren't even allowed on supply ships, let alone warships. I don't claim her story as mine, just that women weren't allowed on ships. Sneaky, huh?

My time at sea was torture. The longer I was away from Helen and the more time I had on my hands, the more my mind returned to my inner problem. Time on my hands was the worst thing I could possibly have. If I didn't keep my mind active at all times, I would soon revert inward to a horrible state of depression. To fend that off, I learned to take along two bags when I went to sea: one contained my clothes and the other held nothing but books. I would read every one of those books by the time I returned. Work on the ship for us was generally "port and starboard" or twelve hours on, twelve hours off. On my time off I was either reading or back at work helping – anything to keep myself from having time to think. It was the only thing I could do to keep my sanity. My three-month TAD tour went agonizingly slowly.

One reason I joined the Navy was to be in the company of men with whom I could identify and find my place in society. I could not have made a bigger mistake. Men in the branch of the Navy that I was in were generally above average intelligence and we got along fine. However, the guys assigned to permanent ship-board duty were another thing entirely. If I had thought that the boys in high school were bad, I hadn't seen *anything* yet. These guys made those Neanderthals look like the peak of high society. I discovered this during my first TAD trip from Rota.

One day when we were getting ready to pull into a port for resupply, I happened along some of the guys talking in the berthing area about what they were going to do on liberty in town. They all had a common goal: to get laid. They couldn't wait. They even set up a contest to see who could do the most disgusting thing to the worst looking prostitute they could find. The more I heard these guys talk about what they planned to do, the angrier I got with them. Finally, I could keep my mouth shut no longer. I looked at the men in total disgust and asked, "How

116

can you guys be saying this?" I pointed to one of the men. "You have a wife at home." I pointed at the others. "You have a fiancé and the rest of you are always talking about your girlfriends back home. How can you even think about going out on liberty and messing around knowing they're back home waiting for you?"

They all glared at me. One of them finally said, "Well, we have needs!"

I just looked at him and replied, "What if your wives and girlfriends have needs? What if they're home right now filling those needs?"

Almost as one, they answered, "Well they God damned well better NOT be!"

What morons! It was ok for them to fool around on their wives and girlfriends when they were so far away from them, but it was unacceptable for their wives and girlfriends to do the same to them. I tried to explain to them how stupid that sounded but was stopped dead in my tracks when one of them asked me, "What's it to you? Why do you care? What are you, a faggot?" They were now all looking at me with contempt.

There was no way I could explain myself to them without getting myself into bigger trouble. To them, if I wasn't looking forward to the same things they were, I was less than a man. Worse yet, I might be *GAY!* It was well known during that time what happened to a sailor who was thought to be gay. Late on a moonless night, a bunch of these real macho types would lure the unsuspecting target to a dark corner on the deck of the ship, throw him a nice blanket party (remember those from boot camp?) and toss his unconscious body over the side into the dark water. No one would even know that the sailor was gone until roll call the next morning; and by then the ship had sailed hundreds of miles. The sailor was almost never found.

117

All I could do was shake my head at the guys and walk away in disgust. The sooner I got away from them, the sooner they'd forget about me. I never heard another accusation from them again and I didn't get a blanket party.

After the port call, I happened along these same men discussing who had won their "most disgusting act" contest. The winner had actually performed oral sex on a really ugly prostitute who was having her period. Suffice it to say, it was *totally* disgusting; and it totally delighted the crowd of men willing to listen to him.

When I returned to Rota, things really hadn't changed much. Although Helen had finally acclimated to the local culture and felt relatively at ease in Spain now, our relationship was still rocky and my arrival at the dock was greeted with forced affection. We were moving further from each other with each passing day.

Life now was very difficult. As much as I had missed Helen when I had been out to sea, I was beginning to look forward to being at work to escape the tension at home. I turned to my guitar and music to relieve the tension as much as I could. This eventually led me to a group of people in Rota that would have an enormous impact on my life.

Just off base in town was a USO compound complete with a small restaurant, game rooms and, most importantly for me, a small thatched-roof building that was affectionately called "The Last Straw Coffeehouse". The Last Straw was a haven for musicians and performers on the base. Operating every Friday night, the stage was open for anyone who had the nerve to get up and perform. The mascot of the Coffeehouse was a frog that lived in the thatched roof. The main and abiding rule of the stage was that whenever the frog started to croak, you had to stop playing so everyone could listen. Someone even made up a picture of the frog sitting on a toadstool playing guitar. He became both our mascot and advertising banner. One of the star performers at the time, a man everyone affectionately referred to as "Track", became one of my closest friends and remains so today. Track played guitar and sang with a beautiful and deeply resonant baritone voice that filled the Coffeehouse. I never got tired of hearing him play and sing.

Another person who sang there regularly was a young girl named Lynne. She had a tremendous voice that was always a pleasure to hear. She also had a very strong, outgoing personality that was quite infectious to all around her. She lived with her parents on the Base where her father worked as a Chief Petty Officer. She was almost 18 and graduating from high school but was still considered a dependent. Helen and I started going to the Coffeehouse soon after I returned from my first trip to sea. After hearing others play for a few weeks, I screwed up my courage and took my turn on the stage one evening. Much to my surprise, I was an immediate hit. I had learned the entire 25-minute version of Arlo Guthrie's "Alice's Restaurant" and performed it on the first night as my final number. It brought the house down. I soon became a fixture at the Coffeehouse which caused me to throw myself into my music to learn more songs and enhance my playing ability on the guitar. It also helped give me something to take me away from the problems at home, if only for a short while. Helen and I came to consider the musicians at the Coffeehouse as close friends. For my part, they were becoming family. We never missed a Friday night, and I never missed a chance to learn and play new material.

After a few months of being back at the base and becoming involved at the coffeehouse, my turn to go out to sea had come up again. By this time, Helen and I had become somewhat closer, although we still argued a lot. We had discovered that she

119

was pregnant again and were really trying to make things better between us. Our marriage was still rocky, though, and when I found out that it was my time to go out again, I asked to be switched with the man who was just below me on the list, with his permission, of course, so that I could have a little more time at home. The Navy, mustering all its understanding and compassion, promptly denied my request.

Before I knew it, I was off for another three-month cruise in the Indian Ocean. But this time it was different. Although I wrote to Helen constantly, I received even fewer letters from her than before. Ever the optimist, I just figured something was wrong with the mail system and I just wasn't receiving her letters. Then tragedy struck. We had been out to sea for about two months and had just left Mombasa, Kenya when I was called into the Executive Officer's wardroom for bad news. I was informed that my wife had just had a miscarriage and was in the hospital. They assured me that she was all right health-wise, but that I had the choice of either staying on the ship to finish my tour of duty or to leave when we got to Karachi, Pakistan in a few days. The Navy was offering to put me on the first flight out of Karachi back to Spain. They also informed me that Helen had told them, oddly enough, that it wasn't necessary for me to come back home. That one was really hard to understand. I was sick with worry and thought that my place was by her side at such a time. We had just lost our second child, for heaven's sake! How could I possibly even think of being anywhere else? How could she *not* want me to be there? Even though I felt that the Navy really would rather I stayed on the ship, I decided that my family was a whole lot more important and announced my decision to leave. When we got to Pakistan, I was relieved of duty and given a ticket back home to Rota via Rome and Madrid.

When I got back home, things were even worse than I had imagined. If my homecoming from the first trip had been cool, this one was positively icy. I felt as if I was intruding in my own home. I wanted to hold Helen and kiss here and tell her that I loved her and that everything was going to be all right. I wanted to let her know that I hurt from the loss of our child just as much as she did. But she was strangely detached from the whole situation. It really didn't seem to bother her at all. And she had changed in other ways. She was dressing differently, less conservatively than before, and wearing much more makeup than I had ever seen her wear. Even her demeanor was different. I couldn't quite put my finger on it, but I knew that there had been a profound change in my wife. That night, the first night I was home after she had suffered a miscarriage, she told me that she was going to leave me.

In the movies when something like this happens all sound stops and there is nothing left but stunned silence. That's how I felt. I could hear nothing and feel nothing. Those words were like a knife in my soul. I just didn't understand. When I regained my senses, I told her that we should really talk about it some more and not rush to any hasty decisions. She had just been through a terribly traumatic thing alone and needed some time to recuperate, both physically and mentally. I was trying to put on a brave face. The music still wasn't playing. We spent the night together in silence.

A few nights later, we had a party that Helen had scheduled before I had returned. She had seen no reason why she should cancel it. Why she decided to throw a party so soon after her miscarriage was a mystery and I wanted to protest but thought better of it. I didn't want to do anything that would rock the boat any more. All I wanted was to find a way to get her to stay. So the party went on as planned. That night I discovered that the person I married was gone. The woman who threw the party was not one I knew. She was wearing a blouse that was cut so low that it left little to the imagination. She wore so much makeup that I hardly recognized her. Seeing my wife painted like this and displaying herself so outrageously made me angry and I suggested that she change her clothes so she didn't look like a prostitute. She just laughed at me and told me what to do with my suggestion. It wasn't a pretty suggestion. During the party, much to my dismay and discomfort, I noticed that she was becoming extremely friendly and "touchy-feely" with many of the male guests, especially with one man in particular named Dennis, who I'd never met. As it turned out, I was going to get to know him whether I wanted to or not. Worse yet, Cal was calling a lot of the men at the party "Daddy".

That night Helen and I had the fight of our married lives. I was shocked and hurt at her appearance and behavior at the party so much so that I could not let this one slide. I didn't want people to think that my wife was the kind of woman that she looked to be that night. I was embarrassed for me and for her. She told me she didn't care and that I should leave if I didn't like it. The arguing and fighting went on until late into the night. We slept apart in the same house for the first time ever in our marriage.

Over the next few days our arguing was incessant. I continued to plead with her to talk to me as an adult about all of this. I wanted to know what was happening to her and to us and what I could do to help fix it. She refused to discuss anything with me. She wouldn't even discuss her miscarriage. She made it quite clear that she just didn't want anything to do with me. I was left to try to figure out what was wrong all by myself. My thoughts ran from the possibilities that she was suffering from severe mental anguish from the miscarriage to the unthinkable alternative: there was another man. I finally summoned the courage to ask her if there was someone else. She denied it and continued to deny everything as I asked again and again over the next few days. I was at the end of my rope. Somehow, I finally talked her into going to the base marriage counselor, a Catholic Priest who had promised not to throw religion into our counseling. Not being religious or Catholic, I was skeptical at first, but he kept his word and God was never offered as an answer to our marriage problems. We never seemed to get anywhere because neither he nor I thought that Helen was being honest at all. We went anyway. I had to do something to keep us together.

One night at dinner she finally decided for some reason that the time was right to tell me the truth. I asked her again if there was anyone else and implored her to be honest with me. She had been feeding Cal at the table and slowly turned to me. She looked straight at me, paused for a moment, and said, "Yes, there is. It's Dennis. Are you satisfied now?"

It turns out they had been seeing each other almost from the moment I had left to go out to sea. Dreading the answer I was sure I'd hear, I asked her the question that I didn't really want to ask: "Have you slept with him?"

Helen glared at me with fire in her eyes and told me in the most venomous voice I had ever heard from another person, "Yes, I slept with him; many times." And just to be sure to twist the knife just a little bit more, she added *with a sneer*, "And I enjoyed it more with him that I ever did with you."

I stared at her, dumbfounded. I don't know what hurt me more, the knowledge that my wife was cheating on me for reasons I couldn't fathom or that she seemed to be taking such pleasure in making it hurt me as much as she could. My mind was screaming at me. I couldn't think. From somewhere deep inside me a rage started to surface that I'd rarely seen in myself before. With a roar of pain, I picked up my dinner plate and threw it across the room. I sat there for a moment trying to control myself with Cal and Helen looking at me in fear. I knew that if I didn't leave the room, I might do something awful that I would regret. I jumped up and walked toward the spaghetti splattered door, barely realizing that I was even moving. I stood in front of the door numbly staring at the doorknob, my mind a cacophony of sound and pain. Something inside me suddenly snapped and I hauled back with a scream of primal rage and put my fist through the door. Totally out of control of my actions, I hit the door a few more times and then started hitting myself on the head with both fists. I slumped to the floor, sobbing hysterically. Cal was now crying, and Helen was standing behind me watching my breakdown in silence. When she reached down to me (why, I don't know), I jumped to my feet and screamed, "DON'T TOUCH ME! GET AWAY FROM ME!" I was petrified that I would turn my rage on her, and I didn't want to take that chance. I would *not* be my father. I threw open the door and ran down the stairs out into the darkened and empty street. I wandered around town for hours that night not knowing what to do. How could I go home to her? She had admitted to the most heinous betrayal of marriage possible and had rubbed that betrayal in my face. I had tried everything to keep our marriage together and it had all been in vain. What was I going to do now? How could I lose her and my son? They were my very life; the anchor for my tenuous hold on my self-identity. I was terrified of being alone. I feared I could be suicidal if I was alone too much. I didn't know what to do or where to go. Somehow, I found myself standing in front of our apartment again. I don't even know how I got there; I had been walking in a complete daze. Not knowing what else to do, I went upstairs, mentally and physically exhausted, let myself in and fell into a deep sleep on the living room couch.

The next few days at home were mostly spent in silence. We were total strangers now. I didn't spend any more time at home than I had to. I couldn't bear to even be in the same room with her. The hurt inside me was so visceral that I felt like I was going to break down crying every time I saw her. I knew that if she actually left, I would be without my son, something almost impossible for me to imagine. For his sake, I tried to talk to Helen to get her to come back to counseling so we could find a way to work things out. I talked to the Priest to get some idea of what I should do. He advised that I move out of the apartment and give her room to think. He said that my pleading with her to stay was only making things worse. So, a few days after her "revelation" to me, I decided to move in with some friends from the Coffeehouse. I packed my bags and left my apartment, my wife and my son. I had never been more miserable in my life.

Later that evening I realized that, in my haste to leave, I had forgotten to take my guitar with me. I walked back to the apartment to get it. I knocked on the door of my own apartment and, when Helen opened the door a mere crack, asked to be allowed to enter. I was met with outright hostility and was refused entry. I explained to her that I only needed my guitar. It was my only solace now. I was told to go away. I couldn't enter the house and I couldn't have my guitar. Inside the apartment, I saw someone move behind her. It was Dennis. He was in my apartment with my wife and son the very day I moved out to give her room to "think". That was the last straw. I shoved the door open and, pushing her aside, and walked in to get my guitar in the living room. As I strode quickly across the room, wanting nothing more than to get the guitar and leave before things got ugly (before I lost control again), Helen followed screaming for me to get out while pounding on my back with her fists. She had gone completely out of her mind. Dennis stood complacently off to the side of the room watching silently. When

I stooped down to get my guitar, Helen's blows were striking my neck and head. Something inside me just decided that I'd had enough. Still stooped, I let go of the guitar case and stood up, swinging my right arm behind me and shouting, "STOP IT!" The back of my hand connected with the side of her face, and she went reeling across the room. Dennis immediately moved in to confront me. "I think you should leave now", he said.

By now I was in such a rage that I could barely think. I screamed at him, begging him to take a swing at me *just once*. I was ready right then and there to take out all of my frustration and pain on him and I know that if I hadn't had at least a little control left I would have done just that. I would probably have a prison record now if I had. I don't think I could have stopped myself once I started. He must have seen the rage in my eyes because he slowly backed off.

As I turned toward the door, I noticed Helen in the corner of the room slumped on the floor and staring at me in disbelief, holding her red cheek in her hand. The realization of what had happened suddenly crashed down upon me. I had done the unthinkable; I had hit my wife. In one moment of unbridled rage, I had become my father. Now I would never get her back. I had ruined everything.

My rage was instantly replaced by almost uncontrollable sobbing. I heard myself begging Helen to forgive me; that I hadn't meant it; that it was just an accident. Dennis, sensing that I was "safer" to approach now, actually came up to me, put his hands on my shoulders and turned me toward the door, telling me that it was best if I go now. I couldn't do anything else. My feet were not my own. I couldn't think. I just kept repeating over and over, "What have I done?"

I left the apartment in a sobbing daze with my guitar still in my hand and walked until I found myself somehow down at the ocean. I had every intention of just walking into the water and continuing until I couldn't feel this horrible pain any more. I remember seeing the dark water looming in front of me, beckoning me with its cold embrace. I don't remember anything else until I woke up the next morning at the home of the Priest that had been counseling us. How I got there, I don't know. I had a shadow of a memory of him leading me to the bedroom but everything else was a blur. I left his house in the morning unshaven, in clothes that I had slept in, barely having said thank you to him. Somehow, I had managed to make my way to work, again without realizing where I was going. I ended up sitting at my desk, staring into space. I didn't even know where I was until my boss knelt in front of me, lightly slapped my face and asked me what was wrong. I saw him through a haze but couldn't answer. No words would come out. I was immediately taken to the hospital where I was given sedatives and sick leave and then taken "home". It was days before I could return to work and function anywhere near to normal.

While in the hospital, I was ordered to see the base psychiatrist to try to get help for my crushing depression. For some unknown reason, during one of my sessions with him after I had left the hospital, I hesitantly told him about how I'd felt all of my life and that it might have something to do with my depression. Surprised, the doctor asked, "Well, you don't really want to have your penis cut off, do you?"

Warning bells were ringing loudly in my head, even through the haze of depression. I knew that my answer could mean my career. This doctor was, after all, a Naval Officer and could very well hold my career in his hands. I shook my head and, in my most convincing voice, I lied, "No, of course not."

127

"Ok, then," he said. "There's no need to go into that. That's not unusual for some people to think, anyway. Let's concern ourselves with the problem at hand."

Inwardly I breathed a sigh of relief. I had come perilously close to outing myself. We talked more about what had been going on between Helen and me and I was prescribed some stronger anti-depressants to keep me from being suicidal and sent back to my temporary home.

* * *

There was only one other time in the Navy that I had let my guard down about my secret. During one of my tours of duty at Goodfellow AFB I was offered the possibility of being able to serve on submarines. It was not well known that Communications Technicians (CTs – changed later to Cryptologic Technicians) were sometimes stationed aboard subs and it was something that I had always wanted to do for some insane reason, so I jumped at the chance. In order to be accepted to the program, I had to have a series of tests, both physical and psychological. I passed the physical exam in flying colors. The psychological exam was a combination of a written test with questions like: 'What do you like to do better – pet kittens or pull the wings off of flies?' The questions were innocent enough until I came to one that stopped me in my tracks. 'Have you ever wanted to be a girl?' I thought about this one very hard. Should I answer honestly? If I do, what will happen to me? I hadn't met Helen yet, so I really had nothing to keep me in the Navy if they wanted to kick me out. With great trepidation, I answered 'Yes' to the question. I was sure that when I sat down to go over the test with the psychologist that this would be a large red flag that would almost certainly be brought up. I was wrong. The psychologist was one of the strangest people I had ever met.

After a few minutes of thumbing through papers and rambling about how they couldn't get him on a submarine if they hog-tied him, he finally proclaimed me physically and psychologically fit to serve on board a submarine. The issue of why I answered that I had wanted to be girl never came up. I never did get to go on submarines, though. It turned out to be something of a "Catch-22" thing; they only wanted CTs with submarine experience on the missions but in order to get experience on a submarine mission you actually had to *go* on a submarine mission. This was the Navy, after all. Nothing was supposed to make much sense.

* * *

I stayed away from Helen now, except to sometimes walk slowly past the apartment to see if she was there and to maybe catch a glimpse of her or Cal. I suppose part of me was also spying on her. I guess I needed to see more to really convince myself that there no longer was a chance for me no matter how much that confirmation hurt. My friends at the Coffeehouse were my only shelter from this pain now and I spent most of my free time with them. My choice of singing material was getting sadder as the days went by. Someone eventually told me that my performances were so downbeat that they wanted to go walk in front of a truck after I was finished. My music was my only outlet, though, and I just couldn't find it in me to sing anything happy.

By this time the Navy was trying to send Helen home. My family problems were disrupting my work and creating quite a scandal around the base. Helen was only in Spain by invitation of the Navy, just as all families of sailors are. The Navy could rescind that invitation at any time. When she found out what was happening, Helen came to me to ask that she be given a second chance. She even offered to go back to counseling with me. For a brief moment I had a glimmer of hope. After a few sessions with the Priest, though, it became clear to both of us that she was only interested in getting back together so she wouldn't be sent away and have to leave Dennis.

The Navy had been waiting for me to sign the papers that would authorize her expulsion from Spain. I signed them with a heavy heart. At the same time, I had gone to a base attorney to ask if there was some way I could get custody of my son instead of having him return to the States with his mother. I felt that, based on her actions of the last several months, she was not a fit person to be raising my son. The lawyer told me that based on the nature of my job sending me out to sea for months at a time, it would be impossible for me to gain custody. When Helen found out I was asking about getting custody of Cal, she threatened to tell everyone about my little "problem" if I persisted. If she had done that, I would have immediately lost my security clearance and been tossed unceremoniously out of the Navy. There was nothing more I could do other than watch Helen and Cal board the plane that would take them out of Spain and out of my life, perhaps forever.

The next time I saw her was about six months later when I took leave to go home and try to talk to her to see if anything had changed. She informed me coldly that it hadn't. I'll never forget Cal answering the door with his hands on his hips staring with wide-eyed glee at the present I had brought him and saying "Well! What have we here?" It broke my heart. I gave the present to my son and left, telling him that I loved him. It was the worst vacation of my life. We were divorced six months later.

* * *

I never knew exactly what it was that caused Helen to become so vicious against me. She never would talk about it or even admit to anything she'd done, regardless of the overwhelming evidence I had to the contrary. I know now that what went on in Spain was not an isolated incident. I learned later from friends of hers with whom she had confided that while I went to work at my second job at night while we were living in Virginia, Helen was not just visiting her mother; she was leaving Cal with her and then going out partying with boyfriends and other friends. At the time I didn't even suspect anything was happening; I was too busy working two jobs to make ends meet for my family.

This has all made me wonder why she married me in the first place. At the time I was convinced she loved me and would do anything to be with me, including standing up to her mother and losing her car. I'm not so sure of that anymore. I've come to the conclusion that the main reason she married me was to get away from her domineering and bitter mother. I'll never really know for sure. It's hard for me to believe that I have been used so badly and, worse yet, that I let myself be used that badly.

My troubles with Helen were not to end with our divorce. She had broken her affair off with Dennis, who confided in me back in Spain of how badly he had been used. He had gone back to see her in the States and was told to go away.

It wasn't long before Helen was remarried. I had been stationed thousands of miles away in another country and had no way to keep in contact with Cal. Even though I was now back in the States, having gotten out of the Navy, I was still so far away from him that there was no way I could have anywhere near a normal father/son relationship with him. Based on my own childhood of growing up with a different name than the rest of my family, I didn't think it was my place to try to get back into Cal's life when the only "father" he really knew was Helen's current husband, Pete. I feared that not only would it be confusing to him, but it might drive an unwelcome wedge between him and his stepfather. I also dreaded any contact with Helen, no matter how brief. After anguishing over this dilemma for quite some while, I came to the conclusion that the best thing I could do for Cal was to allow his stepfather to adopt him, thereby giving him the unity of the family name that I never had.

I had been in touch with Helen each month by sending her support payments for Cal, so I knew where they were living. I screwed up my courage and called her to ask her opinion of my decision. She said she'd been thinking the same thing. It was even more important to her now because she had two more sons with her husband and the disparity in names had started to become a nuisance with schools and within her family. She promised to get the paperwork rolling to adopt Cal into her new family. I promised to pay whatever costs were necessary as a gesture of good faith on my part. Helen was to contact me later to let me know what the legal fees were going to be. I had just agreed to give my only son and child away. It was a horrible decision to make.

Months passed, and I heard nothing from Helen on the adoption fees. After several calls and promises to get back to me later, she finally called to talk about it. She had run into a problem. She had discovered that if she allowed Cal to be adopted by her husband, I would no longer be under any legal commitment to continue making child support payments to her. Because of this, she said she and her husband couldn't afford to go through with the adoption. She actually told me that they "needed my money too badly". I looked at the phone in disbelief. This woman was going to put a few dollars (at the time it was only $100 per month) ahead of our son's best interests and peace of mind. When I reminded her that we were doing this for Cal, she simply brushed me off and told me that this was how it was going to be. She closed with a reminder to make sure that my child support payments were on time.

And they were - until I had trouble finding a job. Instead of just stopping any payments until I could pay, as many delinquent fathers seem to do, I called Helen and told her of my predicament. She surprised me by being very cooperative and telling me to just send what I could until I got back on my feet again. I could make up the difference later. I thought that maybe we were finally going to be on better terms after all. Two weeks after our phone conversation, I received a summons to appear in court for lack of full child support payments. There was no way that she could have gotten the judgment to summon me that quickly. She obviously had this in the works when she told me it was ok for me to withhold payments until I got a job. She had lied to me again, still getting some kind of perverse pleasure out of making me suffer. In court, I explained to the Judge about our phone conversation and agreement, only to be rebuffed and reminded that only the court could make a decision that would alter my payments to my wife. No verbal agreement between us had any legal standing at all. There was nothing I could do. I was reminded yet again that to trust this woman was to court disappointment and humiliation. And she wasn't through with me yet – not by a long shot.

Several years later, I still held to the belief that to insert myself into Cal's life would only cause trouble and tensions in his family. I really believed that it was the right thing to do. The last time I had seen Cal was when he was two. He was eleven years old now and had never really had any other man in his family except for his stepfather. It was doubtful, at least to me, that he even thought about me, if he remembered me at all. It had been the same for me when I was growing up and I didn't think it would be any different for him. I was to find that I was horribly wrong.

* * *

One day I received a letter from my parents. Inside was another letter and a note saying that they thought I might want this. It was a letter from Cal. He had evidently been badgering his mother for information on me to the point where she finally acquiesced and gave him my parents' address in Ohio. She had either lost my address (I was still sending child support payments, but they were sent to by proxy through the Court system) or she didn't want Cal to have my real address for some reason. I had stopped wondering about how she thought about things. The letter from Cal was one of the most heart-wrenching and exhilarating letters I have ever received. He said that he had never stopped thinking about me and wondered if he could meet me sometime. I'd had no idea what Helen was saying about me or, for that matter, if she was talking to him about me at all. There were so many emotions going through me that I didn't know whether to cry for joy at hearing from him or cry in anguish for the years together that we had lost and would never regain. I wrote back to him immediately and promised that we would be together soon.

His family was still living in Baltimore, one street over from his grandmother's house – the very same house that Helen and I had confronted her angry mother and brother in front of so many years before. I was living in southern New Jersey, about a two-hour drive away to the north. When I drove down to Helen's brother's house on the day that Helen and I had agreed to, Cal was standing on the front porch waiting for me. We recognized each other immediately. He looked so much like me it was uncanny. And he had kept pictures of me, so he knew my face by heart. We embraced in a hug that was years late. I was holding my son at last – my son who had been thinking about me for years as I had been thinking about him.

Our first meeting was limited to sitting in his house. I was not allowed to take him off the premises. Helen was surprisingly civil to me and actually seemed happy to see me. She hadn't changed much. Her husband was a short, balding man who greeted me with a firm hand shake. All of the bad feelings of the past disappeared, replaced by the joy at my reunion with my son. Nothing else was important now. We talked for hours, getting to know each other as much as we could after all these years. It was a tremendous reunion. Leaving him there was very difficult.

On subsequent meetings when I was allowed to take Cal with me somewhere, he and I would go around to area attractions and just walk, talking about everything. Eventually, he was even allowed to come home with me to spend weekends. During these extended visits away from his home, I learned more about why he had wanted to contact me after all these years. He and his stepfather did not get along at all. Over time he described incidents in which his stepfather was physically and emotionally abusive to him and to his mother. He tearfully recounted times when his mother was assaulted by his stepfather and he had been helpless to do anything about it even though he tried in his later years only to be threatened with a beating himself. I was aghast at his stories. I thought I had been doing the right thing by staying out of his life. I was discovering that I should have been there all along. It's strange that, with everything that Helen had done to me, I still felt anger at this man that he would lay his hands on her. There was still a part of me that held on to the good times when we were husband and wife.

All I could do was to apologize to Cal for not being there for him. I told him about my childhood, growing up with a different name than my family and with a father that was not my own. He seemed to understand my reasons for not being part of his life until now. He never held a grudge against me for it and I love him all the more for it.

Cal and I would talk about almost everything when we were together. We had so much time to make up for. There was nothing that we wouldn't talk about – almost. The one thing that I refused to discuss with him was my relationship with his mother and what had happened between us. I saw no reason to poison him in any way against her. That was between her and me. But one time, while we were driving home to Ohio to meet his grandparents for the first time since his birth, he asked a question that took me totally by surprise. "Dad", he began, "Why did you desert Mom and me?"

I almost ran off the road.

Everything that his mother had done to me came crashing back on a wave of pain and anger. It was all I could do to control myself.

When I finally regained my composure (and control of the car), I told him again that what went on between his mother and me was not something that I would discuss with him until he was an adult, and even then, I wasn't sure I'd talk to him about it. "But", I said, trying to control my wavering voice, "there is one thing that I will tell you, though, and you can make of it what you will. I did *not* desert you and your mother. If you believe nothing else in your life, believe that. Your mother left me and took you with her and there was nothing that I could do about it. Lord knows I tried everything."

Cal looked into my eyes and must have seen that I was telling him the truth. He said no more about it. I don't know if he ever confronted his mother with this conflicting information but I'm sure that if he did, she would deny it. I still can't believe that she would tell him that I had deserted them no matter how much she detested me. We never discussed the issue again.

Years later, after I had made my decision about what to do about my life, I decided to discuss my condition with Cal during one of his visits. He was old enough to understand and I owed it to him to be honest. I told him everything, how I had grown up, how this had affected me and was still affecting me, and what was going to happen. He sat in silence soaking it all in. When I was done, he looked at me and simply asked, "Will you stop loving me when you're not my father anymore?" That was a question I hadn't expected. I assured him that I would always love him and that I would always be his father no matter what I looked like or what I called myself. He was very supportive of me through my whole process of changing. His family, however, was not.

A few years later, when Cal was engaged to be married, his mother came between us once again. When she found that he had invited me to his wedding, she flew into a rage. Evidently forgetting how much her mother's actions had hurt us at our own wedding, she promised that if I showed up neither she nor any of her family would be there. Cal's stepfather added that if he saw me anywhere near the church, he would beat me up. What a great family. Cal was put squarely in the middle. I told him that I would show up in drag as Rick if that would help keep the peace for his special day. I even told him that I would stay away if that was the only way to help. He replied in no uncertain terms that he was not going to have me there as anything other than who I was, and that there was no way I was not going to be invited. But in the end, he did the only thing he could – he waited until I was away in the Netherlands on vacation to get married. I was very disappointed when I found this out and more than a little angry that he had capitulated to his family's threats in such a manner. But I understood his quandary and forgave him. It was not the last time that he would fold to his mother's demands concerning me.[16] The worst and most hurtful was yet to come. But that's a story for much later. For the meantime, I need to go back to the time just after Helen left Spain with my son and my life.

---

[16] In fairness to Cal, he doesn't remember it this way and wasn't happy to read it written here because he thinks it makes him look bad. I remember it this way, as does my partner, but in any case, my intention was not to show him in a bad light but to show that he was in an unwinnable position, and I don't blame him at all for his decision to handle the situation like he did (as far as I remember it).

Chapter 12
Single Life and Other False Starts

With the advent of Helen's departure, I had come to the decision that my life as a man was, shall we say, a bit less than successful. I felt that I had been a miserable failure at being a husband and a father and, worse yet, neither had changed how I felt inside. I couldn't bring myself to blame anyone but me for what happened to my marriage, no matter how many things I heard after she left about Helen's previous extramarital exploits on the base. And there were many.

One man I worked with, the roommate I had in Texas that had walked in on me and my "guest" in our room, had been overheard *bragging* that he had been in bed with Helen having sex with her when she started to miscarry our baby.

My downstairs neighbor confided in me that while I was gone to sea, our bed upstairs, which had always been squeaky, was making noise almost every night. She said she felt sorry for me and thought I should know. The knife sank deeper into my heart with each revelation.

Another friend approached me at an outdoor party on the base, crying and very drunk, admitted to me that he had been sleeping with Helen, but it wasn't his fault because she had virtually thrown herself at him and he was too weak to resist. He pleaded for forgiveness. If I hadn't been half drunk myself, I probably would have punched him in the face. I even found out that that she had been sleeping with the "friend" that I moved in with when I moved out of our apartment!

Two of my friends at the Coffeehouse told me that they had literally kicked Helen out of their house one evening when, after they asked her why she was treating me so badly, she had responded, "Because I want to make him crawl like the worm he

139

is." She ended up alienating everyone in Rota that we had together called friends.

Even after all of these horrible revelations, I was so blinded by my need for her and so afraid of what would happen to me now that she was gone that I still couldn't bring myself to blame her for leaving. There was always some way that I could find to shift the blame back on myself. So, armed with this misguided self-incrimination, I decided that my only recourse was to start attempting in earnest to see how my life would be as a woman. I could find no place for me as a man in the Navy or in society. Enough was enough. I started cross-dressing at home, experimenting with makeup and mannerisms. It gave me some solace in my now empty life.

* * *

Because my job in the Navy required me to hold a very high security clearance, I had to be very careful about what I did. At that time the Navy was regularly holding what we called "witch hunts" to find suspected homosexuals and expel them from the Navy with less than honorable discharges. There was a thriving underground gay community on the base, complete with closeted doctors and others that could be trusted to keep their secrets. I had many friends in this community and shared their outrage whenever someone was "outed" and discharged. Although I did not consider myself falling into that category, I knew that the Navy would not make any such distinction if they found me out. So, I continued to keep my activities to myself behind closed doors, telling no one what I was doing.

This was the time that I discovered the "Holy Books" of cross-dressers around the world – *Mail Order Catalogues*. The list was endless – Sears, Penney's and Montgomery Wards – all had catalogues from which you could shop in the convenience and security of your own home. With a little courage I was able to anonymously order anything that I wanted with no one being the wiser. With a name like Ricky, I felt that most companies I was ordering from would not suspect that the female clothing I was ordering was going to be worn by a man. But just in case, I ordered everything under the name R. Thompson. In retrospect, I guess that using my initials to order large size women's clothing from a catalogue probably *was* a dead giveaway, but I didn't know or care about that.

My biggest concern with ordering clothes was that I had no idea what size I wore in anything, especially shoes. To make up for this, I would surreptitiously ask women that I worked with that looked to be about as big as me what sizes they wore, all the time trying to keep the questions innocent enough so as not to raise suspicions about why I was asking. That was when I found out that it's really not very sociably acceptable for a man to ask a woman how big her feet are.

My first few orders that I placed through the catalogues were hit-or-miss with sizes but, after sending many things back, I finally got my sizes more or less correct. Undergarments were strangely enough the easiest to get. Bras are basically sized according to chest circumference and cup size. I could easily measure my chest and cup size was pretty much anything I wanted. A lot of beginning cross dressers will go for the truly outrageous and start out stuffing a D or bigger cup. They want BOOBS! I never went beyond a B. The problem I had was what to fill the cups with. Obviously, I had no breasts of my own and had no access to female hormones to begin my own development. That would have been totally out of the question anyway because it would have been very hard to explain why I had breasts while on a TAD trip and taking a shower with a bunch of guys on the ship. It would have also been dangerous. I didn't want to go floating in the middle of the open ocean at night. I decided that it was best to use rolled up socks and tissues for filler. It didn't feel very natural, but it was better than the sad look of empty cups. I tried filling small balloons with water, but they didn't spread out in the cups like I had expected and only became round, cold lumps. They also leaked. I hadn't heard of silicone breast forms yet.

The first time I really cross-dressed in earnest I was as happy as if I was back in my parents' closet at home. I'd forgotten how the clothes made me feel whole. I knew I wasn't and that I probably looked ridiculous, but somehow it felt natural to wear a dress and stockings. I hated wigs, though. The wig that I had bought looked like something the cat dragged in to play with and the dog dragged out because it offended his esthetic senses. I had ordered it through one of those cheap magazines that showed some beautiful starlet supposedly wearing one of the wigs and looking absolutely fabulous. I learned a lot about "truth in advertising" during those days. I had to wear the wig, though. My hair had to be kept short for Navy regulations and it was just too hard to look at myself in the mirror fully dressed with my awful short hair. I also couldn't shave my legs for fear of raising questions that were best left unanswered. So, there I stood in the mirror, bad wig, hairy legs and all, in an outfit that looked like it came straight off the K-Mart blue light special rack, with makeup that hinted it was applied with a spatula and feeling better than I had in a long, long time. Sometimes life is really absurd.

I kept my cross-dressing activities confined to my small apartment, scared to death to venture even one high-heeled foot outside my door. One time when I was dressed, a good friend of mine came to my front door. I went into a blinding panic and started ripping things off yelling, "Just a minute!" I stuck my head under the faucet in the bathroom while scrubbing all the makeup off my face. Then, with one last look in the mirror to make sure there was no sign of makeup left, I threw on my bathrobe and answered the door, drying my hair with a towel as if I had just stepped out of the shower. Later I wondered why I hadn't just acted like I wasn't home. Fear can make us very dumb sometimes.

During this time, something unexpected was happening; Lynne and I were starting to get closer. We sang duets at the Coffee House with increasing regularity and spent more time together practicing material. Our voices just seemed to go together very well, and our duets were becoming the big thing on Friday nights. Since Lynne didn't play guitar much, my accompaniment was just what she needed. I still missed Helen (I wasn't any smarter) and the physical closeness we once had so it was only a matter of time before Lynne and I were sleeping together. For some reason, this budding romance didn't stop my cross-dressing activities when I was at home alone. It just made my inability to see her on occasions that much harder to explain. ("I'm sorry, I can't see you tonight. I've got to put on a dress and parade around my living room.") Finally, I had an idea to end all ideas. Lynne and I were spending almost all of our time together. We seemed to have a much deeper understanding of each other than I'd ever had with Helen. I decided to tell Lynne all about myself and how I felt. It was a big chance, but I just didn't feel like I could hide it any longer. It wasn't fair to her or to me.

I was astounded at how well she took the news, and even more astounded at her suggestion a few days later. Her father was being reassigned back to the States so her whole family was going to be moving soon. She had lived in Spain for much of her teenage years and really loved it. She really didn't want to leave but since she was a dependent in the Navy's eyes even though

143

she was 18, she couldn't stay if her parents left. She suggested a solution that would help us both. After she got back to the States, I would come back for her, and we would be married. Then she would return to Spain with me as my wife so she could stay there legally. In return, she would help me to learn how to be a woman – help with hair, clothes, mannerisms, make-up, anything I needed. When I got out of the Navy in a few years, we would go back to the States where we would get a divorce and I'd be all ready to go on with my new life. This was just too good to be true. Here was a woman that I immensely enjoyed being with who was willing to help me stop from aching inside all the time. I needed her, and I needed this help very badly. Without her I was alone. Alone meant scared and, eventually, suicidal. There was only one thing I could say to her.

I agreed.

This was my dream come true. I now had the promise of real help from someone who wasn't ashamed of who I was. On top of that I had the best singing partner I'd ever known. I was on top of the world. Now all we had to do was convince her parents that it was a good idea for us to get married. I had already been banished from her house earlier by her father who was suspicious of "my motives" with his daughter. Being a Chief Petty Officer, he knew from experience that sailors only wanted one thing and his daughter was *not* going to be my target. After lengthy talks with Lynne's parents about our future (most of it made up or conveniently omitted – we couldn't tell them *everything*), we convinced them that we were serious about each other, and they finally gave us their blessings. They especially liked that we weren't going to get married right away. They thought the time apart would do us good. On the other hand, you couldn't get married in Spain at that time unless you were Catholic, something neither of us was. Non-Catholics had to go to the British territory of Gibraltar to get married. Living together without getting married was also something that was not acceptable, so we didn't even offer that. Besides, we wanted her parents to be part of the wedding. So, it was decided that our getting married back in the States was a good idea.

Watching Lynne leave on the flight back to the U.S. with her parents was hard. I just knew that she would come to her senses while she was gone and that I'd never see her again. I was wrong. We kept in close touch through letters and constant phone calls (there went my paychecks). We set everything up for our wedding. It was to be held at her parents' house in Norfolk, Virginia where her father was newly stationed.

After a few months, I took leave and flew to Virginia to see her. We were very happy to see each other and spent the nights together in her parents' house sneaking into each other's rooms and making love as quietly as we could. This was perfect. Still, there was some little thing tapping at the back of my mind trying to tell me to be careful. As I had before, I ignored all of it. It was just premarital jitters; that's all. And this wasn't going to be a "normal" marriage, anyway. This time everything would be different.

As the day of the wedding neared, we borrowed a car and made the 12-hour drive to Ohio to pick up my mother (my dad couldn't make it). Of course, that meant that we had to turn right around and drive back to Virginia and then I had to do it all over again to get her back home. Since no one had money for air fare, there was nothing else we could do. My Mother was very happy for us. She confided in me that she had never liked Helen and she found Lynne much nicer.

We were married in the living room of Lynne's parents in Norfolk, just like we planned. There were no frills and no fancy stuff – just a simple ceremony with our parents. Neither of us wanted a big wedding that would have saddled her parents with a big bill. Besides, all of our friends were in Spain. Lynne and I spent our wedding night in a Ramada Inn just outside Richmond, Virginia. Our honeymoon was to wait until we got back to Spain.

Our first few years together as husband and wife were happy enough. We had returned to Spain shortly after our wedding to finish out the rest of my naval career. Just as she had promised, Lynne helped me learn to be a woman. I was initially embarrassed for her to see me "dressed" but she immediately complimented me on my appearance, putting me at ease. With one exception, no one had ever seen me like this before. And now for another little time diversion...

* * *

Between the time that Helen left, and Lynne and I became serious, a friend of mine in Spain threw a Halloween party at her house. I got together with some of my closest friends at the Coffee House and we all tried to decide what to go as. The woman named Annie who was the heart of the Coffee House looked at me for a few moments and, much to my surprise, said, "You know, Rick, you'd make a gorgeous girl. Why don't you go like that?" I was both exhilarated and horrified; exhilarated in the thought that she thought I might be pretty as a girl and horrified that someone would see me in a dress, put two and two together and figure me out. I'd be humiliated. But everyone thought it was a good idea and wouldn't hear of me saying no. The women in the group went out to the neighborhood stores and bought me a quite sexy, short blue dress, stockings and a wig. I had to shop for my own shoes on base and finally settled on a pair of gold strap sandals with low heels. The night of the party, my female friends took me into a bedroom at a friend's house and got me ready. I couldn't believe what I saw in the mirror. Staring back at me was a woman that didn't look bad –

146

not bad at all! When I walked out into the living room where everyone had assembled to leave for the party, everyone stopped talking and just stared at me. They were as amazed as I was. I was flattered and embarrassed at the same time. I had to be very careful to play up the masquerade as just that – a masquerade. No one could know that what they were seeing was the real me. I had to constantly talk to myself to calm down and stop sweating from nervousness. No one was going to think that it was anything but a costume. We left for the party.

When we got there, we found that there had been a bit of a hitch. Unknown to all of us in our group, the host of the party had been busted earlier that day for possession of hashish that he had tried to bring in from Morocco earlier in the day. He wasn't thrown in prison but was waiting at home in big trouble with the local government and with the Navy. He understandably didn't feel much like partying, so he got in touch with as many people as he could to tell them to just come over and forget the whole Halloween thing. There weren't any phones in the homes off base, so we hadn't heard the news. We walked into the party in our costumes only to find that no one else was wearing one. How embarrassing! Our costumes and the silliness of it all did brighten up the party, though, and we quickly settled down to having some serious fun. During the evening, a man who was a co-worker of mine wandered over to where I was standing nursing a drink. When he started to make light conversation with me, I realized that he didn't recognize me at all. I remained pleasant, trying not to laugh (or sweat) as the conversation turned a bit more personal. Smiling, he looked at me and said, "I haven't seen you around the base before. Are you new?"

"No", I answered in my softest voice. "I've been here for a few years working out at the Communications Station – the same place you work."

147

His eyebrows went up as he moved closer to me. "That's not possible. I'd have known if someone as pretty as you worked out there."

Everyone in my group had now stopped talking and turned to watch what they had already surmised was happening.

"Thank you", I demurred. "That's a very nice thing to say. But really, I've worked out there for quite some time. We even went on a TAD trip together once."

Now he was getting really confused. Women never went on TAD trips because of the need to be aboard ships and women weren't allowed on ships. He moved away from me a bit, confused, and asked, "Who are you"?

I lowered my voice to its normal pitch (which wasn't all that low to begin with), smiled and said, "Don't you recognize me? I'm Ricky - Ricky Thompson."

He turned pale, set his glass slowly down on the counter and walked away, staring at me all the way. My friends started laughing. Those that weren't in on the little "joke" were told what was going on and they all started laughing. I couldn't believe it. He, along with almost everyone else at the party, hadn't realized that I wasn't in costume at all. They thought I was just another woman at the party. There aren't words to express how happy that made me. I already knew inside that I was really female, and this just proved it. For the rest of the night, the men at the party just stared from a distance. The women came over to me to say how great I looked. I didn't want the evening to end. Of course, my friend who had tried to pick me up at the party steered very clear of me for the next few weeks.

* * *

For the rest of our time in Rota, Lynne picked out clothes for me, helped me with makeup tips and even ordered two silicon breast forms for me from the Sears catalogue. I became so comfortable with her in my female persona that Ricky only really existed outside our apartment door. I hadn't come up with a female name for myself yet but since I'd known a girl when I was little who lived nearby named Rikki, the name seemed to fit anyway. I finally felt I was on my way to becoming a whole person at last.

I got out of the Navy in September of 1977. I chose to be transferred to Norfolk, Virginia for separation because of an offer from Lynne's parents to live with them until we got on our feet. I also had a job waiting at the local Norfolk newspaper to work as a computer operator. For my last two years in Rota, I had been working as a self-taught programmer for a new thing they called a "computer" that we had been given in our department. I had volunteered to take on the job because I was bored doing nothing while waiting to go TAD and I was promised that I wouldn't have to go TAD if I volunteered. It was a no-lose situation for me. I found out I had a knack for programming and, after taking a few classes at the on-base college in programming principles and languages, I soon was tasked with writing programs for the entire Communications Station, one of which was actually reviewed in Washington for use Navy-wide. My job in Norfolk was to work for a short while as a computer operator and then move up to a programmer's position once I was familiar with the system. The pay wasn't very good, and I considered it demeaning work because of my experience but a job was a job, and I really had no real serious college training in programming, so I couldn't afford to be picky.

One of the first things Lynne and I did when I officially got out of the Navy was to find a counselor who might be able to help me for the next stage of my life. When we entered her office, I was more frightened that I'd ever been in my life. More than a little embarrassed, we beat around the bush for the first few minutes of the session about why we were there, rambling about my life and necessary "life altering changes". I think I was afraid I'd be met with derision or, worse yet, laughed at and tossed out the door. The counselor finally looked at me and asked, "Are you trying to tell me that you're considering a sex change?"

I didn't know what to say. It was the first time I had ever heard the term directed at me. It made everything horrifyingly real.

When I found my voice, I explained to the counselor about our earlier plan for marriage, my gender training, our divorce and my uncertainty about what to do next. When the hour was up, I was armed with more information to help me – phone numbers, names and addresses of support groups and doctors in the United States, some in the immediate area, who might be able to help me. Lynne was unusually quiet through the whole thing and remained so after we left. Our relationship quickly took a dramatic change. She became moody and uncommunicative, especially whenever I tried to talk to her about what I should do. She knew very well what we had said we were going to do before we were married but somehow something had changed. Quite a few years later she would finally admit to me that her real goal had been to "get it out of my system" and help me to see that I was better off with her as a man and a husband. She now was starting to realize that her plan wasn't going to work out and that we were really going to be getting a divorce soon. Lynne decided to take matters into her own hands.

As a biological male with all the hormones that drive normal male urges, I was able (and willing) to have fairly normal sexual relations with Lynne. I say "fairly" because most, if not all, of the times we made love, I still fantasized that I was the woman in the act. We had earlier discussed that, because of our plans, children were out of the question, so Lynne was taking birth control pills. Without telling me about it, she stopped taking her pills. Her reasoning was that, if she got pregnant, my sense of responsibility to her and to our child, along with my dread of what I was going to be undertaking, would overshadow my responsibility to myself and make me abandon my dream and stay with her. She almost had it right. As soon as I found that she was pregnant ("The pills aren't 100% effective", she told me), I sat down with her to discuss alternatives. She had to have an abortion before it was too late. What else could we do? I didn't have a decent job, we had nowhere to live except with her parents and I didn't know what was going to happen to me. It just wouldn't be fair to bring a child into the world with such uncertainty and no father. I finally convinced her that it was the right thing to do. We couldn't tell her parents because her mother was very religious and wouldn't understand at all. So, we made up a story about her having to have a medical procedure done to remove a cyst. She had the abortion at a local clinic with no physical complications. The psychological toll was a different matter.

Lynne was depressed for months, partly through guilt about the abortion and partly from the knowledge that she was going to lose me now for sure. There was nothing standing in my way of leaving. I stayed very close to her during this time. After all, regardless of how I felt inside I still loved her and didn't want to see her unhappy. We started making love again. Lightning couldn't strike twice, could it? The pills couldn't fail again, right? It wasn't long until she became pregnant again. This time her plan succeeded. She got pregnant again almost right away. I couldn't let her go through all of this again. I reluctantly abandoned my personal goal and decided to stay and try to find my happiness in our marriage.

She had won at last[17].

---

[17] I was to find out much later that she had lied to me all along. The first time we had sex she said she'd never done it before. Turns out she had – with a friend of mine. If I had known, I would have known better than to have trusted what she said about wanting to help me. Our children would have never been brought into the world and there would be two fewer people to hurt in my life.

Chapter 13
If At First You Don't Succeed, Fail, Fail Again

Our daughter Julie was born on October 1, 1979. I had left my computer operator's job at the newspaper after only 2 months for a much better paying job as a programmer for a major software development company in Norfolk. We had moved to a nice apartment in Virginia Beach. Lynne's father had retired from the Navy and moved the family back home to West Virginia where he had been raised. Lynne had taken a job with a large credit reporting firm in downtown Norfolk. I was also working part time in the evenings at a local fast-food restaurant as a night manager to help bring in more money. But even with our combined salaries and my night job, we were barely able to keep ahead of our bills. In fact, we were falling behind fast. I had never been able to handle money very well and Lynne had no experience with it at all. We were in trouble with the IRS because we had both listed all three of us for tax withholding purposes where we worked. It was the first time Lynne had ever really had a job and never thought to ask me what she should do about withholding for income tax. When tax time came, I found that we owed over a thousand dollars to the government because we had claimed a total of six dependents from our employers. I didn't know what to do. We just didn't have that kind of money to pay the IRS and there was no way I was going to be able to get a loan to pay it. A thousand dollars was a whole lot of money at that time. Much to my surprise, I was able to make a deal with the IRS to pay the money back in installments. Just after that agreement was made, however, the software project I was working on was lost to a rival company. My company was starting to lay people off. Some of my friends had returned to their original company up in southern New Jersey which was doing similar work and had asked me to give them my résumé. Even though I had been assured by my management that I was not going to lose my job, I'd had no solid assignments for months and was getting nervous. It was approaching the Christmas holidays and people were being let go right and left. I did not want to be one of them, so I went to southern New Jersey to interview for the job. I was hired right away.

This turn of events actually turned out to be a good thing for us financially. We decided that Lynne and Julie would go to West Virginia to stay with her parents. We wouldn't have to pay rent for an apartment because my new company would put me up at a hotel for a couple of months until I could find a place for us to live. I had a lot of vacation time on the books at my old company for which I would be reimbursed when I left. Plus, I got a signing bonus from my new company and a substantial raise to boot. We were going to be able to pay off all of our bills and start over with a clean financial slate in our new home in New Jersey.

Or so it seemed.

That's when *The Law* hit us right between the eyes – Murphy's Law, that is. The day I was to leave my company, the IRS quietly put a lien on my final pay. Somehow, they had found that I was leaving and figured I was skipping the State to get out of my debt with them – a thought that had never crossed my mind. I may not have been good with money, but I was honest to a fault. Good grief, I was only going to New Jersey, not moving to another country. Maybe the IRS thought they had too much extortion competition from the mob in Atlantic City and might not get their money back. Whatever the reason, they decided that they wanted all of their money now while I had it rather than trust me to pay them in installments as we had agreed and as I had been faithfully doing. Without even telling me about it beforehand, they took all my severance pay, including my final paycheck and vacation reimbursement. I had no money at all. I also had a car that wasn't running particularly well with four bald tires that would not last the five-hour drive to New Jersey. And I had bills to pay – lots of bills. My new company had paid for airline tickets for Lynne and Julie to go to West Virginia, so I didn't have to worry about them, but I had to do something. All my carefully made plans and dreams of a fresh start were crashing down around me. I had no choice but to call home and do something that, as a child, I had always dreaded. I asked my father for money.

Much to my surprise, my father didn't ask any questions other than how much I needed and where he should send it. Aliens had evidently kidnapped my father and left this pod person in his place, but I didn't argue with him. I was, however, grateful to the aliens. Within two days I left for New Jersey with four cheap, new tires, a bunch of mollified creditors and some money in my pocket. I just had to manage for a few weeks until I got my first paycheck. Then I had to find a home and figure out how I was going to get Lynne and Julie to New Jersey.

* * *

My new job in New Jersey was good. I had plenty of work to do and did such a good job at the start that, before long, I ended up practically running the group I was working in. I had driven to West Virginia to pick up Lynne and Julie. Everything went well on the trip home until a stranger in a car next to us at an intersection in Cumberland, Maryland frantically waved at us and shouted that our car was on fire. I immediately pulled into a bank parking lot to look. Sure enough, my right rear wheel was blazing furiously away. I first attempted to put the fire out with

155

a gallon bottle of something that I'd found in my trunk. It turned out that it was watered down anti-freeze that hadn't quite been watered down enough. The fire blossomed into a raging inferno. Someone from the bank came running out with a fire extinguisher and put out the fire. We were shaken but unhurt. I was able to slowly drive the car to a nearby service station and we checked into a motel just across the street to settle in and try to figure out what to do next. We had no money and no way to get back to South Jersey.

Desperate, I called a friend at my new company who actually volunteered to drive down to pick us up. We were a good four hours' drive from home, but it didn't matter to him. He was a very good friend. He arrived the next day and we piled into his car, leaving our damaged car behind to be repaired. It turned out that a wheel bearing had seized, causing so much friction in the wheel that it actually got hot enough to catch the brake fluid on fire. I had basically destroyed the right rear axle. And since the car was a Triumph Spitfire and I was in the middle of basically nowhere (my apologies to the good folks of Cumberland), right rear axles for British sports cars weren't exactly lying around. The guy at the service station had to go looking for one.

About a week later he finally called to tell me that he'd found a right rear axle for my car, but it was going to cost me a total of about $400, not including labor. I was being fleeced. I'd had problems with my car's split rear axles before and knew of a place near where I worked where I could get one for about $80. Since I didn't have $400 and I knew how to replace the axle myself, I called the service station in Cumberland and told the guy not to touch my car. In return he told me to get it the hell off of his property. I assured him I would be there the next day. My friend again volunteered to drive me back down to Cumberland and help me fix my car. We arrived in the late morning and pushed the car across the street to the parking lot behind the

Motel we had stayed at weeks before. I jacked the car up and got to work – just as an almost blinding snowstorm hit. Did I mention it was winter and we were in the mountains? I actually managed to fix the car just fine after a few hours of lying in the deep snow and drove the car home without further incident, except for frayed nerves that expected something to go wrong at any moment.

* * *

Lynne and I finally got settled down in New Jersey, but things started to go wrong right off the bat. Our money problems hadn't gone away. We still had all the bills we'd had before we came to New Jersey, thanks to the IRS. On top of it all, we didn't have Lynne's paycheck any more. Even though I was making more money, it wasn't enough to cover our combined salaries in Virginia. Worse yet, for some reason that she wouldn't share, Lynne refused to get a job. She wouldn't even go to get a New Jersey driver's license. She insisted that she needed to stay home with Julie – she didn't trust day care centers. Our bills started to pile up even more. The more money we owed, the more I tried to talk Lynne into going back to work. Finally, she did do something – she stopped using birth control without telling me. Again. This time, instead of pills, she was using a diaphragm with spermicidal jelly. She simply decided to stop using the jelly. She got pregnant almost immediately – again. Now she *really* couldn't go to work. Nine months later on October 15, 1980, our son Michael was born with us on the verge of bankruptcy.

Then we discovered something truly horrible.

Michael was different than his little sister. He cried all the time and didn't eat well. When Julie was born, Lynne fussed and fretted over her constantly, always worried if she made the slightest little unusual noise. Michael's behavior threw her into overdrive. She called me at work several times a day about little things that Michael was doing that scared her. We visited our pediatrician's office so often during those times that we almost lived there. No matter what the doctor checked for, he couldn't find anything wrong. We heard the term "colic" a lot, but no prescribed medicine seemed to help at all. Michael's almost non-stop crying and Lynne's constant worrying was driving us both crazy.

Finally, one day she called me at work to tell me that she thought there was something wrong with Michael's breathing. His breaths had become startlingly rapid and shallow. I left work and we rushed him to the doctor's office. The doctor listened to his chest, moving slowly from one place to another and concentrating intensely on what he was hearing. When he was finished, he looked at us with a worried frown and told us to get Michael to Children's Hospital in Philadelphia right away. He would call them to tell them we were coming. He told us to try not to worry; that it might not be anything at all, but the doctors at Children's Hospital would be able to tell us more with some tests.

When we drove up to the hospital entrance, they were waiting for us. They rushed Michael into a room where they ran a few tests on him, including an emergency cardiac catheterization. We could do nothing but sit in the waiting room, trying hard not to fear the worst. Hours later, the doctor came out and asked us to come with him to his office. We sat down and steeled ourselves for news that no parent ever wants to hear – our two-month-old son was gravely ill. The catheterization had revealed that Michael had an atrial-septal defect in his heart as well as a deformed mitral valve. In layman's terms, he had a hole between the two chambers of his heart and a valve that wasn't closing enough to keep blood from rushing back out of his heart instead of through it. His heart was pumping furiously to try to get blood to his body, and his lungs were almost rigid from the increased pressure, making it difficult for him to breathe. They admitted him right away and immediately put him on medicine to slow his heart down and stabilize his breathing.

The first night Michael was in the hospital his heart actually stopped beating. Lynne had been sitting by his bedside when his lack of movement caught her attention. She ran screaming down the hall for help. Luckily, they got Michael's heart started again and he survived the night. The rest of his week-long stay in the hospital was less dramatic and we took him home with the dark knowledge that our son was going to have to have open heart surgery some time before his fifth birthday. The doctors didn't want to operate now because they wanted to wait until he was older and stronger to operate. We weren't convinced that he would last that long.

From the day Michael came home from the hospital, he was dependent upon very precise doses of heart medication to keep his heart beating as normally as possible, antibiotics to keep him safe from illness – the slightest of which could be life threatening to him – and diuretics to keep him from retaining too much water because of the heart medication. As time passed, Michael's constant crying had stopped, and he seemed at least to be stabilized for the time being. But it was obvious that he was far from well. By the time he was a year old, it was becoming clearer that he was going to have to need surgery much sooner than expected. He wasn't growing normally and still couldn't eat well. His lungs were still so rigid from the errant blood flow that breathing was difficult, making the simple act of eating so

159

exhausting that he would fall asleep before he could eat much. We were watching our son begin to die. We had only limited medical insurance at the time which would have only paid a portion of the astronomical costs of open-heart surgery. I was becoming increasingly essential at work and needed more and more time off as time went by. Things had never looked darker. I was worried for the life of my son, the mental health of my wife and for my job. Ironically, I was so worried about everyone and everything else that, for the first time in my life, my inner problem had disappeared.

When Michael was one and a half years old, we found we could wait no longer. Thanks to the Deborah Heart and Lung Center in Browns Mills, NJ, Michael had his surgery for no cost to us. No one expected him to survive the operation; not even his surgeons. Before the surgery could proceed, we had to read and sign a statement listing the risks of this surgery and that we understood that he might not survive. Then I had to write out the same statement freehand on a separate piece of paper and sign it again. They wanted to make sure we had read and understood every word. On the day of the operation, Lynne and I were allowed to carry Michael with the nurse as far as the operating room doors. The hardest thing I've ever had to do was to pry him away from my near-hysterical wife and hand him to the nurse, knowing that we might never hold him again. We watched, both of us sobbing, as the nurse carried him through the operating doors and to whatever fate awaited him.

* * *

Much to everyone's surprise and delight, Michael survived the surgery. He wasn't out of the woods yet, but at least he was still alive. He was immediately placed in the Critical Cardiac Care Unit where he was to stay until he was stabilized. He was listed as critical but stable. The first time we saw him after the surgery, Lynne almost fainted. They warned us of what we were going to see when we entered the room, but the warning wasn't enough. There didn't seem to be a patch of skin on Michael's entire body that didn't have some kind of wire or tube sticking out of it. He was on a ventilator to help him breathe, a heart monitor to watch for trouble and about a thousand other things that were just horrible to see protruding from his helpless little body.

His recovery went slowly, and he spent much more time in the CCCU than was usual. On a day that allowed us to finally breathe again, he was taken off the critical list and moved to the non-cardiac Intensive Care Unit where we witnessed the most astounding change we had ever seen. With each passing day, Michael visibly gained strength and vitality. The surgery had been a complete success. The doctors had found not one but two holes in Michael's heart, one of which was dangerously close to the major nerve bundle in the center of his heart that regulated its beating, making the surgery even more dangerous than even they had originally thought. If they had even so much as nicked that nerve bundle, Michael's heart could have been irreparably damaged. Both holes were successfully closed, allowing his blood to pass properly through his heart. They repaired the deformed mitral valve, keeping the blood from backing up out of his heart with each beat. For the first time in his life, Michael's heart was normal. As it turned out, the type of heart problem that Michael had was very unusual for a child not born with Down's syndrome. If he had been born with both problems, I honestly don't know if we would have authorized the surgery. It would have seemed kinder somehow to just let him slip away naturally. We'll never know. Luckily, that wasn't a decision that we had to make.

Michael's recovery was nothing short of miraculous. With each passing day, he was more animated during the day than we had ever seen him, eating voraciously at every meal and sleeping well at night. We had a normal son and we had Deborah Heart and Lung Center to thank for it. We never received a bill for their services. Their payment came from whatever the insurance companies would give them combined with charitable donations given to the hospital. They had saved my son's life and asked nothing in return. We are eternally grateful for their skill and their kindness.

* * *

Michael was in good health and growing for the first time in his life. Julie's health was never in question, and she was fast becoming a small version of her mother, even at age three – very outgoing and self-assured. Our money problems, however, were getting worse with each passing day. Lynne still didn't have a job and we argued long and hard over the need for her to help with our finances. Nothing I could say did any good at all. The only way Lynne helped with the finances was to run up hundreds of dollars in phone bills each month to her mother in West Virginia and to keep the thermostat in the winter turned up to 75 no matter what I did to keep her from doing it. I spent a lot of time on the phone with the telephone and gas and electric companies begging for them not to turn off our service. Left with no other options, I filed for bankruptcy. It was the only thing I could do, and it was the last thing I wanted to do, but I had no choice. A few months after filing, it was official. It was almost seven years before I got any credit again. I felt like a total failure.

I had hoped that with the bills gone our marriage would begin to bounce back. With Michael's health problems behind us, Lynne no longer had a valid reason not to work and I was finally able to talk her into getting a driver's license and a job. She found a job without too much trouble but most of her salary went to day care for the kids. It was still a good thing because it got her out of the house and allowed us to start saving some money. I had to admit that, even though I was ashamed of having to file for bankruptcy, it was nice to have a fresh start again.

With Lynne's new job came an independence that she hadn't felt before. During Michael's hospitalization and recovery, she spent most of her time in the hospital and I had to spend most of my time at work trying to keep my job. I'd had to force myself not to let Michael's problems overwhelm me and risk losing our only source of income and medical insurance. I had to be strong for my family. Lynne misunderstood this to be a lack of caring and, no matter how much we discussed it, she never forgave me for not being there with her more often.

Other problems between us were surfacing all the time. We never seemed to agree on how to raise the children. Whenever I would discipline them, all they had to do was run to Lynne who would then negate everything I had said or done. In the evening I would put them to bed and scold them several times for playing instead of going to sleep. Lynne would come home late and both kids would hop out of bed to greet her. When I told her they were supposed to be in bed, she'd tell them it was all right and let them stay up later. I ended up having no say whatsoever in how they were raised. I was only allowed to punish them when punishment was needed. This went on for a long time, even in front of my parents when they came to visit one time. They were appalled. One night it just became too much. When the kids jumped out of bed for the umpteenth time and Lynne overrode what I had told them, I snapped. I roughly put Julie and Michael back in their beds (too roughly due to my anger) and then turned my attention to Lynne, yelling at her for contradicting everything I did with the kids. I even pushed her down on a futon bed behind her when she started to tell me how unfair I was with the kids and, in my rage, even kicked the futon a few times with her lying on it. I was very nearly out of control. When I realized that, I left the house and drove around for hours trying to collect myself. I even called the therapist who I'd been seeing to get me to calm down. When I returned home, Lynne had barricaded herself and the kids in the kids' room and wouldn't come out. I finally convinced her to open the door and let the kids come out so I could talk to them. I hugged them and explained that I loved them very much and that sometimes Mommy and Daddy have arguments. I apologized to them for my outburst. I apologized to Lynne only for the violent outburst; not for losing my temper. Our marriage was truly falling apart around us.

Lynne found that she liked getting out and working after all this time and started to enjoy herself. Her new-found independence became a convenient way to move further away from me. She even started talking to me about cute guys at work that she found extremely attractive. Instead of coming together, we were drifting further apart. I desperately wanted things to be better for her sake and for the sake of the kids, so I had gotten a phone number from a friend of a counselor named Bob in Philadelphia and made an appointment to go see him. Surprisingly (to me, anyway), Lynne really didn't want to talk to him even though that was the reason I had gone to him in the first place. We saw Bob together as a couple only a few times. During one of those sessions, I told him about how my "problem" had interfered earlier in the marriage but that it was under control, and I wanted to make this work out. You could see the lights going on in his eyes. He asked to see me by myself to talk about this further. I was hesitant at first to say yes because I had dabbled in seeing therapists before. Every one of them had told me that I really didn't have this problem; I was simply confused because of what kind of a person my father had been and how he had left us. I have to admit that in those sessions, I was so afraid of what might happen in my life, I hadn't been totally honest with them about how I felt. And their rush to judgment about what was wrong with me and their professed "ease" at treating me over lots and lots of sessions made me suspicious of their motives (money) and their abilities (few). It's like signing up at a karate school that guarantees that you'll get a black belt if you pay them a lot of money up front. I never saw any of the other therapists more than a few times. This time I promised myself it would be different. This man seemed to understand what I was going through and really wanted to help me. With my marriage crumbling around me, I was determined to finally take the plunge and take my first steps into the unknown. I was terrified of what I would find.

Pictures

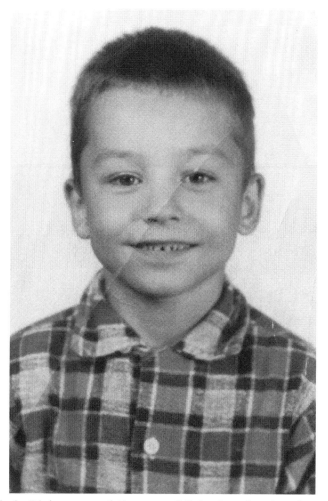

This is Ricky around the age of 5 during the time he was sitting in the field looking for the first star. You can see the Native American in me here.

Family picture of all of the family kids when I was about 8. From the back, left to right, Ricky, my brother Danny. In front, my little brother Tim and my sister Debbie.

This is Ricky around the age of 12 when the bullying and
name calling were just starting.

Ricky in the 8th grade in a new school with a whole new set of tormentors ahead of me. I would learn to find refuge from the bullying in the piano room during lunch class when I got into high school.

This is my graduation picture from 1969. The original picture was in color. They airbrushed the zits from my face and colored my hair red. They also captioned the picture in the Senior Yearbook as "Rock Thompson". Not only was Ricky not really me, the picture was not even Ricky.

This is the Bryan, Ohio, courthouse where we played as children in the elevator. At Christmas time, lights strung from all four corners of the spire. People can see it from miles around.

I was barely 19 here and stationed in the Philippines
where I ended up living with my friends in their on-base
house taking care of their 2-year-old daughter. I've never
been in a hotter place in my life.

This is the last picture of Ricky ever taken. I was a department manager here in 1990 with my entire career going nowhere but up. I had a great salary, a wonderful fiancé, and everything going for me. But I gave it all up to find myself.

This is my first picture ever - taken at night in a coin-
operated photo machine in front of a K-Mart. It was at
night because I was afraid to go out during the day yet.
Looking at this picture after I took it almost made me
change my mind about going any further. I couldn't
imagine that I'd ever look any better than this or that my
life was going to go anywhere but down.

Dr. Michel Seghers (1932-2014) standing in front of his home in Brussels, Belgium. Dr. Seghers was a great surgeon with a wonderful sense of humor who made me laugh even when the stitches hurt when I did.

This is my very first company Christmas Party. I had my hair done specially, bought a beautiful outfit with heels to match. It was the first time I ever got to shop for Rachael for a special occasion. I felt gorgeous for the first time in my life!

My friend Aine and I in Dublin, Ireland. When I went for my second surgery in 1994, I stopped in Dublin first to see my dear friend Aine. We bounced in and out of every pub near the Ha'Penny Bridge all night. It was wonderful!

In 1998 Marilyn and I went to Amsterdam for the Gay Games where I participated in and judged the martial arts competitions. After the opening ceremonies we lost each other and ended up going back to the hotel in the city separately and in a panic.

This is me in New Jersey in 2005 just before the tick bite that put me in the hospital in a coma and changed my life forever. I thought one life-changing event in my life was enough. Evidently the fates didn't agree.

In 2008 I was still recovering from my bout with the tick but living quiet happily in New Hampshire. New Hampshire is a lot friendlier than New Jersey. Up here they wave at you with ALL of their fingers.

Chapter 14
The Journey Begins...sort of...

Lynne and I tried to see Bob together for some time to try somehow to find a way to make our lives together work at least for the sake of our children if for no other reason. That came to a screeching halt at one particularly raucous session in which Lynne had been complaining about things that I did and how they made her crazy. Bob let her talk and get it out of her system and then asked her to tell him what she thought *she* was doing wrong in the relationship. She thought about this for a few seconds and, seemingly from nowhere, said, "The only thing I'm doing wrong is putting up with all this crap. I understand now why Helen treated him the way she did."

I was horrified and speechless at this attack. I couldn't believe she'd said that. She knew how much Helen had hurt me and it seemed that *she* wanted to do it, too. What in the world was wrong with me that made these women want to treat me this way? For a moment, that time with Helen came crashing down over me again along with all the pain and humiliation. I started to shake. Bob stood up, red faced, glared at Lynne and told her to wait outside. When she tried to protest, he yelled,

"GET OUT! I NEVER WANT TO SEE YOU IN MY OFFICE AGAIN!"

Lynne, outraged that anyone would have the audacity to speak to her in such a way, left the room in a huff, slamming the door behind her. Bob turned to me and asked if I was all right. I broke down crying. After a few moments, I regained my composure and told him that I was OK. I wasn't ok, but what else could I have said? I wasn't looking forward to the ride home at all. Lynne never set foot in Bob's office again. Our marriage was over within the space of the year. We filed papers for an uncontested divorce with a Separation Agreement giving her custody of the children with full visitation rights for me – or at least that's what the paper said.

With the Separation Agreement in effect, Lynne took a job back in Virginia. On a bright, sunny day I loaded up pretty much all of the furniture in the house along with all of hers and the kids' belongings into a rented U-Haul truck and moved her and the kids to a small apartment in Virginia Beach. When I returned to New Jersey with the empty truck to my empty house, the first thing that caught my eye was the back yard where a few of the kids' toys that had been left behind were scattered. I sat down and cried for hours. Once again, I had failed miserably and once again I was alone.

* * *

I started seeing Bob twice a week. My insurance covered fifty percent of the charges for outpatient psychiatric care for what he diagnosed (for the insurance company) as depression. If he had said I was being treated for "Gender Dysphoria", they would not have paid anything for my sessions. According to the insurance companies, who certainly know medical and psychiatric needs better than doctors and therapists, Gender Dysphoria is not a real problem; it's all made up and should just be ignored. Most insurance companies to this day still will not cover anything having to do with this condition. In some ways we're still living in the dark ages. Anyway, Bob and I talked about everything in my life; my relationship with my parents and siblings, my childhood, my friends, my inner feelings – everything we could think of to try to come up with some way to help me beat these feelings that would not die. At one time, he tried putting me into group therapy to help me to be more open about myself and not feel so ashamed. It was a disaster.

During my first night with the group, I listened as the others in the group talked about their problems and fears. I didn't understand some of their problems, but I felt for them and the pain they experienced. Some of them even had made up alter-egos for themselves to help cope with their problems. When that issue came up, Bob looked at me and asked aloud, "Rick, you have an alter-ego, or another name, that you use to help you, too, don't you?"

Although I really sympathized with the others in the group, I didn't feel that anyone there had a problem anywhere near as life-changing and serious as what I was going through. I just didn't relate to them at all and felt very uncomfortable being there. I just nodded to Bob and said, "Sort of." I didn't feel any need to elaborate even though I knew he wanted me to. I just didn't feel comfortable talking about my identity crisis to a group of people who were fighting with agoraphobia and other personal fears. My group sessions lasted only a few weeks. Bob agreed that it had been a bad idea.

One of the main problems I had with Bob, and with most other therapists, was that I knew more about my condition than he did. I read every book and article on transsexualism that I could find, even some that were decidedly against even admitting that the condition existed, all in my insatiable desire to learn what was wrong with me and how I could fix it. Most therapists just didn't have any background in this sort of thing. I was becoming impatient. It didn't feel like we were getting anywhere, and I had been seeing Bob for quite some time. Maybe this guy really didn't know how to treat me for this condition after all. But he had tried everything he knew. Bob even had his wife, who was also a therapist in an adjacent office and who had never met me, give me a battery of psychological tests. Even she could come to no specific conclusion about what was wrong with me. The tests did, however, show that I had a proclivity towards feeling I was the wrong gender. That was at least some comfort. One surprising thing that the tests showed was that my depression was so severe that most people on the same scale were either hospitalized or unable to function well in society. It seems that my learned ability while in school to throw myself into my studies or work to get my mind off of how I felt actually turned out to be of great benefit to me.

With both of us becoming increasingly exasperated, Bob finally brought in an associate of his to get a second opinion. Richard was a soft spoken, handsome gay man who worked more with sexual problems, especially in the gay and lesbian world. Together, Richard and Bob sat down with me, and, in a two-hour session, we discussed everything in detail; how I felt, what Bob had tried and what he thought about it. When we were finished, Richard took Bob aside and told him that he believed I was, in fact, suffering from Gender Dysphoria and that he believed that he could help me. He didn't believe that there was any other kind of therapy that would be effective. From that time on, I saw only Richard. And I'm glad I did.

* * *

Before we go on, we have to go back a little. While I was seeing Bob and trying to convince myself that I could beat this thing and make it go away, a few most interesting things happened. One of them had to do with my mother. While I was in the Navy and going through my divorce with Helen, I had shared my secret with my sister, Debbie, desperate for someone to talk to. I didn't know at the time that she was going through severe personal upheavals herself at that time. Her husband had been cheating on her and she was leaving him, taking their three young children with her. She was having enough trouble handling her own problems and just couldn't handle mine. She shared what I had told her with our mother. Mom's response to the "news" was to write to me to tell me that "the grass wasn't greener on the other side of the fence." She thought that this whole thing that I had been going through was all in my head as an attempt to run away from the hurt that I'd faced in my life with repeated rejections by women. I had told my sister about my birth certificate discovery and, of course, my mother heard about that, too. In response to this, she did something that I didn't think was possible – she went to the local town Clerk's office and asked for my official birth certificate. Then she pointed out to the clerk that a mistake had been made. The birth certificate said I was female when she knew for a fact that I was obviously male. They had made a mistake when I was born, and she wanted to fix it. And while they were at it, she thought it would be only right to have my name updated from Ricky to Richard. Unbelievably, she seemed to have the right in Ohio to do that until I was 21. At the time I was only 20. She was my mother. So, she had them make the change and no one thought anything of it – except me. I now have a correction paper attached to my official birth certificate stating that my gender and name were corrected as she had requested. I was now fully and legally a male name Richard Eugene Thompson. When she first told me she had done this, I was upset. How dare she make changes without my approval? I was an adult, after all. But after thinking about it, I came to the conclusion that this might be a good thing after all. Without the gender error and girlish sounding name hanging over me, maybe this would help me be male after all. It was worth a try.

* * *

With Lynne's absence I started to convince myself that I was finally in control of my life and of my destiny. So, I started dating. This was interesting experience number two.

My first dating experience found me in a very odd relationship. I began seeing a woman at work named Bonnie. The first strange thing about the two of us being together was our size difference – I'm almost six feet tall and Bonnie was four feet nine and one-half inches tall (she was very precise about it). We looked like a very odd couple indeed. She was a manager, as was I, and very sure of herself and her ideas. She had no problem dressing someone down who didn't do their work properly or praising someone who had done well. She was driven to always do an above-average job and constantly pushed those around her to do the same. She also didn't have a problem with going in and yelling at her boss (something I would never consider doing). She was exceedingly pretty, outgoing, vivacious and a very sexual person. But she had some problems of her own. She was extremely self-conscious of what others said or thought about her. After dating for some while, we moved in together but only after she extracted a promise from me that I would not tell people at work about our living arrangements. She did not think it would be appropriate or good for her career to be found living with someone outside of marriage – and with a co-worker at that. So, I had to keep our cohabitation a secret. I was never comfortable with that. I never did like lying to people.

The strangest thing about our relationship didn't come to me until long after we had split up. Bonnie didn't cook; she didn't clean, and she definitely didn't do windows. Her idea of a walk in the Great Outdoors was crossing the parking lot to Macy's. We didn't go out much, especially to do the outdoor type of things that I enjoyed so much. She was a city girl, tried and true. She was used to calling out for dinner and having someone come in to clean. Of course, I wasn't used to that and, in fact, enjoyed doing those things from so long ago when I helped my mother at home. So, I ended up being the housekeeper and cook in our household. I didn't mind at all.

Bonnie was also very moody. One minute she would be praising me for being great in so many ways and then get me in bed and screw my brains out; the next minute she was verbally abusing me and telling me how stupid I was for some small thing I had done wrong. She would bring me flowers and then, not an hour later, storm out in a rage over something I had said or done that had somehow offended her. I was often left standing with my mouth open watching her slam the door and wondering what I done. Strangely enough, though, I found myself enjoying this relationship in spite of the sadomasochistic overtones that I didn't really even see at the time.

Our romance ended when she decided to take a job out on the West Coast. I was going to college in the evenings trying to get my bachelor's degree in Computer Science as well as another in Foreign Languages Specializing in Chinese and was very close to graduation from both. I just couldn't find it in myself to stop in the middle of all that to follow her, only to have to start all over again somewhere else where my hard-earned college credits might not be accepted. I realize now that I was also subconsciously telling myself that this was a good place to make a break. We had a very emotional and tearful breakup and she left for the West Coast.

The *very* strangest thing about our time together was that, looking back on it sometime later, I was amazed to realize that my relationship with Bonnie was almost identical to my mother's relationship with my birth father, with the exception of the physical violence. I had been the proverbial housewife, kept at home, kept happy and kept firmly in my place, punished when I did something wrong and praised in an attempt to make

187

up. It had been the 1950s all over again and *I had been happy with the role.* That realization was quite a shock to me. Was that really what I thought of gender roles and how I felt I'd find happiness? It seemed horribly self-destructive. My inner problem never really surfaced much (except during sex when I could fantasize out being the woman) because my mixed-up emotional needs seemed to be met. I knew that I had to think on this a lot more. I didn't want to have my mother's life. It had been too late for her, but it certainly wasn't for me. In later years when I saw Bonnie again during a business trip to California, she apologized for the way that she had treated me and said that she didn't blame me for not following her out to California. It was nice to hear but way too late.

With that breakup, I found myself alone again with no prospects for companionship and no knowledge of where my life was going. It was getting to be very familiar territory. Again, I had a lot of time to sit and think about myself, which was never a good idea if I wanted to keep from thinking bad thoughts about my condition and my continued existence. When the loneliness became almost too much to bear, I broke a rule that I had finally set for myself after Bonnie – I looked for companionship.

* * *

I had talked one evening to a very sweet woman named Barbara who worked at a local store in customer service and, on an impulse that my common sense couldn't deter, I asked her out on a date. Our relationship quickly became physical and intense. We were both people in desperate need of someone in our lives. I wasn't lonely any more but the closer we got, the more insecure I started feeling about my identity. All of my old thoughts started flooding back and, in a panic, I broke off the

188

relationship before they got any worse. Poor Barbara had done nothing wrong and didn't understand. I couldn't tell her the real reason we couldn't go on and so I ended up hurting her terribly. The thought of that is still a knife in my heart. She didn't deserve such treatment. I felt even worse now than I had before we had met.

Sometime after that breakup when I had gotten my head back together (and forgotten my pledge not to date again), I was introduced by a friend at work to his sister Kate. By this time, I had been alone again for a sufficient enough amount of time that my thoughts were starting to scare me again. Suicide was never far from my mind during those days. But, as always, I knew that if I threw myself into something else, I could get my mind off of problems and, at least for a while, they would go away. I agreed to meet her. We immediately hit it off very well. Kate and I had everything in common that Bonnie and I hadn't. We both enjoyed backpacking and bicycling and all other manners of outdoor things to do. Before long, we found ourselves becoming closer than I had initially expected or even wanted. We had fallen in love. Kate was so different from the other women I'd known (or married). She was very intelligent, independent and very loving without being critical of what I did or said. She was like a breath of fresh air. We soon found ourselves spending all of our free time together cycling all over southern New Jersey with friends in a local outdoor club. I was actually having fun with someone close to me for the first time in my adult life. The more time we spent together, the further into the shadows I was able to push my inner turmoil. I began to honestly believe that I had finally found the person who could make me whole. But there were signs to the opposite that I continually ignored.

One of the missed signs had to do with bicycle clothing. The black spandex shorts with the padded rear were very tight and

189

showed the central bulge between my legs in great detail. On one club cycling trip, one of Kate's girlfriends remarked to her about it with me standing right there. They both had a good "nudge, nudge, wink, wink" laugh about it. Because I'd always been embarrassed by my "size", I was thoroughly mortified and sped off on my bike so they wouldn't see my face go crimson. I don't think it worked. They did think that my reaction was amusing, though.

Kate and I had grown so close that we finally decided to move in together. She was renting the bottom floor of a small duplex house in nearby Collingswood, and I was still renting the small apartment that I had secretly (except everyone knew) shared with Bonnie. It didn't take much to convince me to move out of there with its empty rooms and confused memories. Kate's house was situated in a quiet little neighborhood and, although it was small, had plenty of room for the both of us.

Our first few months together were very happy. I even took her home to meet my parents in Ohio. They were thrilled with her. They had not been happy with my choice of Helen, especially after she lived with them for the six months I was in the Philippines, and they were very much against Lynne who they correctly saw as a clone of Helen. Kate was very different, indeed. My parents took an immediate liking to Kate as she did to them. I couldn't have been happier. However, there was one little glitch. While we were home visiting my parents, I decided that our relationship had come to the point where she needed to know everything about me. One evening as we were lying in bed, I swallowed my fear and tearfully told her about how I'd felt for all those years. She took it fairly well although she was obviously shaken by the news. She asked me how I felt now. I told her that she was the only thing that was important to me and that all that other stuff was behind me. I wanted to make sure that there weren't any secrets between us. We talked through the night until she seemed satisfied. I didn't know it at the time, but I was lying to her. I really had convinced myself that I had found the one person who would make me forget forever and be happy with myself. I still didn't realize that this was not the sort of thing that would just go away by itself. That would come in time. Complacency in my life would see to that just fine.

As I said, our lives were very happy together. We talked of marriage but only a little. Neither of us was ready to make that plunge yet. We brought Michael and Julie up to visit every once in a while from Delaware where they were living with their mother and they would stay with us through the weekends. They loved her, too, and she was very good to them, treating them as if they were her own. I had it all. I was great friends with her brother at work and, with his fiancé and his and Kate's mother, Flo, I really started to feel like I was part of the family. But my inner identity just couldn't be squelched that easily. The more content I became in our relationship, the more I felt the old feelings start to creep back in. I guess without the giddiness of a new relationship masking everything else, my mind had more time to ponder other things. Without telling Kate, I started seeing my therapist, Richard, again. It was difficult to keep that kind of secret from someone I was living with, so I finally ended up telling her about my sessions. I explained that there were just a few things that I had to work out. I told her not to worry – I just needed a "fix" from my therapist to help.

Richard immediately set to work with me by introducing me to *Renaissance*, a support group for men with psycho-sexual problems that met in the outskirts of Philadelphia once a month. It was originally founded for transvestites (TVs) or cross-dressers (CDs) as they preferred to be called, so that they had a place to dress up and mingle without fear of discovery. They eventually expanded their outreach to include transsexuals and

191

had allowed a small group of them to get together during their monthly soirees. This was a mixed blessing for me. Most transsexuals don't think of themselves as transvestites; as a matter of fact, they consider being called one a supreme insult. Transvestism and transsexualism are at opposite ends of the spectrum. TVs are usually either married straight men who get a sexual release from dressing up as women or flamboyant gay male female impersonators. In either case, a transvestite would never consider having his penis removed. Transsexuals, or TSs, on the other hand, would like nothing better. They are not people posing as the opposite sex – they are posing as the sex into which they were born. Neither understands the other. So, at a place like Renaissance, the two groups stayed far apart with the exception of the occasional curious person sitting in on group conversations, not even beginning to comprehend why *these people* are like they are. It was all very confusing.

I agreed with Richard that it might be a good thing for me to go check this group out so, one Friday night, I screwed up my courage and drove the 45 minutes to where the meetings were held. I was very afraid that first night – afraid of being associated with the group, but more afraid that I just might find out that I was a TV after all. I didn't dress in women's clothes – I just went as Ricky, curious to see what I would find. The first person that I met at the door was a very large man dressed in a black leather dominatrix outfit complete with spiked heels, fishnet stockings and a bad wig. He took out a blank name tag and asked in a deep voice, "What would you like to be called?"

* * *

I actually had considered names prior to this encounter. I had come to an earlier conclusion that my name would be Karen Stewart, a name that I continued to use from time to time when I wished my true identity to be hidden for some reason. I liked the name Karen – it seemed to fit me somehow – and my favorite actor growing up was Jimmy Stewart, ergo "Stewart". The name just sounded right. I finally chose not to use it, though, because of problems if I ever decided to go through with everything. During the transition period in which I would be dressing and living as a woman, I would have to change all of my identification documents. It wouldn't do to have to show my male ID to someone while I wasn't dressed as a female. That would be embarrassing. So, I thought it might be easier to change my name, at least for the time being, to something that would start with the initials of my birth name – R. E. Thompson. I bought a book of baby names and started scanning. My middle name wasn't a problem. Originally, I was given my father's middle name of Eugene. My mother's middle name is Evelyn. What better way to honor my mother than to base my new life around her and take her middle name? (I was to find later that my mother was not honored in the least.)

My first name was a bit harder. I wanted to find something that started with 'R' and went well with Evelyn. I settled on Rachael. I chose that spelling because the spelling of "Rachel" just didn't seem right to me. I've since discovered that about half of the population expects the name to be spelled with the extra 'a' as I had chosen, and the other half expects it to be spelled without. In the end it didn't really matter much.

So, it was settled. My name was going to be Rachael Evelyn Thompson. Now I could get all of my personal identification documents – credit cards and the like – changed to R. E. Thompson and it wouldn't matter how I was dressed.

* * *

I looked at the faux dominatrix standing in front of me and said, "I'd like to be called my name – Rachael". He rolled his eyes and gave me an "Oh, no. Not another one of *those*" looks, wrote the name down on the name tag (misspelled) and handed it to me. I asked him where the TS group met, and he pointed toward a door across the crowded room. That was when I got my first good look around me.

The main room of the psychiatrist's office where the club met was full of men in all sorts of various clothing that most women wouldn't be caught dead in. Although the Dominatrix theme seemed to be very popular, there were all manners of other fashion styles present. There were evening gowns, prom dresses and heavy makeup everywhere. There was even a very large, very hairy bearded man wearing a yellow polka-dotted Suzie-Homemaker-from-the-50s-type dress complete with frills around the collar. The stockings he was wearing showed the matted leg hair beneath them with stunning clarity. Everything inside me said, "RUN!" but I steeled myself and pushed politely through the crowd, hoping that no one would hear the screaming that was coming from inside me. The mere thought that I might find out that the feelings that I had struggled with all of my life might turn out to be nothing more than a sexual fantasy and that I was really just a transvestite that could be part of this crowd was horrifying to me. I just couldn't be one of these guys standing around in drag talking in deep voices about sports and auto maintenance, all the while making sure their press-on nails look just right. I held my breath and moved further across the room toward the door.

I'm not sure what I expected to find in that room. I had never met another person who believed that they were transsexual. What I found took me pleasantly by surprise. Instead of the garish female caricatures that I had just passed, I saw a small, inviting, quiet room with a few casually dressed women in jeans and blouses – hair done nicely (or at least good wigs) and no heavy makeup. It was the exact opposite of what I had just seen. At first the women in the room were a little startled to see a man walk in but when they saw my name tag, they knew why I was there. I was immediately welcomed by everyone and told that I had nothing to fear – I was with friends. For the first time in my life, I finally got to meet other people who were going through the same thing that I was and let myself talk openly about how I felt. It was one of the most tremendous and enlightening nights of my life. These were real people struggling with the same thing that I had lived with all my life. They were in different stages of change – some just starting out, some already post-operative – but I felt an immediate kinship with all of them.

This night was also one of the most difficult for me. I guess I had expected some sort of closure in my life by meeting these people. Instead, I discovered a new yearning. I realized that I wasn't alone in my feelings and that I could actually be a whole person if I just had the courage to go forward. I didn't know how I would ever find that courage, though. Worse yet, I had to go back home and face the woman I loved and tell her how things went without scaring her. I hoped she'd understand. She had known that I was going and wasn't happy about it at all, but she figured, as did I, that it might do some good, so she acquiesced. When I returned home in the early hours of the morning, she was in bed but not asleep. I felt very embarrassed and uneasy, but we talked a bit about the meeting. I could only bring myself to tell her about the outlandish transvestites I had seen and how utterly ridiculous they looked. We didn't talk about it much more that night, but I could tell that our relationship was already beginning to crumble.

195

My next session with Richard was very interesting. When I told him about my severe discomfort with the men in drag at the meeting, he understood perfectly. I was close to tears with the thought that I might be one of those people. He tried to comfort me with the knowledge that he didn't believe at all that I was a transvestite, or that I had ever been one. That did make me feel better. I trusted his judgment. He finally suggested to me that if I felt too uncomfortable there, I could go to a different group that met in the city. It wasn't in a location as posh as the psychiatrist's office where Renaissance met but it was all TS people. The group was called the Philadelphia Transsexual Support Group. I decided to try them.

My first encounter with the PTSG was on a rainy summer evening in a tiny dark room donated by a local gay-friendly Catholic group (I hadn't known there was such a thing). Inside I found a small group of people, some in transition, and some not, but all there for the same reason as me – to know that they were not alone and get solace and hope from each other. It wasn't the type of meeting where someone would stand up and say "Hi! My name is {insert your name here} and I'm a transsexual". It was very informal and moderated by a woman named Denise who was further along in the process and a little more centered than most of us. If you wanted to talk about your current situation, you could. If you didn't want to, you didn't have to. Many just sat and listened, especially for their first few visits. The good thing was that whatever your problem at the moment might be – fear, anger, abandonment, etc. – someone in the group was either going through it or had gone through it and would understand. Some people I'd met from Renaissance were there, too, so I didn't feel totally alone.

My first shock at the meeting was a small, pudgy, balding man sitting up front. I remember him specifically because I felt so sorry for him that he would have a horrible time trying to pass as a woman. I just couldn't imagine how he would pull it off. Then I found out that he was a Female-to-Male TS who was going through transition. This guy used to be female! I was floored – and impressed. He was having some problems, though, and was there looking for some answers. It was not the only time I saw "F-to-M"s there, though. In time there were so many coming to the meetings that they decided to split off into their own group. The last thing these guys wanted to do was sit around listening to a bunch of women giving each other makeup and fashion tips.

My second shock was something that didn't really hit me hardest until the next day. There was a woman there who was just starting her transition to full time status living as a female. She was the biggest, most masculine looking woman I'd ever seen. All I could think at the time was, "My God, that poor person is going to be in a living hell trying to pass." But the longer the evening wore on, the more I started to see myself in her. Not feeling like a particularly feminine looking woman to begin with, I often looked into the mirror only to see a man in drag looking back. I had broad shoulders, was tall and had a bit of a lantern jaw. The more I looked at this woman, the more upset I started to become. My thoughts had started to tell me, "I'm going to look like that, I'm never going to "pass" and MY life is going to be a living hell." By the end of the evening I was just short of an official basket case.

The next day at work I found myself unable to concentrate on anything. I couldn't get the image of that woman out of my mind. I teetered on the verge of bursting into tears at a moment's notice – not a good thing to do at work, especially considering I was now the Department Manager of the group. It would have been a little hard to explain being found in my office crumpled on the floor crying hysterically. The last thing I wanted to do was to have to explain why I was so upset. As the urge to cry became more desperate, I called Richard and, barely able to control my shaking voice, pleaded to see him right away. He told me to come in right away, so I left work immediately to take the train into the city.

The moment I set foot in his office the dam burst. I broke down like a little child, as I had before so many times. After I regained some sort of control over myself, I recounted my experience the night before and how it had made me feel. By the time my hour with Richard was over, he had convinced me that I had no idea how I was going to look or how people would react to me when it came time for my transition, if it ever came to that. He pointed out to me that my features weren't anywhere near as masculine as the person that I had described. I was just being hyper-critical of myself (I've heard that often about myself). Worrying about that now would be self-destructive. I had to hold onto that though if I expected to remain sane. With my eyes still red and swollen, I left Richard's office feeling better and returned to work. By the time I got back, I had totally regained my composure. I have to admit, though, that I was beginning to wonder if my fragile hold on sanity was beginning to slip. It took a lot of work keeping my depression at bay.

I never told Kate anything about this near breakdown. Our relationship was already on shaky ground. She understood that I had to have some help but when she confided in one of our friends who happened to be a lesbian about my predicament, she told Kate that what I was going through was very similar to being gay – it was never going to go away, no matter how much help I got for it. Kate was beginning to worry. I was secretly (or so I thought) buying female clothing again that I would put on at the meetings – never at home. I had gotten my left ear pierced earlier and Kate had given me a diamond stud to wear. She went away on business for a week once and I pierced my other ear.

198

She couldn't help but notice even though I tried hard to hide it. The clincher came when I ordered a pair of silicone breast forms by mail. They came one day in two separate packages with the name of the prosthetics company I'd ordered them front printed in big letters on them. Kate just happened to be home that day when they were delivered. It didn't take a rocket scientist to figure out what they were, especially when I wouldn't tell her.

Within a few weeks, I knew that I needed to go further to see if this path was the right one for me. The pain was beginning to become unbearable. It was raining the night I decided to tell Kate. The last thing in the world I wanted to do was to hurt her, but I didn't know how it was possible for me not to. I quietly slipped out of the front door and walked around the neighborhood, oblivious to the cold rain that was drenching me. I couldn't remember ever having been this depressed. My wonderful life with Kate was only going to be a dream. It was never going to happen. I tried to tell myself that nothing was certain – that I could actually try out this new life I'd been contemplating and find it wasn't for me – but deep inside I knew that wasn't true. Even if it was true, the chances of Kate taking me back afterwards were probably close to nil. I wanted to lie down and die right there in the rain. It would have been so much easier.

I found my way back to our house and watched as my feet carried me through the front door. When Kate saw me, she was shocked. I was soaking wet and crying. She got me a towel and we sat down to talk. When I finished explaining to her how I felt and what I thought I was going to have to do, she got very quiet. Then she told me that she'd had her suspicions that it might come to this. She told me that it just wasn't possible for me to experiment with this and still live with her. She just couldn't watch. She told me firmly that I had to leave as soon as I could manage it. If I got this out of my system and wanted to come back, she would consider it.

I spent the next few weeks looking for an apartment and moving out of the house and out of her life.

THE MASK AND THE DARKNESS

It's dark inside.
    There is no place for light here;
        It doesn't belong.
            The light is afraid of this place.
There is no sound where she hides.
    The silent agony pierces her soul
        Like a knife longing to taste blood
        And certain that it never will.
She screams for freedom,
    But softly, for no one must hear;
        No one would listen anyway.
            She's afraid of hearing herself.
In times of deafening solitude
    She can slip free of the Darkness
        If only for a moment.
            The Darkness knows she will return.
Her heart soars on wings of hope;
        She revels in Being.
                She is Alive!   She is Free!
                    The Darkness smiles and waits.
But there is something wrong.
    The mirror is broken.
        It reveals the Lie of the Truth and
            Opens the wounds that none can see.
And so, she is back with the Darkness,
    Wrapped in the arms of Despair.
        She has known no other lover;
            She is certain she never will.
The Mask is firmly in place again;
    No one must ever know she lives.
        She cries as the knife kisses her soul.
        She is so alone.

R. E. Thompson

Chapter 15
Fear, Self-Loathing and Lots of Other Really Helpful Things

My new apartment was nothing to shake a stick at. It was just a featureless one-bedroom place in a typical apartment complex not far from work. The front door faced a hundred other apartments just like it. The sliding door in the dining room faced a small tract of woods just behind the complex. Kate had been kind enough to help me move out of "our" place and into this one. It must have been horribly difficult for her. I know it was for me. I tried my best to make it a home, keeping in mind that Kate and my dream life – my safety net – were only fifteen minutes away. I steeled myself for the very serious task of finding out once and for all if I had any chance of making the change that I'd wanted all of my life. No matter what happened, part of me was going to die. That was a very frightening prospect for me. I had lived with Rachael all of my life and, although she had made my life miserable, I didn't know if I really wanted to see her go. She was a part of me. She may even *be* me. In that case, I would have to let Ricky go. Either way, I wouldn't know unless I let Rachael see the light of day in earnest. I started a diary with the title: "1989 – The Year Rachael Thompson Lives...or Dies". I was ready to start the search for my soul come hell or high water.

* * *

I started off by changing the name on all of my credit cards to R. E. Thompson as I had planned. Much to my surprise, I had few problems making this change. If I'd have been changing my name, I would have had to go to court to have it done legally

202

and then supply the papers with each name change application. Because I was only going to my initials, no one really asked any questions – except for the New Jersey Department of Motor Vehicles. The DMV was very strict about having a person's full name printed on the license and wouldn't allow me to change to just my initials. This meant that I would have to be supremely careful driving while dressed as Rachael. If I was stopped and had to present my driver's license that said my name was Richard and that I was male, and it wasn't Halloween, I'd die of embarrassment. Richard helped out in this with a signed letter that I carried at all times explaining that I was under his care and that cross-dressing was part of my therapy. In retrospect I guess the letter wouldn't really have done me much good, but it made me feel better having it. I never was stopped so it was a moot point. But in some way, the letter gave me "official sick-o" status instead of just "run of the mill sick-o". Hey, it was something.

One thing that helped me through this frightful period was my school work. I was still attending evening courses at a local university after work and, just as I had done when I was in high school and feeling bad about myself, I threw myself into my studies. It really seemed to work on two levels – two or three classes each semester kept me preoccupied enough not to constantly dwell on my misery, fear and loneliness, and I ended up receiving the university's Computer Science Student of the Year award during one of my school years and finally graduating Cum Laude. In addition, I was concurrently taking classes at another college at the same time in Foreign Languages specializing in Chinese and had a 4.0 GPA there.[18]

---

[18] NOTE: I would like to take this moment to say that I do NOT recommend experimenting with transsexualism to anyone who is trying to improve their grades at school. Transsexualism should only be attempted by professionals who have lived with it all their lives.

* * *

My first forays of putting Rachael into the light of day, or rather the streetlights of night, were tentative and hurried. I would spend hours picking out just the right thing to wear (which was almost always the wrong thing to wear if one wanted to "blend in") and standing in front of the mirror trying to make myself look as believable as possible. Then I'd sneak hurriedly outside, taking great care to make sure my neighbors weren't around so I wouldn't be seen, and then drive around, sometimes stopping at a McDonald's. I wasn't comfortable enough with my appearance to go into the restaurant and order in person, so I would just use the drive-thru window, which turned out not to be such a good idea after all. No matter how hard I tried to change my voice, I would always end up being called "sir" by the person inside. That didn't do much to bolster my confidence. It would be quite a while before my voice would stop giving me away.

As I became braver, I started showing up at the PTSG meetings as Rachael. This was a really big deal to me because there were only two ways to get into the city – drive or take public transportation. Since the trains and buses were brightly lit, they wouldn't do; someone was bound to notice me. So, I had to drive. Parking in Philadelphia, like any other city, is never easy. I almost always had to park quite some distance from where the meetings were, forcing me to walk several blocks at night in the city by myself. It's funny that I wasn't as worried about being mugged or raped as I was about being discovered, or "read" as we called it. In retrospect, if I had been jumped by someone and they found out that I was physically male, chances are I would have been beaten or killed. I should have been more worried about reality.

At the PTSG meetings I got a lot of tips on how to make myself more presentable in public, both in dress and mannerisms. Most TS people start out dressing either way too flamboyantly or way too formal. Their makeup is too heavy, and their wigs look awful. Their walking gait is either an over-exaggerated hyper-female mince or an unthinking normal male swagger. All of these things broadcast loud and clear to passersby to "LOOK AT ME!" without ever having said a word. People pick up on these subtle things without even realizing it. Their subconscious nudges them to notice that something's not quite right here. It's not really surprising that beginning TS people have problems in these areas considering that we didn't have anyone to help us learn these things as genetic girls (GGs, or cis-gendered (non-transgender) women as we call them) have when they're growing up. But, like most things, you learn by doing and try to develop a thick skin when you fail.

The more often I went out the better I felt about myself and my ability to "pass". I even started taking voice lessons from a speech therapist in Philadelphia to learn how to make myself sound more feminine without having to resort to anything as drastic as vocal cord surgery. A friend of mine went that route because she just couldn't seem to make her voice do what she wanted it to. When she returned from her surgery, we were mortified at the results. The doctor had actually wound her vocal cords tighter to make her voice higher, just like one would tune a guitar string to a higher pitch. Not only was she awake during this surgery, she had to talk while the doctor was tightening the cords. When her voice got to the pitch she was looking for, he tightened them just a bit more to account for post-operative relaxation of the vocal cords. When she first said hi to us, she had a voice that sounded for all the world like Minnie Mouse – very high pitched and cartoonish. We were horrified for her, thinking that her voice would stay that way. It didn't, though, but she had to put up with sounding like that for quite some while. The surgery did have a lasting effect on her by making it nearly impossible for her to ever sing again.

This was definitely not an option for me. I was always afraid that if I went through with this change, I would never be able to sing again without my male voice giving me away. Instead, I was able, because of my extensive language and music background, to change my voice naturally. It was really only a matter of softening my voice, which was never really low to begin with, and changing inflection and phrasing. Think of the actresses Bea Arthur (TV's "Maude") and Patricia Neal. They both have very low voices for women, but you'd never think that they were anything other than females when you heard them talk, even if you didn't see their faces. I didn't stay in voice therapy for very long. I felt comfortable with my voice after only a short time. I wasn't being called "Sir" at the McDonald's drive-in window any more. Each success made me feel just a little more confident about myself.

* * *

Of course, everything wasn't always a bed of roses. One time after one of the PTSG meetings I was asked to go to a nearby bar to give the keys to the building where we met to the bartender, whose boss owned our building. That meant that I had to walk several blocks in the heart of the city and then go into a very public place. As I walked down the street in the early evening, I passed by two small groups of people. The first was a couple of older men standing by a shop. I steeled myself as I walked by them. To my amazement, they whistled at me! I was on top of the world, smiling as I turned the corner toward the bar. Then I saw a group of young people on a stoop just ahead of me.

Feeling a bit more confident, I strolled past them trying to be as inconspicuous as possible. As I walked by, I heard one of them exclaim, "Hey! That's a guy!" I quickened my pace as my good mood sank into the gutters. After I dropped the keys off at the bar, I found a different way to walk back without having to pass by the jeering group of young people again. Of course, it didn't take me by the whistling men, either.

Bummer.

Another problem I had was trying to make sure that I was "butched-up" again before I went to work the next day after one of my meetings. I would stand in front of the mirror and study my face carefully to make sure that there wasn't one speck of eye makeup left on my face. I would scrutinize my nails (I had stopped calling them fingernails – a very male thing to say) for any hint of leftover color. I even had to stop playing basketball during lunchtime with my friends because of the trouble I would have trying to explain my shaved legs. There was a constant fear that I would be found out somehow – that I would miss some little thing that someone would see, and I wouldn't be able to talk my way out of. That actually almost happened to me one day when I was shopping for shoes for Rachael in a mall near where I worked. A friend of mine from the office saw me standing in line to pay for a pair of pumps that I was holding and laughingly asked me who they were for. Trying hard to choke back embarrassment, I told him that they were a present for my sister. He laughed and just said, "Right." I didn't know if believed me or not. The shoes were size 11, not exactly the usual size for GGs. I was very careful from then on about where and when I shopped for clothes.

* * *

207

Richard asked me during one of our sessions if I would be interested in joining him for a talk about my "condition" with a group of students at a city nursing school. Although I was starting to feel more confident about myself, I had really only been out in the evenings and even then, usually only with others like me. I had never been in a fully lit room surrounded by non-TS people who knew who and what I was, let alone sit there and tell them about my life. Because I was feeling better about my appearance by that time, I found the strength to say yes. I don't think I've ever been more frightened of doing anything in my life.

On the night of the class, I rode the train into the city – a first for me – trying hard not to make eye contact with anyone around me. I was dressed in an understated knee-length dress, my hair, nails and makeup done to the best of my limited ability. No one bothered me on the train. When I got off the train, I walked to the university building where the class was to be held and, to my great relief, spotted Richard almost immediately waiting in the hallway for me. He smiled broadly at me, complimenting me on my appearance, and then opened the door and escorted me into the classroom. I took a deep breath and walked in. The classroom was full. Every face turned to look in my direction. With a nervous smile, I took my seat next to another woman there to talk to the class, an older woman who had had gender reassignment surgery years before. Her presence there helped to calm me. I wasn't the only one in the spotlight.

Richard introduced us to the class and the other woman began by talking about her life. Unexpectedly, she turned out to be hilarious. She told her story in such a way that it dissolved any discomfort that anyone in the room may have felt, including me. She had us all in stitches with her off-color and very human stories. I was to later use this approach, although not nearly so

208

bawdy, when it came my turn to speak to classes on my own. Humor was natural to me and I had always been able to use it very effectively in teaching or leading what would be otherwise horribly dull meetings.[19]

When it came time for me to tell my story, I started very timidly. This was the first time I had ever bared my soul to "normal" people, and it wasn't easy. I ended with how nervous and afraid I was about how I looked and the consequences I always feared of being "read" or discovered to be a man dressed in women's clothing. When the class was over, several of the students came up to me and told me that they were very impressed with my courage to come and talk to them. They also assured me that I had nothing to worry about concerning my looks. Some even asked tips on how I did my makeup. I went home feeling incredible. I had survived the evening with dignity and even a few compliments. I had expected only the worst. I was actually starting to feel comfortable in my own skin for once.

My euphoria didn't last long. Reality came crashing down on me when I least expected it. One evening I was all dressed and ready to go out into the world as Rachael when I heard a knock on my front door. I wasn't expecting anyone. When I asked who it was, a familiar voice responded, "It's Kate." I was panic stricken. If I had any hope of ever getting Kate back if this trial period didn't work out for me (part of me still held out that hope), I couldn't let her see me like this. But I couldn't just tell her to go away. Instead, I said the first thing that came to my mind.

---

[19] I once wrote a memo to upper management that hardly used any English words. It was full of acronyms in my feeble attempt to say "ENOUGH!" to these things. Working in government applications, they're everywhere. One of my boss's bosses thought it was one of the funniest things he'd ever read.

"I'm not myself, honey," I said to her through the door. There was a moment of silence followed by the realization of what I was talking about.

"Ok. I understand," Kate said in a choked voice. She turned and left. I peeked through the curtains and watched her hurry to her car and drive away without another word. I didn't go out that night. I just sat alone and cried. In that brief instant she had brought the enormity of what I was doing crashing down on my head. If this turned out not to be the right thing for me, how could she ever trust it never to come back and break us up again? I stood a very real chance of losing her for good. I don't think it ever had sunk in before as much as it did that night.

Not long after that night, my world really fell apart. I came home to my apartment late one January evening after school, put my key in the lock and pushed the door open. Strangely, the door wouldn't open completely. Somehow, it had become chained from the inside. I had no idea how in the world this could happen but, without thinking about it much more, opened the door with a slight push. The security chain hadn't been fully engaged and fell away easily. I figured it must have somehow just swung up and caught itself when I had closed the door to go to school. Then I went inside and discovered that all the lights were on. "That's odd," I thought. "I don't remember leaving the lights on." The next thing I noticed was that it was very cold inside the apartment. I had left the heat on so that shouldn't be. That's when I noticed that my patio doors were open – wide open. It finally started to dawn on me what was going on. As I looked around the apartment, I saw that my stereo set had been pulled away from the wall and that several tapes and records were strewn across the floor. I walked into the bedroom and my knees buckled. The entire room was in shambles. My clothes (both Ricky's and Rachael's) were scattered everywhere. The dresser drawers were hanging open with bras and underpants, slips and t-shirts thrown about the room. Even my breast forms had been tossed on the bed. My closet had been ripped apart and even some of the heater vents had been pulled literally right out of the walls. My sea bag that had held all of my Navy clothes was gone – the clothes were dumped on the floor – along with my suitcase and all of my pillowcases. My brand-new computer was gone as well as my guitar, my cameras and a lock box that contained my wedding rings, my collection of coins gathered from around the world and four-star sapphire gems that I had bought in Pakistan several years earlier. Someone had been in my home not minutes before I returned and had gone through everything I owned. They stole just about everything that wasn't nailed down. They even took the darts that were in my dartboard beside my front door. I was told by the police later that those were meant for me in case I walked in on them early. How frightening was that? I picked up the phone and first called the police, then Kate, and then went into the bathroom, also ripped apart, and threw up.

When the police arrived, Kate and her brother Peter were right on their heels. It was bad enough having to talk to the police about what had been done and to have them going through all the lacy underthings that were lying around my wrecked home. For all they knew, they were my girlfriend's. But for Pete to be there was unthinkable. He was not only one of my closest friends at work but one of the best and most reliable section managers I had working for me. I couldn't let him see the bedroom with all the unexplainable things lying around. So, I feigned anger at the whole situation (not much acting involved) and practically yelled at him to stay in the living room. I felt bad for being so brusque with him, but I figured he'd just write it off as the understandable passion of the moment. It seemed to work. He did as I requested and didn't ask any more questions.

211

Pete finally left, and Kate stayed behind to see if there was anything she could do to help. There was. I couldn't stay in the apartment that night. I was frightened out of my mind and angry as hell all at the same time. I asked her if I could stay at her place for a few days. She said yes and, for the first time in months, I went home with her. We even slept together that night with her holding me. It was very nice to feel her next to me again, even under the circumstances.

As it turned out, it was a couple of kids that had broken into my house by smashing the small window in the kitchen. They had stuffed all the small things they could get their hands on in my seabag, my suitcase and all of my pillowcases and carried them out the patio doors. Anything bigger was stashed in the drop ceiling of a nearby empty apartment. A maintenance man found the items when he went in to do some work and saw that some of the ceiling tiles were askew. The police were called, and the place was staked out. One of the boys was caught a few days later sneaking back into the apartment to retrieve the larger items from the ceiling. I ended up only recovering my guitar and my computer. Everything else was gone forever.

Also gone was my peace of mind. I had to explain things to the police and, worse yet, Pete had almost discovered my secret. My confidence was totally shaken. I started to hate what I was doing and what I was becoming. I couldn't bring myself to become Rachael any more after that. And because my nerves were shot, I started spiraling back down into another deep depression. This time it was so bad that Richard sent me to a medical doctor to be put on Prozac. Within a few months I had managed, with the help of a lawyer, to break my lease with the apartment complex out of fear for my safety. I bought a condo in a nearby town from some friends at work and quickly moved in. It was the first home that I had ever owned, and it took every cent I had but it was well worth it. I wasn't paying rent to anyone any more. The mortgage papers would come back to haunt me later.

After I moved into my new home, I resolved that I had been taking my life in the wrong direction and convinced myself that I was going to give up on the idea for good. It had been a nice try but I'd shown myself that I couldn't do it. I wasn't able to handle the stress and humiliation that was certain to come if I went any further. I could barely handle it now. This new resolve was based mostly, as you can probably tell, on fear and not on what was best for me. It was also fortified with that wonder of all wonder drugs, Prozac. Sometime after I had started taking Prozac, it dawned on me that I didn't feel so depressed as usual. The old feelings were gone – or at least going away. I found myself thinking less and less about wanting to die so I could stop the pain that I lived with every day. The pain was quite simply disappearing – or at least fading into something so much in the background that I almost forgot it was there. It was an amazing discovery. With each passing week, I felt better about myself. Kate and I tentatively started seeing each other again. I convinced her that my "problem" was a thing of the past. I even convinced myself.

Before long we were back together and closer than ever. We took a trip to Montreal and, at the end of a sumptuous and expensive dinner, I proposed to her with a poem and a ring. In the poem, I talked about how I had slain my dragons for good, attributing that conquest in part to her and asking her to be in my life forever. When I presented her with the ring, she immediately said yes. I don't think I'd ever been happier.

I don't think I'd ever been more wrong.

THE PASSAGE

Darkly the Passage beckons:
Rest for the Weary,
Comforting embrace.
Sorrow takes wings against the gloom.

Softly the Passage beckons:
Come quickly,
Come gently.
Tread the path lightly, inevitably.

Ever the Passage beckons:
Sweet surrender,
Sweeter peace.
Courage will come in time.

Now the Passage beckons:
Release despair,
Heed the call –

"Sleep with me tonight."

R. E. Thompson

Chapter 16
What doesn't kill you...

All was fairly well with the world. Kate and I were back together and finally engaged, the Prozac was helping me to feel better than I had in a very long time, and I was a respected manager at work with nowhere to go but up. It was nearing New Year's Eve 1990. Kate and I had decided to do something really different this year and celebrate the New Year in style. We made reservations for a nice dinner and a showing of "The Phantom of the Opera" on Broadway in New York City with the plan to join the celebrating masses at Times Square to watch the New Year's ball drop.

Our trip to New York City was uneventful – a short drive to a train station in New Jersey and a ride into the city from there. Dinner at the restaurant overlooking Times Square was sublime. The air was festive and charged with excitement. Kate looked wonderful and I felt on top of the world with her by my side. We walked to the theater after dinner and settled in to enjoy the show. It was my first time in a Broadway theater, and I was in awe of the décor and the wonderfully dressed patrons all around us. The show itself was spectacular and we left very happy that we had come. Something in the back of my mind was bothering me, though and I wouldn't put my finger on what it was until we returned to New Jersey much later that night.

After the show, we made our way through the crowded streets in the frigid December night to find a place to stand so that we could see the ball drop. There were so many people there that the closest we could get was about five or six blocks away, and it was not even eleven o'clock. We could see the ball, but it was very small sitting so far away on top of its spire. The crowd was the largest I'd ever seen. There were almost a half million people standing almost shoulder to shoulder. There were colorful hats and noisemakers, confetti and alcohol and the unmistakably sweet smell of marijuana wafting through the air. This kind of thing wasn't exactly our cup of tea, but we found the revelry and party atmosphere to be contagious. We were having a wonderful time in spite of ourselves and the cold.

The countdown for the last sixty seconds finally began. When the ball finally dropped, signaling the start of 1991, a deafening roar went up from the crowd. "Happy New Year!" Everyone turned and hugged complete strangers. Kate and I held each other in the cold and kissed the New Year into being. Then, surprisingly quickly, the crowds simply began to disperse. I guess we weren't the only ones tired of standing in the cold. As we walked back to the train, my thoughts began to turn back to the nagging discomfort that I had felt during the show, trying to sort out what it was that was wrong. We spent most of the trip back in silence, happy just to hold each other. We were both cold and tired, so Kate didn't seem to notice my mood all the way home. Feigning a headache, I dropped Kate at her apartment and drove home alone.

Inside my small condo I undressed and sat on my bed thinking. What was it that was making me feel so uneasy? I'd just had the most wonderful evening with the woman that I loved and everything in my life was finally looking up. I wasn't unhappy any more about myself so what could it be? My mind turned back to the show and my awe of the beauty and grandeur of the place and the people. What could have possibly upset me during such a grand time? I tried to replay the experience in my head – the wonderful play; the soaring music; the beautifully dressed women. A feeling of sadness descended over me in a dark cloud. I finally knew what it was. I had been looking around admiring all of the stunning outfits being worn by the women around me, their glamorous hairstyles, their carefully sculptured faces and nails – all the while with one subconscious thought running through my mind:

"I'm never going to have the chance to look like that. Never."

The realization of that thought was, in retrospect, one of the most devastating things to ever happen to me. Here I was finally happy, with my entire life to look forward to. I was taking pills that I thought were going to make this all go away once and for all, and yet the feeling was still there under it all. Not only was the feeling there, but right under it was a profound and crushing sense of loss; loss of the person that I had always felt I was and never would be. I hadn't noticed it because it was all tempered by the Prozac from what would have been a searing, familiar pain to what I now realized was just a dull ache. I had gotten so used to the ache that I hadn't even realized it was still there. I really had thought it was gone. This was just awful. It was dawning on me that I was going to have to live with this empty feeling for the rest of my life no matter what drugs I took, no matter how successful I was, and no matter how much love and success I had in my life.

I sat on my bed and sobbed in desperation. I had never felt so lost and so alone. I cried for being born this way. I cried for the unfairness of it all. I cried because I had done everything I knew to do, and it was still there.

I cried because I knew I just couldn't take it anymore.

I don't know how long I sat on my bed sobbing but before long, a strange calm came over me. I stopped crying and sat staring into nothing. My mind was working in a fog. I heard my own thoughts as if they were coming from somewhere far away. I knew that I had done my best. I knew that I had fought long and hard and that I'd finally had enough. I had hit the wall and it was just too high to struggle to get over any more. I had no more strength left.

Through the haze of my red and blurry eyes, I watched with detached interest as my legs raised my body from the bed and took me into the bathroom. I stood watching from the sidelines while my hands opened the medicine cabinet and pulled out every bottle of pills inside. I felt my feet shuffle my body slowly back to the bedroom and sat back down on the bed staring at my hands as they opened the bottles, spilling the pills out onto the bedspread. I sat there with the mound of pills in front of me, calmly wondering what I was going to do next. Somewhere in the recesses of my numbed consciousness I knew exactly what was about to happen, but it was like watching a movie – this really wasn't happening to me; this was happening to someone else. There was no panic in me; no fear, no concern of any kind. It just was.

I returned to the bathroom and brought back a large glass of water. I began to sort through the pills, culling them out into smaller piles based on what I thought were the most lethal of them for my first course. With the unnatural steadiness that accompanies complete calm, I picked up a few of the specially selected pills, put them in my mouth and washed them down with a drink of water. I remember that the water tasted cool and sweet. It was a very nice sensation. I picked up another handful of pills and sat back with my eyes closed, wondering what this was going to be like. Would it hurt? Would I get violently ill and just throw it all up? Oh God, I hated throwing up more than anything else in the world. I managed somehow to convince myself that if I took too many pills too quickly, that's exactly what would happen. I put the second handful of pills down. If I was going to do this, at least I was going to do it right.

As I sat there waiting (for what?) I wondered how long it would take for anyone to find me. I wondered if anyone was really going to miss me all that much. The main thing that had kept me from doing this through all these years of suffering was the worry of what it would do to my mother considering what she had gone through with Ernie so many years ago. The thought fleetingly crossed my mind again, along with what Kate would think, but neither really had any consequence any more to the empty thing that I had become. I rationalized that somehow my loved ones would continue on even if it did hurt a little at first. Their hurt couldn't be as bad as what I had gone through all my life. They'd get over it. I silently apologized to them both and wished them well. I reached for the second handful of pills once again.

Then an odd thought came to me. My friends at the TS Support Group had been there for me for all the time that I had associated with them, and I owed it to them to thank them before I left. It was around three o'clock in the morning, but I picked up the phone and called Lisa, one of my best friends at the time and a post-operative TS from the support group – the one who had had her voice surgically altered. We had remained friends even after I had decided to go back and try the "normal" life one more time. She was asleep with her boyfriend in their home in Flemington, about a two-hour drive to the north. When she sleepily answered the phone after a few rings I apologized right away for waking her but told her it was important.

"What's the matter?" she asked, concern creeping into her voice.

I said, "Nothing's wrong. I just wanted to call you and tell you that I'm leaving. I wanted to thank you for all that you've done for me and for being my friend."

There was a silence at the other end of the phone. "Ricky, what are you talking about? Where are you going?" There was another silence as realization sunk in. "What are you doing?"

I explained to her what had happened in New York, how I now just felt numb and that it was time to go. I told her that this was for the best and I wanted her to know how much her friendship had meant to me. She was totally awake now. "I'm going to come down there to stay with you. Don't take any more pills."

"Lisa, it's three o'clock in the morning and you have to go to work in the morning," I said. "You can't drive all the way down here now."

"You're not thinking clearly right now," she tried to explain. "You need someone to be with you. It's no trouble." She was up out of her bed and already starting to get dressed.

We argued for some time about this. The last thing I wanted was to put someone out on my account, especially at this ungodly time of night. She asked me to call Kate and have her come over, but I couldn't do that. I didn't want to wake her or give her the chance to try to talk me out of what I knew I had to do. I only wanted to say goodbye to my best friend. In my diminished state I must have thought that my phone call wouldn't really cause her any alarm at all. Or maybe I was asking for help and didn't realize it. Whatever the reason, I was confused at Lisa's reaction.

We talked for almost an hour on the phone. We talked about life and what it meant to us. We talked about how difficult it was for her to make the decision to change her life and how happy she was for having done it. I told her about how I wouldn't ever be able to find the courage to do what she did, and I couldn't imagine how she had found the courage herself. At some point in the conversation, I started crying again. We talked until the haze in my mind had started to lift and I was more in control of myself. My pleading with her not to drive all the way down to my place in the middle of the night had finally worked as she realized I was becoming more rational. She promised not to come if I promised not to take any more pills and call her the very first thing in the morning. I told her that I would, and we hung up the phone.

I looked down at the bed and its remaining piles of brightly colored pills. The ones I had taken didn't really seem to be doing anything. I didn't even know what they were. It was just as well. Somewhere inside of me I found the momentary strength to scoop up the remaining pills, walk back into the bathroom and flush them all down the toilet. As they swirled in the bowl and started to disappear down the drain, part of me inside was screaming, "NO!" at the prospect of having to face another day. Another part of me knew that what I had been considering just wasn't an answer at all. It was nothing more than a cop-out – a moment of unparalleled weakness that had passed with the help of a good and caring friend. The more I thought about that night, the more I came to regard my life as an interesting book. I wasn't ready yet to put the book down because I still hadn't found out what the ending was yet. It may not have been much of a rationalization, but it was something I could hold onto to keep myself alive.

I started to feel the first twinges of nausea, so I went into the kitchen and fixed a pot of coffee. I drank the entire pot over the rest of the early morning. I sat in my living room watching the sun come up to start a new day that I almost didn't get to see. I never got physically sick that night, so I guess what I had taken wasn't all that lethal after all. For once I was glad that I hadn't done something right.

Now I had to figure out what to do next. Where do I go from here? Which direction do I take my life? I never said a word of this struggle to anyone but Lisa. As promised, I did call her the first thing in the morning. She was relieved and happy to hear from me.

221

Day in and day out I wracked my brain trying to decide what I should do but it was useless. No matter how badly I had felt that night I still couldn't quite close the door on my life. I knew that the Prozac could make the depression tolerable but was that enough? What kind of life was I going to have with Kate if I was just going to settle for "tolerable" for myself? I couldn't go through another divorce and the loneliness that came with it. I certainly didn't want to hurt another person who said she loved me. By the end of February, I was still going around in circles, my emotions at war with my logical side. I finally decided that the one thing I needed most, strangely enough, was solitude – the very thing I had feared so much. I needed to be away from everyone and everything – no opinions, no distractions, and no temptations. I needed time for myself to think clearly. I called Kate and made up some reason that I had to be out of town for a weekend. Then I headed out to the Pine Barrens of New Jersey in the dead of winter with my camping gear. Not surprisingly, there weren't any other campers at the State Park I had decided on. The Ranger at the front gate must have thought I was completely nuts going out there in the sub-freezing temperatures alone with my tent and sleeping bag. I couldn't tell him that I was trying to find a way *not* to go nuts. I wasn't worried about the cold because of my experience with winter backpacking and I knew no one else would be out there. The Ranger took my money and waved me on. I set up my tent at a nice spot overlooking the drained lake in the park and sat down alone in the wilderness to think.

The only distraction I afforded myself out there was a book on philosophy. I wanted to be able to read all weekend to find some words of wisdom that might help me make my decision. I chose the best book I knew – The Analects of Confucius. I guess there aren't many people who would think to find answers in an ancient Chinese philosopher's writings, but I didn't know of anything better. I had been very impressed with what I had read of these during my Chinese Studies. They had been around for almost 4,000 years and were still being used faithfully by billions of people, so I figured that there had to be something to them. Some people might have taken a Bible to read but over the years I had come to think of God, if God existed at all, as an uncaring and cruel being that had allowed me to be born into this life of non-ending suffering. I questioned why a god would allow that to happen. I had always been told that God constantly tests us. I did not appreciate this forty-year-long test. It had almost killed me. No, a god couldn't be an answer for me. I had to find my answer by myself. If God had anything to do with it, then He (or She) gave me the reasoning ability to work this out. I was determined to do just that.

At first, I found nothing. Confucius talked a lot about how a person was to act in life toward parents (filial piety), work, government and religion. It was not exactly exciting stuff. But I kept reading hoping to find some kernel of wisdom that I could grasp hold of. I read late into the night, stopping only to watch the full moon rise majestically over the trees as nature around me literally hushed to share the spectacle (I later wrote a poem about this). I read until I couldn't read any more. I crawled into my sleeping bag and slept soundly.

When I awoke in the morning, I made myself some coffee over a small backpacking stove and sat down again to resume my reading. Something had been tugging at my mind from the things that I had already read but it wasn't quite strong enough to come to the surface yet. By the afternoon I had it. I also had snow; lots of it. But I had found what I needed to learn. It's funny how sometimes some of the most obvious things can be so thoroughly hidden in plain sight. It's like my mother always liked to say: "If it was a snake, it would have bitten you." This was more like a mosquito – a seemingly insignificant kernel of truth that repeated itself over and over in the book until it became big enough to hit me right between the eyes. Of all the things that Confucius talked about, the one constant that finally got through to me was really one of the simplest. It boiled down to this:

"You have to love yourself first before you can love anyone else."

Duh! What a simple concept that was! What a blind idiot I had been for not seeing it before. I had never really thought about it. I know I didn't love myself. Hell, I didn't even *like* myself. It's no wonder that none of my relationships ever ended in anything but disaster. I started out happy, trying hard to make *this* the one that would fulfill me, but I always ended up spiraling down into bitterness, prone to outburst of anger, then falling into severe depression and, finally, alone. I tried to use the love that someone else gave me to fill the emptiness that I had inside me. I never realized that without self-love, that emptiness can never be filled. There was always something missing.

* * *

During my group therapy fiasco in the past, the therapist asked everyone to describe something they did "to be nice to themselves". When it got around to my turn, I couldn't answer. I honestly didn't understand the question. I spent so much time trying to keep my mind occupied so I didn't have time to think about myself and my problem, that the very concept of doing something "nice" to myself just didn't register with me. That should have been a clarion call to me that something was horribly wrong, but I was so wrapped up in self-loathing that I couldn't see it. I never did answer that question. I left that particular session confused as hell.

After my winter camping epiphany, the $100,000 question was, "What do I do about this?" By the time I left the woods that weekend, I knew what I had to do. My revelation, along with the memory of forty years of pain, my abortive suicide attempt, and the certainty that it would happen again if I didn't act soon, answered everything for me. I now understood why my friends in the TS Support Group who had gone through this process in trying to find themselves couldn't explain to me how they had found the courage to do it. *Courage had nothing to do with it.* That's why I couldn't find it. It wasn't courage after all. It was conviction – conviction that I really was a valuable person who didn't deserve to live in such horrible pain and that if I didn't lift myself up and go forward with my life, I would, quite simply and quite literally, die. It was a matter of life or death. Mine. I had spent far too much time contemplating how I could end my life and make it look like an accident – looking for just the right tree to run my car into at night; searching for an opening in highway guard rails to crash into a bridge abutment or stopping my car on a railroad track in front of a speeding train.

There it was. My own personal version of the Vision Quest of my Native American ancestors had revealed to me what I needed to know after forty years of searching for the answer. This would be the year that Rachael Thompson quite literally either lived – or died. There was no other outcome possible. I had to find out. I was ready.

It was time.

THE DARKNESS WITHIN

Enduring Existence alone,
Each day seeping more slowly into the next,
Filled to overflowing with nothingness
She waits for sleep to numb the pain.
Wondering how long this can go on,
Fearful of the alternatives,
Dreading the rising of each new sun
That only shows more clearly the darkness within.
All hope is dashed.
Nothing remains but tears and memories
Embraced with empty arms;
The future reveals no kinder face.
Somewhere far into the darkness
A solitary light burns with hope.
To touch that light is the task at hand;
To hold it an unreality.
Sadness has ever been her solitary lover.
All others were not meant to be.
She struggles against that destiny
Knowing the day of reckoning has come.
She must now answer to the emptiness;
Face the darkness and strive for the light
Leaving everything behind
And risking everything ahead.

Rachael Evelyn Thompson

Chapter 17
The Journey Begins...Really

I had made my decision. I was frightened to death to go ahead but I knew that I couldn't face any more of the life that I had lived even if it meant losing everything else dear to me.

My first step was to break the news to Kate.

I called her a few days later and invited her to dinner at my place. It was nothing special – just a nice, relaxing dinner at home with a bottle of wine. I was going to need the wine.

After dinner we watched TV for a while with Kate lying on the couch and me sitting on the floor next to here. At her normal insistence, I began to massage her feet. It was one of her favorite things. Inside I was a wreck. If I hadn't been massaging her feet, she would have probably noticed how badly my hands were shaking. Finally screwing up my courage, I turned the TV off and looked into the face that I loved so very much. I knew I would probably never see it again after this night. I kissed her and told her how much I loved her. We held each other for a few minutes. Then I sat up and gazed into her eyes. My heart was beating so hard in my chest that I could barely hear anything else. I was sure she'd hear it soon.

"Honey, there's something we have to talk about," I said. She looked up at me as a hint of worry crossed her face.

"Ok," she said hesitantly. "What?"

I swallowed hard and tried to calm my heartbeat. "I've been doing a lot of thinking lately. You know what I've been through and what I've been trying to fight all of my life."

Her eyes started to slowly get wider. "What's going on, Rick?"

For the first time I told her how I'd felt on New Year's Eve, what had happened when I got home and my winter camping trip to find myself. Then I laid it all out. "I've got to go through with this. It's never going to be gone and I've got to find out if it's the right thing for me. I can't live like this anymore. It's not fair to you and it's not fair to me."

She sat up like a shot and, without another word, hurriedly started putting her shoes on. She was already starting to cry. I moved to put my arms around her, pleading with her to try to understand and telling her over and over that I loved her. She pushed me away and rushed to the door. I implored her to please say something to me. She never stopped moving; she just grabbed her coat and opened the door. On her way out, without even looking back, she simply said, "Don't call me anymore." The door and my old life slammed shut behind her.

I cried for a while, but it surprised me that I didn't cry that hard. I felt terrible that I had just deeply hurt the woman I loved but a part of me felt so numb inside that the pain was dulled. I felt horribly alone but this time it didn't scare me as much as it would have just a few months earlier. I guess my revelation at the park had affected me more deeply that I thought. With the knowledge of what I had to do came a resignation to what I was going to have to go through. This was just a necessary start no matter how much I hated to do it. It seemed horribly cruel, but it really wasn't. It would have much crueler to go on living the lie that I had lived for so long and bringing yet another innocent person into it.

The next day at work I told Kate's brother Pete that it was over between Kate and me. I didn't offer any explanation and, thankfully, he didn't ask for one. I told him I was sorry but we both had thought it was for the best. Much to his credit, Pete never showed any displeasure or anger to me even if he felt it. I still consider him to this day to be my friend. I hope that never changes.

* * *

Now that the ball had started rolling, it was time to give it another push. The previous Sunday's newspaper had an advertisement in it from a very well-known cosmetic surgeon in the area. From previous trial forays outside "dressed" I knew I didn't feel very good about how I looked so I thought that it might be possible to get some help. I called and made an appointment for a consultation.

When I walked into the doctor's office, I was a bit disconcerted to see a number of people with bandaged faces sitting around the waiting room. It looked like a war zone. *One of these days*, I thought, *that will be me sitting there*. I went up to the receptionist's desk and told her that I was here for my appointment. She gave me some papers to fill out and asked me to have a seat. As usual for doctors, the cosmetic surgeon was about a half hour late in seeing me. He led me into his office, and I sat down across from him at his desk.

"Mr. Thompson," he began. "What can I do for you?"

Here it comes, I thought. *Be strong and don't worry about what he might think.* My voice didn't have a trace of nervousness in it. "I want you to make my face look more feminine," I said. "I'm going to have a sex change operation and I don't want to look so male." I never thought that I would ever hear myself publicly disclosing what was happening to me.

He stared at me for a moment as if he was unsure of what to say next. Then he got up from behind his desk and came over to study my face. His fingers ran over my features and, after a few seconds, he said, "Ok. I think we can help you. We'll start by taking up your eyelids, then we'll give your cheeks a little more definition, make your nose a little narrower and do a little liposuction under your chin. It won't be hard to do at all."

I was grateful for his professionalism. I don't know how many people like me he had ever seen in his office but if he was surprised by my request, he really didn't show it much. I guess part of me thought that he would say that he couldn't help me and semi-politely show me to the door. Instead, he worked up a few numbers on his desk pad and told me that he could do the whole thing for $3,000. I had worried that it would be a lot more than that, especially since my insurance wouldn't cover one cent of it, so I was happy and relieved to say yes. We scheduled the whole thing for the beginning of May. I would go into the hospital, have the surgery, and then stay home for the next two weeks to recover. Of course, I had to let someone at work know that I needed the time off and that some "small" changes were coming. That was *really* going to be hard.

During that time, I was also seeing an endocrinologist that a lot of the other M-to-Fs (male-to-females) were using in Center City Philadelphia. And elderly man with a small practice who has since retired, he always treated me with great gentleness and respect. He had me taking a very small oral dosage of Premarin, a female hormone made from, of all things, horse urine. It's very popular, especially to limit hot flashes in women who have gone through menopause. I was expecting to see growth in my breasts start soon after starting on the Premarin, just as any girl who is going through puberty would. Given time, the hormones were also supposed to help my body fat redistribute so I would have a more feminine figure, make my pores smaller so my skin would be softer and also lighten and diminish my body hair. They would do nothing, however, to raise my voice or to get rid of facial hair.

It's not fair.

When Female-to-Male transsexuals take male hormones, their voices deepen, and they start to grow coarse body hair along with full beards. Of course, their surgery is a lot more involved and expensive, so I guess it works out in the end.

The hormone dosage I was on was so small, however, that nothing was happening. The doctor was being very conservative in his approach and didn't want to increase my dosage too quickly. I finally became impatient and went to another recommended doctor who I had been told gave intramuscular injections of Premarin. I began to see results almost immediately after seeing him.

I was thrilled. What had started to happen to me when I was an adolescent was happening again only this time, I wasn't afraid. It started as a small area of discomfort around my nipples that made them so sensitive that I had to wear an undershirt to minimize the rubbing of cloth on my chest. I never wore undershirts but it's not like I could wear a training bra at work, you know? To actually see the changes start was worth the minor discomfort. Day by day I saw my breasts grow. The more they grew the more tender they became until they were downright painful. The first time I hugged one of my friends from the TS Support Group after I had started growing, I cried out in pain and pulled away. They all laughed at what they called my "tender tips." They'd been there themselves and knew exactly what I was going through.

By day I was male. At night, that male was left at the office. Rachael was now the only one actually living in my apartment. Ricky kept his clothes on one side of the closet, but I had my own on my side. Funny as it seems, that's exactly how I was coming to think of my predicament. The more comfortable I got in my new role, the further away Ricky seemed. It was getting harder and harder to have Ricky walk out the door in the morning to go to work. I began to feel like I was going to work in drag. I must have been subconsciously giving off signals because one day I was headed into the men's room when one of my wise-cracking friends, who happened to be walking by at the time, stopped and told me I was going in the wrong door. He was always joking about my sexuality, but guys do that, and, after all, I had longer hair than was usual and was probably looking more feminine all the time. I laughed but inside I was worried that somehow everyone knew what I was up to.

Work was the next hurdle – and it was a big one. Since I had my cosmetic surgery scheduled, I figured that my next step was to let people at work know what I was about to do. I was going to have to take time off from work. I could have just said I was going away on vacation, but I was determined to tell no more lies. This was by far the hardest decision I had yet to make, and it presented a bit of a special problem. Most people I knew who went through this sort of thing quit their jobs and went to work somewhere else in their new identity. The only alternative to doing that was to stay and transition at work where everyone knows you. The former allows for complete anonymity and a chance to start fresh with no one being the wiser (or so you'd hope). The latter is fraught with potential discrimination from the company and derision from other employees.

By this time my hair was getting quite long. I didn't want to cut it, but it had so much gray in it that when I got it styled at the hairdresser's in a perm, it made me look old. At a party one evening someone asked a friend of mine if I was the mother of someone there. Part of me was thrilled that someone thought I looked good enough to be mistaken as someone's mother. Another part of me was horrified that someone actually thought I looked *old* enough to be someone's mother. So, I tried to color my hair. When I was born and through the first thirty years or so of my life, my hair was very dark. Because of this, I chose a dark brown hair color for my new look. I found, however, that dark hair just didn't look natural on me anymore. The difference in my appearance was stark. If I was a bit self-conscious about my long hair at work, I was even more so with my hair dyed. Of course, my friends and my boss didn't hesitate to rib me about it.

My position and history at work made it difficult for me to leave the company. I was an upper-level manager and hadn't worked in any technical area for many years, so my technical skills were slipping as the computer industry evolved around me at light speed. The only companies in the area that did the same kind of work that I did basically worked on the same projects so we all knew each other. There was really no chance for me to stay in the same profession in this area and expect to retain any degree of anonymity. Another option was to physically move to a new area to start over. But with the job market at the time, no one would have wanted to hire an upper-level manager coming from such a specialized field. I saw résumés across my desk all the time with people looking for those kinds of jobs. They just weren't there – anywhere. So that option really didn't seem very good. That left me with only one other thing I could do – I could quit and go to work in an entirely different field. That wasn't going to be possible, either. I had worked in the computer industry for over sixteen years and really didn't have any other talents that could pay me the kind of salary I was making at my company. Money was going to be a real problem. I had to pay for everything that I was doing out of my own pocket because insurance wouldn't cover any of it except for part of my psychotherapy. Even then they were starting to wonder why I was still going for therapy after such a long time. (Richard had to write to tell them that I was still suffering from "depression" and needed more therapy). I had to pay for my hormone therapy, new clothes, electrolysis and, eventually, the surgery and all of its associated costs with no help at all. I was making a good salary where I worked and was very unlikely to find anything even remotely similar in any other field.

In the end I was left with only one real prospect: stay in my job and swallow all of the trouble that I was bound to get from people. I knew things were going to be hard but the reality of actually starting to go through with it was finally starting to sink in. I knew what I had to do, though, and part of it was being strong and trying not to care what others thought. For the first time in my life, I had to put aside making other people happy and do what I had to do for myself. No one else could matter until this was taken care of.

I made up my mind to stay.

* * *

In my current position as Department Manager, I did a lot of face-to-face work with our customers, something that I thought might become difficult during my transition. My company had been good to me through the years, and I didn't want to do anything to embarrass them or put them in an awkward position. I also thought it might be best for me not to be so much in the public eye until I was really comfortable in my new role. I reasoned that the best of both worlds for me was to keep my job at my company but step down from my current position and take an out-of-the-way technical role on another project in another building where I wasn't known quite so well.

So, it was decided. That's what I would ask for from my superiors. Of course, they could just outright fire me. Although there were laws in New Jersey prohibiting companies from discriminating against people because of their sexual orientation, there were no laws anywhere in the country that even mentioned the term "Gender Dysphoria", let alone what rights should be afforded to someone suffering from it. I was open game for the open door. It was an enormous risk. If they fired me, I'd be out on the street trying desperately to find some kind of job that would pay me enough that I wouldn't have to wait another forty years to have my surgery. That was something I really didn't even want to contemplate. I had to make this work. I decided to talk to my boss.

Making the decision on what I needed to do was the easy part. The hard part was actually talking to my boss, Ed, about it. Ed was always an imposing presence. He was very tall and quiet and all business all the time. When he made a joke, you were never really sure if it was a joke or not. He was very hard to read. This was *not* going to be easy. The morning that I decided to tell him, I asked my secretary to hold all of my calls and not to disturb me for any reason. I closed my office door and just stood looking out the window at the lake across the street. I knew full well that what I was about to do was not something that I would be able to take back once it was done. My life was literally going to change forever the moment I opened my mouth in his office. Up until now everything that I had done had been done in secret. I could walk away from it all right now and no one would ever know the difference. But once I told Ed about this, it would no longer be a secret from anyone. It would be final and irreversible.

I stood and stared out the window for hours trying to find the courage I needed and to try to make my hands stop shaking. By eleven o'clock I knew I couldn't wait any longer. I called Ed and asked if I could talk to him. He told me he wasn't busy, and I could stop in right away if I'd like. I took a deep breath, opened my office door and walked the long hallway to his. It was funny that I'd never thought of the hallway to his office as ever having been this long before. This time it seemed to go on forever, but I was at his door in seconds. The hallway wasn't long enough after all.

I entered Ed's office, closed the door behind me and sat down across from him. "There's something that I have to do that I have to tell you about," I said to him. "It's not going to be easy for you to understand but it's literally a matter of life and death for me. Please hear me out before you say anything."

Ed became very still and then nodded slowly for me to continue. God only knows what he thought I was going to say but I dare say that nothing he could have imagined could have prepared him for what he was about to hear.

I told him the whole story. I recounted my youth, my trials and my failures. Then I told him what I had to do and why. Without pausing I offered my idea of moving to another position to keep from causing any problems with our customers. Then I added that if they couldn't find me another job out of the public eye that I would stay right where I was and make the best of it. I was determined not to leave. They would have to fire me. It was a big gamble, but I felt I had no other choice. I didn't think that they would have wanted me to stay in my current very visible position. They were either going to find me something else or show me the door.

When I was done, Ed just sat and stared at me in silence. He had recommended me to take his place as the Department Manager when he moved up and I literally owed him my career. He had confidence in me to do the job or he never would have offered it to me. He had even given it to me over a person who was working for him as a Section Manager but already held the title of Department Manager. He thought I could do a better job. I tried hard not to feel like I was letting him down.

Finally, as the silence was starting to become awkward – perhaps only a few seconds but time felt it was moving through molasses – he started to speak. "Okaaaaaaay", he said slowly. "You really know how to drop a bombshell, don't you?" We both let out a little uncomfortable laugh. "Are you sure this is what you want to do?"

I told him that I knew it was and that I knew I no longer had any choice in the matter. He looked at me and said, "All right, then. I'll get in touch with Human Resources and let them know. I really don't know how to handle this but I'm sure they'll be able to come up with something. I'll call you when I can get something set up."

I thanked Ed for his patience and left the room. It was done. I had just quite literally changed the course of my life. There was an enormous weight that seemed to have lifted from my shoulders but, at the same, more than a little dread was creeping in on what was to come next. I went back to my office and sat down at my desk.

Not five minutes passed when I got a phone call from Ed saying that Human Resources wanted to see us right away. That was fast – too fast, maybe. My fear of being fired outright had a lot to do with the fact that I held a Department of Defense security clearance, much the same as I had in the Navy. There might just be something in the regulations that said,

"Thou shalt not change thy sex and still be able to maintain thy security clearance."'

Who knew? All I could do was screw up my courage one more time and face the future. I put on my coat and met Ed at the door. We walked in silence across the parking lot to our

Personnel Building and then to the office of the Head of Human Resources, a very nice man name Tom whom I knew well.

Tom welcomed us in and closed the door behind us. We all sat down, and he looked at me very seriously. "Ricky, I know you well enough to know that you've thought this through a great deal."

I shook my head in agreement.

He went on, "So I guess it's not going to do me any amount of good to ask you why you want to do this or to try to talk you out of it. You know a lot more about the subject than I do."

Again, I nodded. "I know this is difficult for everyone to understand," I said, "but I've been going through this all of my life, and I can't continue like this anymore. I've been terribly depressed over the last few years, and I have to do something about it now."

It was his turn to nod.

"This company has been very good to me in the past," I continued, "and I think that I've been an exemplary employee during my twelve years here. I've never asked the company for anything other than a chance to excel at my job and to be the best that I could be. I have to ask for something now. This is very important to me."

Tom studied me for a moment and said, "You're right about your value to us. But do you think that making this change here is going to affect your work afterwards?"

It was a good question. Even though I really hadn't thought of it before, the answer just rolled out of me. "If you think I've been a good employee while I've been so horribly depressed all this time, just think of how much better I'm going to be when I'm not depressed anymore."

He smiled and said, "Good point." Then he was quiet for a few moments. "Ok. Here's what we're going to do," he said. I'm going to assign one of our senior people to this and we'll see what we can do for you. Maybe we can find you something at one of our other groups in the immediate area, so you won't have to go through this here with everyone knowing about it. I want to make this easy on both of us."

What a relief to hear this from Tom! I told him that I understood and appreciated his help. We stood and shook hands. He then took me to see his associate, Ivy, and returned to his office. I had never met Ivy before and had no idea if she was going to be understanding or uncomfortable or outright hostile. I didn't expect the very first thing she said to me.

"I won't pretend to know the first thing about this," she explained, never letting her eyes drift from mine. *"But I want you to know that I will put my job on the line before I will allow this company to discriminate against you in any way."*

I was floored. Here was a complete stranger telling me that I was going to be all right. Of course, that didn't mean that the whole company was going to be behind me but at least I had the assurance of someone with some say being on my side. This was more than I could have hoped for. If this had been a movie, beautiful music would have started playing in the background, the sun would have come out and all the birds would be singing. Although it wasn't really happening, it was sunny and musical inside my little world at that moment.

Ivy and I talked for a while about what I'd gone through in my life, and I finally got around to telling her about my plans for cosmetic surgery and time off from work, finally coming back to work as Rachael. This was the first time I'd ever told anyone outside my support group my adopted name. She thought it was nice, especially the part about my taking my mother's middle name in tribute to her. Of course, I was going to have to work with Ed on letting everyone know about my resignation from my Department Manager's position (if that was going to happen) and then find a replacement for me. I wasn't going to worry about that yet. For now, I just wanted to make sure I was going to have a job to come back to.

* * *

A few uncomfortable weeks passed, and I still hadn't heard anything about another position. My company had several other branches in New Jersey, none fairly close by but none so far away that it would have made commuting terribly difficult. I was hoping for one of them. No one knew me at all at any of these places because they did totally different kinds of business in the programming world than what we did in Moorestown, so I would basically be able to start all over. When I finally did hear from Ivy, though, it was to tell me that there were no positions available at any of those other offices. She was still looking. We were all starting to get nervous. None of us wanted me to stay in my current position. Transition would be hard enough for me without having to constantly worry about what people were thinking about me and, even worse, believing that I might have an adverse effect on my company's relations with our customers.

Then one day, Ivy called me and told me to go talk to another Department Manager over at one of our other buildings in the area. It was for a job on the same contract that I was working on, but in a different department with a lot of people I didn't know. It was as close to moving away and being unknown that she could find for me. The Department Manager that I went to see turned out to be a long-time friend of mine named Rick. I walked into his office, shook his hand, and then proceeded to tell him why I was looking for a new job. When I finished, he looked at me for a moment and then burst out laughing. When I didn't laugh back, he stopped and just stared at me. "You're serious, aren't you?" I never know when you're being serious and when you're not."

"I'm dead serious," I said. "I want you to put me in an office by myself with some programming task that will keep me challenged. I need to be out of the limelight for a while."

Rick shook his head in disbelief, still not quite sure I wasn't pulling his leg. He had been told a little about why I was coming to interview but hadn't quite believed it. He believed it now. Then he told me of a position that he had open that he could use my specific set of skills on. I gratefully accepted. We discussed when I would be leaving my current job and coming back to work and what my new name was going to be. He shook his head and laughed a bit again. "That's going to take some getting used to," he said.

I also told him that I planned to have an open-door policy to answer any questions from anyone because I knew that some people might not take this well. I'd rather they heard straight answers from me than gossip from someone else; not that gossip wouldn't be rampant, of course. And, oh boy, was it ever.

When we were done talking, he shook my hand and said, "You never cease to amaze me. You've got a lot of courage to do this. I sure hope you know what you're doing."

For the first time in my entire life, I honestly *did* know what I was doing. And as everything was finally coming together for me to start my new life, I was getting more nervous and more excited at the same time.

GHOSTS IN THE ADDICT

Something stirs in the darkness
Long thought dead, buried and forgotten,
Packed away in dusty memories.

The dragon stretches with claws yet strong
Readying himself for the battle anew
Knowing he will eventually kill his foe one way or
another.

With fetid teeth razor-honed and
Hungering for an innocent soul,
He has no conscience beyond his own ends
And cares nothing for the life he would destroy.

The monster has lurked in the shadows
For far too long now.
He will be free from his aged and rusted chains
Or he will perish and take his victim with him.

The victim prepares for her destined role
Knowing there is no defense left
And bracing for the inevitable.

Perhaps there is something more on the other side
Perhaps not.
It doesn't really matter.
The pain must stop, and the dragon must be fed.

Rachael Evelyn Thompson – 1991

Chapter 18
Easy as Falling Off a Log...From About a Mile Up

With the days of "buy and purge" behind me, I could now actually concentrate on a real wardrobe for my days ahead. My first step was to do something about my hair, though. As long as it was, it still wasn't quite long enough to really do anything terribly feminine with it. That didn't stop me, though. There was no way I was going to go back to wearing that ridiculous wig any more. It itched, and it looked like partially combed out road-kill – not exactly the look I was going for. So, I decided to go to my favorite hairdresser, Carolyn.

Carolyn and I had been good friends for some time, and she knew what I had been struggling with. We were kind of confidantes at the hair salon. She had her problems and I had mine. Talking made us both feel better. I don't know what it is about a hair stylist's chair, but it seems to me that a person could make a lot of money as a hairdresser with a psychologist's degree. "Now, tell me how you're feeling, and will that be just a little off the sides today?" Two birds killed with one very expensive stone.

Carolyn probably thought that there wasn't a whole lot that I could do that would shock her after all of the personal talks we'd had in the past. I was about to prove her wrong. One day I went into my closet and picked out a nice pair of slacks, a pretty white blouse and some matching shoes and earrings to go with the ensemble. I carefully did my makeup and played with my longish hair until I thought it looked at least a little feminine. Then I picked up my purse, took a deep breath and went to the salon just down the road – in broad daylight.

When I walked in, Carolyn recognized me immediately. Actually, she stopped breathing. All eyes were on me, trying to

243

figure out what was going on. The first words that stumbled out of her mouth were," Are those new earrings?" She told me later that she didn't know quite what else to say. She had known exactly who I was, of course, and so had all the other hairdressers in the salon. But what they all saw was Ricky in drag. Bad drag at that. This is one of the many nasty little memories that surface in my mind sometimes of something that I did that was so embarrassing to remember that the smart side of my brain gives me a little ice pick jab in the eyes trying to get even for not having been consulted before I acted. I had to give all of the ladies at the salon credit because not one single person laughed. Maybe they were just too shocked.

I sat down in Carolyn's chair and asked her to find a way to make my hair look nice. She did her best with what she had to work with, but it didn't turn out a whole lot better than what I had done to it myself. In the meantime, she finally found her voice and quietly asked me what the hell I was doing. I told her the whole sordid story about the weekend in the woods, my breakup with Kate and my talk with the people at work. I told her that this time it was for good. She wished me well and told me that I would always have her support. She has always been true to her word. She also told me that I should not ever again wear polyester pants. I took her advice immediately.

When I left the salon, I imagine there was a whole lot laughing and talking about me but, strangely, I didn't really care. I'd found the courage to go out and do what I had to do and it felt good. My knees felt like jelly, but it was good jelly. I had just gotten my first hairdo. Ricky Thompson never got his hair cut again. At this writing, Carolyn is still my hairdresser, and we still talk about all the weird things going on in our lives. We still remain good friends.

* * *

Now it was time to deal with rest of the things going on in my life. The first was the concert/marching band I played with. It was a basic 40-or-so member band made up of adults that missed playing instruments from their days in school. I had been playing the Sousaphone with them for a few years now and was well known by all the other band members. We played in local concerts around the South Jersey area and marched in parades at various times during the year. I was good friends with the conductor, Jim, and at times I took over conducting when he wasn't there. I was now going to test our friendship to the max.

Once every month the band's Board of Directors got together to discuss matters of importance to the band – where we were playing, equipment and music, potential new members, etc. I had asked permission to sit in on the next one in order to bring up something that was going to have an impact on the band. I told them it was best that I didn't elaborate until the meeting. The night of the meeting, Ricky didn't show up; Rachael did.

At first everyone was confused. Then they spiraled right down to disbelief and beyond. The first problem of the meeting was when they called for names of all participants. They put me down as Ricky. I corrected them on it later.

When it came my time to talk about new business, I got up in front of them and tried to put their minds at ease. "I know this seems a bit odd to you all," I explained, standing in front of them in my long denim skirt. They all laughed nervously. Continuing, I gave them the condensed version of my story and what I planned to do. I told them that from now on, I would be taking Ricky's place as a member of the band and that if they felt uncomfortable with it, I would understand and regretfully resign. I really enjoyed playing in the band and liked the people immensely. Leaving would be heartbreaking but I didn't want to do anything that would hurt the group's cohesion.

After a little discussion, it was decided that at the next band practice I would talk to the whole band and see how they took it. If they decided that this was just way too weird for them then I would simply wish them all well and walk away. Out of all the people at the meeting, only Jim seemed to be uncomfortable. I found out later that he was a born-again religious sort that didn't really think too kindly of this sort of thing – not that he'd ever seen it before, mind you. Much to his credit, though, he kept his thoughts to himself and left me in peace.

The evening of the next band practice was yet another of a long string of "swallow hard and walk in the door" events that were to become the mainstay of my life for some time to come. I walked in and sat down in my usual chair with my Sousaphone. Only this time instead of wearing jeans and a shirt I was wearing a flowered skirt and blouse. At first everyone thought I was playing a joke and they laughed and told me I looked "very nice". Then Jim got up in front of the band and told me that I had an announcement to make to them all.

Most of the people in the band were blue collar workers and I didn't expect to get much sympathy from them. I stood in front of them in my makeup and pantyhose and told them what I was going to do and why. I asked them to please give me a chance and let me stay in the band but that if they couldn't I would understand. I finished speaking and waited nervously for someone to say something. No one did. Then, breaking the prolonged and shocked silence, one person stood up and started to applaud slowly; then another, and another until the whole band was on its feet and clapping. By this time, I was crying. I had really expected most of them to be uncomfortable to the point of showing me the door. Instead, they were showing their support for something that they had never faced before and were very likely told in Sunday sermons was wrong. I was overwhelmed. Every last one of them, except for Jim, came up to me at our break in rehearsal to either give me a hug or a kiss or to shake my hand. They applauded me for my courage and even told me I really did look nice. I stayed with the band for a number of years after that and quit only after a broken love affair (which I will go into later). But I never forgot my friends' support. And I never will.

* * *

As frightening as it was, there were a lot of fun things about getting ready for my change in the world. I was still going through the horribly painful ordeal of electrolysis, or, as I like to refer to it, follicular torture. Picture having the hair burned out of your face with an electrified needle slid down the shaft of each individual hair, one hair at a time. That's pretty much what electrolysis is. It was a really swell thing to go through and only slightly ahead of dentistry on the Masochism scale. In the end, I figured it was my payment for not having had a period every month of my life from puberty like genetic girls have. Believe me, I would rather have had the periods. I know a lot of women might disagree with that, but they really need to have an hour of electrolysis on the hairs at the base of their nostrils some time. They'd change their minds real fast.

I was still getting monthly shots of female hormones in my rear and enduring the changes in my body, both in the tenderness in my chest and the hot flashes that would take over at the end of the month a few days before I was due for my next shot. Sometimes the hot flashes (or *power surges* as I now call them) were so severe that if it was cool inside the house, my glasses would fog up. My doctor thought that was pretty funny. I didn't quite see all the humor in it that he did.

As a result of the voice training that I'd received and constant practice into a tape recorder reading from books and listening to how it sounded, I'd gotten so used to the higher register and way of talking that I was passing the "telephone test" all the time now. When I first started my transition, people on the phone would almost always refer to me as "Sir" until I told them my name. Then they would usually apologize and call me "Ma'am" from that time on. I compensated for it by introducing myself first so I could pre-frame their mental view of the gender of the person who they were talking to. My voice training has been so successful that I can no longer get down to the lower register of my old voice without working very hard at it – or unless I have a bad cold.

* * *

Being able to make my voice sound more feminine was another enormous thing for me. When even thinking about making the change to Rachael I got very good at coming up with all sorts of reasons why I couldn't do it – none of them earth shattering, but it was easy to make a mountain out of a molehill when you're frightened to death. One of the most important of these "reasons" was my singing voice. I was convinced that, if I made this change, I would never again be able to play guitar and sing without making people look twice at me. It was a deal-breaker for me for a long time. It finally became unimportant in the grand scheme of things, especially after having taken voice training. However, that fear never left me. My trial by fire came later – literally around a fire. I had been teaching a Basic Backpacking and Wilderness Survival course with the local

248

Outdoor Club of South Jersey for years and, at our camping adventures with students, would always bring along my guitar and sing around the campfire. After I had made my final decision about changing my life, I had to also decide if I was going to remain as an instructor with the course. Like playing in the band, this course was something I thoroughly enjoyed doing and was very reluctant to give up. So, I steeled my nerves and, just like in the band, Rachael showed up at our instructors' meeting to explain what was happening. Again, I had to face the likelihood that I would not be welcome. Instead, after recovering from their initial shock, every instructor stated that they wanted me to stay.

When it came to the hiking trip where I would usually bring my guitar, I hesitated, but felt that this was as good a chance as any to see how I'd do. I brought my guitar along and, like I had so many trips before, sat around the campfire and played and sang for the students. It was a complete success. Some of the students even told me later that they had enjoyed my playing and complimented me on my singing voice. They were *complimenting* me on my singing voice! They might as well have told me that I had just won a million dollars. One of my most fearsome obstacles was behind me. It never bothered me again.

* * *

Of course, I was continuing to go to psychotherapy once a week. My therapist's job was mainly to keep me on my feet every time I got knocked down. He picked me up an awful lot in the years that I saw him. He became my rock as I went through life test.

* * *

Let me take a moment to explain what "life test" is. Not that long ago, all a person had to do to get what was called a sex change operation was to find a surgeon who would do it (usually out of the country), pay him, take a chance that you might get mutilated, and go home to your new life. Unfortunately, some people didn't survive the surgery – or the aftermath. When it was discovered that post-surgical people seemed to be dying at an alarming rate, a study was done to find out what was happening. It turned out that a whole lot them were, for some unknown reason, committing suicide within the first few years of their transformation. A doctor named Harry Benjamin decided to do something about that. He came up with what is known as *"The Harry Benjamin Standards of Care"*. These standards were written partly to provide a blueprint for anyone who wanted to go through gender reassignment surgery but mostly for the doctors who would treat them. The main point of the Standards is to ensure that the underlying problem of the prospective patient was, in actuality, Gender Dysphoria and not something else. It seemed that a lot of the people who were going through with surgery were not transsexual at all. Some of them were actually gay men made by society to feel so ashamed of themselves that they couldn't live with being a man loving other men. So, they found a doctor and had their penises removed in an attempt to conform to society, regardless of what it did to them. Instead, it ruined their already tenuous self-identity and many of them ended up jumping off bridges. There were a lot of other reasons why people would have sex changes and, unfortunately, a lot of them turned out to be big mistakes. Once you have the surgery, there's really no going back. There is no penis to sew back on. For males to females who try to go back to being male again, there's no sex or using a urinal ever again. For females to males, breasts have to be restored with implants, they have to go through electrolysis to remove facial hair and, in a lot of cases, sex is no longer an option for them, either. So, having gender reassignment surgery is a pretty drastic thing to do. Doctors were starting to realize that there was more to this than just a "nip and tuck" job and the patient goes away happy.

Dr. Benjamin's Standards of Care start out with the requirement that anyone requesting surgery has to have had a long history of psychotherapy before actually having the surgery. Any surgeon worth his or her salt will ask for, among other things, a signed note from at least one psychotherapist and one psychiatrist. They also want to see a signed note from the person's medical doctor that he or she has undergone hormone treatments for at least a year. But probably most important of all is the note from the psychotherapist certifying that the person has lived, worked and socialized exclusively in their new gender role for a period of no less than one year – quite often two or more depending on the personal requirements of the surgeon. This period of time is called *"Life Test"* by those of us who have gone through it. It is a time to get used to living in your new role and being treated as any other person of that gender. For "M-to-F"s, it means getting used to complete strangers calling you "sweetheart", treating you like you have fewer brain cells than the average chimpanzee, and, in a lot of cases, taking a pay cut for doing the same type of work you've done all along in your life. For "F-to-M"s, it means putting up with public scratching, spitting, sexist and obscene jokes and not saying anything when their companions talk about their wives and girlfriends as personal possessions or sex toys. It's a very important and enlightening time to go through. A lot of people find that they can't take it and stop before the surgery makes everything irreversible. Then, of course, they have to find a way to live the rest of their lives with their "problem". There are also those who find during this time that they "pass" in public so badly that they decide that the pain of Gender Dysphoria is actually better than the pain of the public humiliation that they feel from constantly being stared at and made fun of. Again, they have to find a way to live with the problem. Some don't.

In most cases, though, Life Test is just one more affirmation that what the person is doing is the right thing to do. For me, it was a case of "never look back". I knew I was doing the right thing and I knew that even if I didn't always pass very successfully, in time I would. Part of passing is not so much how one looks as how one acts. A friend of mine who was going through this would make herself up to look very attractive in nice clothes and hair but when she walked, she had the glaringly obvious gangly walking gait of a man. Tell-tale signs like that make a person on the street who would otherwise not take notice, take a second look at you. And when they take that second look, they often see what you don't want them to see. So being out in public in a nice summer dress and loudly hocking up a giant loogey on the sidewalk is right out. You just can't do that and look feminine at the same time. People will stare. Not that I ever did anything like that myself even *before* my change, you understand.

* * *

By May of 1991 it was time to start my own Life Test. I announced to everyone in my department that I was leaving to take another position in another department and another building. Of course, they all asked what I was going to do but I just told them it was a technical position that I couldn't talk about because it hadn't been confirmed yet. That managed to keep most people from asking too many questions, but some didn't find it very convincing. The last thing I wanted was for people to find out about what I was going to do before I was ready.

The day I left my department, my employees and friends threw me a going away party. We had a great group that always got our work done on or ahead of schedule and pretty much better than any other department at the time. I was very proud of them. The other departments hated us because of our successes that constantly made them look bad. But we were a family and not only was it hard to leave the family, I felt bad on top of that for having to lie to them all. At the luncheon party several people got up to say something about working with me – usually highly satirical. I expected no less from them. Everyone was having a good time. One of them even gave me a coupon for a free haircut at a local barber. Very funny. Then they gave me a present from the entire group. I was horribly nervous as I opened it. I had this terrible feeling that they all knew what I was going to do and that the present was going to be something that would blow the whole thing wide open. As it happened, my present was a beautiful gold desk clock which I still have in my home. But everyone noticed my shaking hands as I opened the package and were quite puzzled. I laughed it off by telling them I wasn't sure if it was going to explode or not. I offered my thanks to everyone and told them that I would keep in touch when I got into my new job. I was going to be taking a few weeks off first and then they'd hear from me. None of them suspected that they would never talk to Ricky again.

Chapter 19
Life Test and Other Masochistic Things

The time had come. I had cleaned out my desk and had taken a few weeks' vacation. My friend Denise from the PTSG drove me to the hospital in Philadelphia where my cosmetic surgery was going to be performed. Before I knew it, I was lying on a gurney being wheeled into the operating room. Oddly, I wasn't scared at all. I was actually excited. I was now on the road (or the hallway) to the biggest adventure of my life. They moved me onto the operating table and made me comfortable. The anesthesiologist told me he had just given me a shot and asked me if I felt anything. I thought for a moment and said, "N…".

I woke up to a strange sensation in my head. I felt like I was wrapped up like a mummy and partially suffocating. Touching my face, I found out that I pretty much was. I had stitches on my eyelids, my nose was covered with a stiff, shaped form and stuffed with gauze and I had a compression bandage wrapped from the bottom of my chin all the way over the top of my head. Other than that, I felt just fine. The nurses had been a bit concerned because I wasn't answering to my name when they tried to awaken me after surgery. They were calling my old name. Even then my psyche was changing. I vaguely remember someone calling that name but not knowing what to do about it. Someone looked at my chart and suggested that they call me Rachael. They said I responded at once and opened my eyes.

After an hour or so I was allowed to sit up and get dressed. I called Denise to come pick me up and then waited for her. As I sat in the waiting room, I noticed people staring at me like I was some grotesque monster. I certainly felt like one. The other thing I noticed was that it was becoming increasingly hard to breathe.

Because of the bandage around my face, I couldn't speak very loudly so all I could do was wave my hands. A nurse finally noticed my frantic gesturing and came to see what was wrong. I told her though my clenched teeth that the bandage around my chin was getting tighter and very uncomfortable. She called the doctor.

When the doctor came into the waiting room to look at me, he removed the bandage from my head and his eyes went wide. Evidently, he had nicked a blood vessel under my chin while doing the liposuction. The skin under my neck was literally filling up with blood. I looked like a balloon. That's why the bandage was getting so tight. Then he did something that he immediately regretted – he squeezed my neck to try to get some of the blood out. It came out, all right – it gushed out, spurting all over him and across the waiting room floor in all directions. He jumped back and, after regaining his composure, sent someone over to clean me and the floor up. Then, after checking that the bleeding wasn't profuse, he put the compression bandage back on me a bit tighter than it had been originally. The bleeding had stopped but they made me sit there for another half hour to make sure it wasn't going to start again. Between the bandages and the fully HazMat-suited janitor sent in to clean up the waiting room, I was now being avoided completely. The only reason I bring this up is because this was to be a pattern in my life. There was not one time that I had any surgery from this point on where something didn't go wrong. It was really something to look forward to.

Denise showed up and drove me home. I spent an extremely uncomfortable night because my head was bound and my nostrils were packed. My breathing was labored and sometime in the middle of the night I woke up feeling that I was going to asphyxiate. I had to mentally grab hold of myself and calm myself down before the rising panic I was feeling hit me full force. I felt like screaming. I managed somehow to get control of my breathing and the panic subsided. It was not a fun night. But it was the worst that I would have to endure.

I spent the next few weeks healing up to the point where my bandages and stitches were removed. As I sat in the doctor's office for my final visit in my nice blouse, skirt and heels for my final checkup, they called for Richard Thompson. I sat still. They called again. I didn't move. Finally, as nonchalantly as I could, I got up and walked over to the receptionist's desk where I quietly informed the woman that I was there but not to call me Richard any more if she didn't mind. She turned a bit red and apologized. I spoke of it to the doctor, and he assured me it would never happen again.

When I first visited the doctor's office, he had several black and white pictures taken of my face from all angles. With my healing nearly complete, he took more pictures for comparison. There was a noticeable difference. It wasn't a startling change but just enough to soften my features a bit and give me a little more confidence. The doctor asked one of his associates to come take a look and offer his opinion. He fawned all over the "radical" change in me, staring in disbelief at the "before" pictures. What was he going to do, tell me he didn't notice any difference? I knew that most of the compliments weren't really very sincere, but they were nice to hear, anyway. It sure beat the hell out of hearing, "Oh my God! What an ugly broad!"

I was now healed up and ready to start my new life in earnest. It was time to go back to work as Rachael; something I never thought in my wildest dreams would ever happen. I remembered all the times that I had wanted so badly just to come into work as Rachael and tell everyone just to deal with it. I knew I couldn't do that, but the urge was sometimes so great that it was almost unbearable to go into work as Ricky. I wasn't going back to work as a total unknown, though. One of the things that Ivy had discussed with me before I left my Department Manager position was how they would prepare my new co-workers for my "coming out". I didn't see any reason to tell anyone anything. There was a new woman coming to work. What else did they need to know? The Human Resources people didn't see it as quite so innocuous. They were afraid that there would be a lot of concern about something I hadn't even thought of – use of the ladies' room. I still had male genitalia. If anyone found out that I had been using the ladies' room while still being physically male, the uproar might be overwhelming. So, they decided it was best to let everyone know about it ahead of time. They brought in a local "expert" on transsexualism to talk to the people in my new building the week before I came back to work. I was not invited to the discussion. They thought it might be better for people to be able to discuss the situation openly without being afraid of hurting my feelings. So, the people at work found out not only *what* was coming to work, but *who* that thing used to be.

News spread like wildfire. I started getting phone calls at home almost immediately after the briefing. Most of the calls were from friends who didn't believe what they'd heard. Others were well-meaning friends trying to talk me out of it for various reasons, mostly religious. I would hear those kinds of things again, over and over.

Between the time of the briefing at work and my actual first appearance, rumors abounded, and tempers flared. One woman at work was seen going from office to office screaming profanities about how much unmitigated gall I had to anyone who would listen. "How DARE he think he can just click his fingers and be a woman!" she and others would say. *Rumor Control* was going full force. Everyone had an idea of why they thought I was doing this. One of the funniest of them all was that

I had been having a homosexual affair with a cute mail delivery boy with long blond hair who seemed to always stay in my office to talk before moving on. We enjoyed talking to each other – that's all it was. The rumors said I was having a sex change so we could be together as husband and wife. I was old enough to be his mother. He thought that was pretty funny, too. With all these rumors and some of the backlash that I was hearing, I discovered that people found it really hard to accept this sort of thing, especially when they never saw any outward signals at all from this person they'd known for years. Some even felt that I had lied to them. They didn't understand that I didn't lie – I couldn't tell anyone about myself without subjecting myself to ridicule and worse. A lot of people who have gone through this hide their inner feelings by going overboard in their birth gender role. They'll act overly macho so no one would ever suspect how they felt inside. I wasn't like that, though. I mostly kept to myself, something I learned to do from my youth. If I didn't get too close to people, then I didn't run the risk of making them wonder about me. It was a lonely way to live but it was safe.

As Ivy suspected, when the expert came to talk about me – what I was and, more importantly, what I *wasn't* – one of the first things to come up was my use of the ladies' room. There was a very vocal minority of older women who refused to have me in the ladies' room with them. They listed three things that caused them overwhelming concern.

Number one: I was going to ogle them while they were in their stalls. For those of you of the male persuasion who haven't ever been in a ladies' room, let me describe them to you. There are no urinals – that could prove to be messy. Instead, they only contain toilets, each of which are contained within their own high-walled stall with doors, just like the toilets in the men's room. The only possible way I could ogle anyone (even if I wanted to) would either be to stand in front of the stall door trying desperately to get a peek through the cracks of the door frames, or to stand on the toilet seat in an adjoining stall and peer over the wall. Neither would be particularly clandestine, and both would be ridiculous to even imagine. Besides, I don't care what they're doing in there as long as they don't bother me.

Number 2: I might sexually attack someone while in there. After all, I was still properly equipped, wasn't I? By the time I came back to work in my new persona, I had been taking female hormones for quite some time. My "equipment" was only functional for pointing where I wanted to pee, an ability that comes in quite handy, I might add, when backpacking in the wilderness. By now I was basically "chemically castrated". I could no more have an erection than give birth. The female hormones had seen to that quite nicely. It was not something I missed.

Number 3 (and my personal favorite): they were afraid that I would leave AIDS on the toilet seats. This one hardly deserves comment. When I heard this, it was all I could do not to break out laughing at the unadulterated ignorance of the thought. But ignorance won out even though the expert they'd brought in tried to explain away all these misconceptions.

The final decision to rectify this "problem" was particularly inventive: brackets were attached to the door of the only ladies' room I was allowed to use (there were three in the building) so I could slide in a large 8 x 12 bright red sign I had to carry with me every time I needed to use the toilet that read in giant white letters:

DO NOT ENTER
SCARY TRANSSEXUAL INSIDE

259

Ok, the second line really wasn't on the sign, but it might as well have been.

I was supposed to carry my sign to the ladies' room, knock on the door, and open it a bit to declare to anyone inside that I wanted to come in. Then, if there was anyone in there and she didn't mind my being there, she'd call out for me to come in. Otherwise she'd tell me to wait until she came out. If I received the second response I had to stand in the hallway like a preschooler, trying to look nonchalant while holding my gaudy red sign and trying not to dribble down my legs if I really had to go badly. When I was finally allowed to go inside, I had to slide my sign into the brackets on the door, enter, do my business and then remove the sign as I left to go back to my desk. It was very humiliating. I put up with this for a couple of weeks before I went to Ivy and told her it was too much. If I had to have a sign, could it at least be a bit less flamboyant? She agreed, and I was issued a much smaller 3 x 5 white card that attached to the door via a small piece of Velcro. It was still a sign saying:

DO NOT ENTER

but it sure beat the giant red warning banner. I thought the whole thing was so silly that, from time to time, I would make up my own version of the "warning" and tape it over my little sign. If I had to use the sign, I was going to have some fun. Usually it would say something like:

COME ON IN – THE WATER'S FINE!

People actually started to look forward to whatever silliness I had written on my sign. I had several of them so people wouldn't get bored. I had discussed the unreasonable demand to use this demeaning sign with my therapist and told him how embarrassed it made me feel. He explained that this was the only way the women who objected had any control over an uncomfortable situation they felt that they were being forced to endure by the company. All I had to do was put up with it for the period of my Life Test and then, after my surgery, I would never have to worry about it again. If they still didn't want me in the bathroom afterwards then they'd have to go someplace else. It was their problem, not mine. In the meantime, he thought my playing with what the sign said was very therapeutic, and quite funny.

Most of the women at work didn't have any problem with me being in the ladies' room with them. It seemed to be only those women who were older and/or less feminine looking. I think that I was somehow a threat to them. Perhaps they felt that, with my non-terribly-feminine appearance, someone might think that they were TS, too. I can only imagine how they must have felt but I had to keep telling myself that how they felt about themselves had no bearing on me. However, I did send out an email to everyone at work on my first day back telling them that my door was open at all times and that I would be more than happy to sit down with anyone who wanted to know more about what I was going through and put their minds at ease. During the entire year of my Life Test, only two people actually came to see me. The others there who had trouble with my existence were probably much more comfortable with gossip and half-truths. They weren't about to let silly things like facts interfere with their opinions.

But speaking of silly, I want to go back to a few years earlier with my first few "outings" as a clandestine female.

* * *

261

Lynne and I had been invited to go to a Halloween party at a local fire house in New Jersey where my boss at work was a fire chief. I always liked to go overboard at these types of things. Once I went to a party wearing a full chimpanzee mask that I had to glue onto my face in two pieces, put makeup on just like a real movie makeup artist, glue fake black hair on my hands and feet, paint my fingernails and toenails black, and wear a black wig. Then I rented a large-sized wedding gown, wrapped up a bouquet of bananas in a ribbon and went as "The Bride of the Planet of the Apes." I won best costume at the party.

For this party, I decided to go as a Playboy bunny – a PREGNANT Playboy bunny. Starting to see a pattern? I got the entire outfit complete with a body stocking, bunny ears and tail, and then stuffed a pillow in the front to make it look like I was 9 months pregnant. It was hilarious, and I felt great doing it because 1) I was going out dressed up as a woman, and 2) it was so silly that no one thought anything about that I was going out dressed as a woman

The party went on just fine although I did cause more than a bit of consternation having to use the bathroom, walking into the men's room like that. I didn't drink much that night because going into the bathroom just once was all I could take.

When the festivities were over, Lynne and I went out to get into the car to go home. The car we were driving was an incredibly beaten-up old Plymouth that I had bought from a friend at work for literally *one dollar*. He was doing me a favor because my car had broken down and I had nothing to drive and no way to afford a new car. The engine in the car worked just fine but outside it was rusty and the interior, especially the rear seat, was torn up to the point where we put blankets on the seats so we wouldn't feel TOO much like white trash driving it.

I pulled out of my parking space and started to turn around to head back out onto the road. Then a horrible thing happened: I had no brakes. I kept pumping them, but the car wouldn't stop. I wasn't going very fast, but this car was a behemoth and rolling slowly into ANYTHING just couldn't be good. Except that I was rolling right toward the fire station bay doors. Luckily there was something in the way – a brand new Pontiac Firebird that one of the firemen had just bought. All I could do was watch in horror as my car broadsided his. The door crumpled, and glass broke out all over everything. After I made sure Lynne was all right, I went inside, called the police, and then found the man who owned the car. When he came out to see the damage, he understandably wasn't too happy. As we exchanged insurance information the police office showed up. We talked for a bit and II told him what had happened. He got into my car and pumped the brakes, then told me not to worry. It was obvious what had happened, and that it wasn't my fault. He didn't issue me a ticket.

A friend drove Lynne and I home and we had the car towed to get the brakes fixed. But the story doesn't end there.

Of course not, silly.

About 3 weeks later got an interesting lesson in the mail about how the New Jersey police system worked. I got a ticket from the same officer who came out the first station saying THIS time that I WAS at fault for the accident because I had been driving an "unsafe" car. I had the choice of paying for the ticket (several hundred dollars) and getting points on my driving record or contesting the ticket in court. I couldn't believe what I was seeing. This was outrageous! I was NOT going to let this stand.

I called the police department and asked why I'd gotten this ticket when just a few weeks earlier I'd been told I wasn't going to be issued one. I was told that all officers had 30 days in which to change their minds and issue citations if they decided to. I got this ticket just three days short of that 30-day window.

I decided to go to court.

A few weeks I was summoned to go to court. I'd never contested a ticket before, but this was just so unfair there was nothing else I could do. When my case started, the prosecution (the city) had their own lawyer. I had me.

Uh, oh.

The prosecution presented its case first and called the police officer who didn't write me/wrote me the ticket. He first asked the officer, "Do you see the defendant in the courtroom?"

The officer replied, "Yes, but he looked different at the accident scene. He was at a Halloween party."

"Oh?", asked the attorney, "What was he dressed as?"

Now, someone with a real law degree would have stood up and said, "Objection! Irrelevant!" Keep in mind I'm not now nor have I ever been a real lawyer although I have watched people on TV playing lawyers. I sat there and didn't open my mouth, ready for the embarrassment that I knew was just moments away.

"He was dressed as a Playboy bunny," the officer said. He added, "a PREGNANT Playboy bunny".

The courtroom, including the judge, erupted in laughter.

The judge looked at me and said, "I'll be you wished he hadn't asked that question."

I shook my head sheepishly, my cheeks bright red.

When the laughter died down, the attorney continued to ask questions about the accident and why the officer thought my car was unsafe to drive. He explained that it looked like it was about ready to fall apart, describing the obvious cosmetic

264

damage that he'd seen, and then said that, in his opinion as a mechanic, total brake failure like that just didn't suddenly happen with no warning.

The prosecution rested its case. It was my turn...and I had an idea.

My first question to the officer was how it was that he "knew" my car was unsafe just because of how it looked. I told him I had 4 brand new tires on the car and a state inspection sticker that was only a few weeks old.

He said he hadn't noticed that.

I turned to the judge and offered to go out to the car to get my inspection certification if he needed it. He said he didn't.

Turning back to officer, I got to the meat of my defense. But I did something no lawyer is supposed to do – I asked a question to which I didn't already know the answer. I was taking a chance based on a hunch I had and asked him where he worked on cars.

"I work on them in my garage at home for myself and for friends", he explained.

"So, you don't work at any certified garage?", I asked.

He responded, "No. Just at my home".

I then replied, "So you're not actually a licensed mechanic. What you do is just a hobby."

"Yes."

Got him! "So", I continued, "you're not really qualified to say that brakes don't "just instantly" fail because you're not an expert mechanic, are you?" (I'd actually had this happen to me once in another car.)

He had no choice but to admit that I was right.

I looked at the judge and said, "I have no further questions", and returned to my seat.

The judge dismissed the case, and I didn't have to pay for the ticket. Perry Mason would have been proud. Or at least the writers for Perry Mason, anyway.

And now back to our regularly scheduled memoir.

* * *

There was one bit of business that I had to tend to before I could formally start work as Rachael. Since we all had security clearances at work, we were required to prominently wear badges with our pictures and our full names displayed on them. I had already changed all of my credit cards and accounts to R. E. Thompson, but I couldn't do that with my badge. It had to be my full name. Unless I wanted to have Rachael's picture on my badge with Richard's name under it, I had to legally change my name.

I went to my local town clerk's office to inquire how a name change was done. He simply gave me a few stapled pages with instructions on them and told me to follow them. All in all, it was a pretty easy thing to do. I had to first put a notice in the local newspaper stating that I was changing my name. This was done so that it was a matter of public record that anyone could see in case there was any objection. It cost about thirty-five dollars. As soon as the notice was printed, I had to send a copy of it to the courts with a check for their costs. I then received a court date in the mail for the hearing which I had to announce once again in the newspaper (for another thirty-five dollars) so that anyone with objections could show up in court to, well, object after notifying the court that they were going to be there. No one called to say they had any problems with it, so I didn't even have to show up at the court hearing. I was simply sent a letter from the court authorizing my legal name change after a thirty-day waiting period. I had to put up another thirty-five dollars to advertise my final authorization in the newspaper and then do nothing else until the waiting period was over. It took just over two months to complete the entire transaction.

After I got my name legally changed, I thought it would be a good idea to get the ball rolling on changing my driver's license and having my Social Security card updated as well. I took my legal name change papers with me to the Social Security office first and filed for the name change. I was a bit nervous, but it was something I had to do. To my surprise and relief, the woman I spoke to at the agency didn't seem to mind at all. She did balk, however, at the extra change that had been made on the form. Along with changing my name from Richard to Rachael, I had indicated that my gender should be corrected from M to F. Nothing ventured, nothing gained. When she saw the change, she explained that she wasn't sure if she could do it but she'd find out. She went to the back of the office to talk to her boss. I watched as the two of them pulled out one huge book after another, thumbing through each of them to try to find some directive that covered this sort of thing. After a few minutes of head scratching, she came back to her desk where I was patiently waiting and told me they couldn't find anything that said they couldn't change my gender along with my name. She said she would try it. The worst that could happen would be that the government wouldn't do it. If I wanted to make a stink about it, I did have my official birth certification saying that I had been born female to back me up. Of course, I'd have to explain to them why it said Female in the first place with a male name on it. One thing at a time.

Within a week I received my new Social Security card in the mail with my new name and my correct gender on it. Sometimes the government *can* actually work for you. With this success under my belt, I confidently headed to the local Department of Motor Vehicles office.

I showed up at the DMV in a nice feminine business suit armed with my new identity papers and my legal name change authorization. I filled out all the paperwork, including changing my gender, and handed it to the clerk at the main desk. In a few minutes a call came over the loudspeaker. "Ms. Rachael Thompson, please come to Counter Six."

I walked up to the counter marveling at how fast this had been and smiling in anticipation of yet another success. In true bubble-bursting form, the clerk looked at me and asked why I was changing my name. I told her. She stared at me for a moment, not quite sure what to say. Then she asked, "Have you had your surgery yet?[20]"

I answered, "No, but I will be having it in about a year." I explained to her what Life Test was all about and why I was doing this.

When I was finished, the clerk looked at me with more than a bit of disdain and said, "I'm sorry Ms. Thompson, but until you have your surgery and bring back a note from your surgeon verifying that the surgery is complete, we can't change your gender on your driver's license." This meant that for the entire year that I was working and living as Rachael Thompson, there would be a big, bold, dark 'M' for MALE on my driver's license for all to see and wonder at. This was just not going to be acceptable at all. I showed her my new Social Security card and my birth certificate, both of which said I was female, and told her that the U.S. Government already legally had me listed as female. But the poor U.S. Government was no match for the Great State of New Jersey. They had their own rules, and no stinking Federal Government was going to tell *them* what to do.

---

[20] By the way, don't EVER ask this of a transgender person. Not only is it exceedingly rude, it's none of your business.

No matter what I said or how much I pleaded with them, I was doomed to having male designation on my license right under my undeniably female name. It seemed like they were determined to make sure that someone would get a chuckle for the next year if I was ever stopped for anything in my car. It wasn't enough for them to have your driver's license picture make you look like a convict when you've asked them specifically not to. It was maddening and humiliating. I left the DMV dejected but determined to obey every law of the road until this was fixed. Ok, I always did, anyway, but this made it all that much more important. It would not be my last encounter with the DMV.

* * *

My first day of work as Rachael went surprisingly well. I had chosen a very professional looking blouse, skirt and jacket and had carefully done my makeup and hair. I took one final look at myself in the mirror, took a deep breath and walked out my front door to the first day of my new life. I was amazed that I didn't feel all that nervous. I knew that this was the only option left to me so being nervous wouldn't really serve any purpose. I just told myself not to be. For the most part, it worked – sort of.

My first stop at work was to go to our security department and get my new picture identity badge. Although the people in the office were expecting me, there were more than a few raised eyebrows but also quite a few compliments from friends that I'd known in that office for years. I walked out with the first official picture of Rachael Thompson ever taken. It was a great feeling. Getting back in my car, I headed to my new building, my new office and my new professional life.

When I got to my building, a man entering just before me held the door for me and said with a smile, "Good morning."

What a nice way to start my first day! Going upstairs, I walked into my new boss' office and told him I was ready to start. He looked at me in shock. A month before, a man had walked into his office asking for a favor. A woman was now standing in front of him to collect it. I could tell that he was having trouble getting words out but when he finally could, he told me that I really looked nice. That was a start; and a good one at that. We talked for a little while about how ready I was for this and what he was going to want me to do in the department. Then he walked me around the office to meet my new co-workers. Everyone already knew who (and what) I was but for the most part they seemed friendly enough if not a little stunned or bemused. I was shown to my office and sat down to start work. My big red bathroom sign was already waiting for me in the top drawer of my desk. With the exception of having to start using that, and the basketball-sized lump in my throat, the day went pretty much without incident. When I returned home that first evening, it felt unbelievably good to not have to change out of my work clothes into something more feminine. I just changed out of my work clothes into something more comfortable like any other professional woman would do.

At the end of the week, I stopped into my boss' office and asked him how things were going in the department now that I was there. He smiled and said that the only thing he had heard was that some of the other women were jealous of my clothes. He said that everyone was amazed at me and he was pleased at how well everything seemed to be going. No one really knew what to expect seeing me that first day. I think most of them thought they'd see a man in drag with no fashion sense. Instead, they saw a professional woman that fit in pretty well. It was a good week. I knew I was on the right track.

* * *

I was so ecstatic with the way things were going that I had some pictures taken of me at a nearby photo studio and sent them to my parents, explaining what I was doing and how happy I was. A week later I received my pictures back along with a note saying, "We love you but don't ever come home like this." My worst fears were coming true: my own parents didn't want any part of me any more – just when I needed them the most. I wrote them a long and angry letter explaining to them that even parents with children in jail for murder don't turn away from their children and I hadn't committed any crime. I got a phone call the next week from my little brother, Tim, who was very angry that I had talked to our parents like that. I explained to him that I hadn't meant to hurt anyone – I was just incredibly hurt myself and didn't understand how they could turn their backs on me like that. He seemed to understand after a while, but I promised him that I wouldn't upset Mom and Dad like that again. I eventually ended up breaking that promise years later.

* * *

Work during this time was a blessing. I had to learn a whole new and complex computer language just to start the project. Much as I had done as a social outcast in High School, I lost myself in it to help keep my mind off the tension around me. A lot of people went out of their way to be friendly but still more went out of their way to avoid me like the plague. I got cards of encouragement from fellow employees, some I barely knew, stating their pride at my courage and promising their help if I needed it. From others I got anonymous biblical passages left on my desk describing such things as "God's design for men and

271

women" as determined by their particular religious organizations. Those I could have done without. I was pretty sure that there wasn't anything in the Bible that specifically said, "Thou shalt not change thy gender" but that didn't stop these people from doing a little free interpretation of their own. One of my friends from my old department sent me a "Congratulations! It's a Girl!" card that made me smile. It was from the same guy who had seen me in the store buying a pair of shoes for "my sister".

Time crept along slowly at first but seemed to speed up as I got more accustomed to my new life. During this time, I had already started looking into making arrangements for surgery. As you can tell, sometime during all of this my thinking had changed from "see if this is right for me" to "I know this is right and I'm going through with it". I don't really know when that change happened; it may have been there all along. With this conviction in mind, I didn't want to waste any more time than I had to. I was determined to have my surgery as soon as possible after Life Test was over. I was living in a sort of self-imposed limbo socially. Although I was now living twenty-four hours a day as a woman, I had made a pact with myself not to date anyone. Until I was anatomically correct, I didn't think it was a good idea to get involved with anyone. I'd heard far too many stories about people who had been beaten almost to death when the person they were dating found out there was a little "something extra" in the package. It was safer just to be on my own for the time being. It was only for a year, and I had the rest of my life to date afterwards.

I got an interesting question in that vein from a friend during this time that got me thinking. After I had my surgery, was I going to date men? I realized that I honestly didn't know how to answer it. I'd never been physically attracted to men at all but in the back of my mind I always thought that might be because I didn't have the right plumbing. Plus, I couldn't imagine myself as a gay man. Did that make me homophobic? I really didn't want to be close to a male body. I'd had enough closeness of my own in that regard. Dating and marrying women in my previous life got me closer to the female body that I always wanted for myself, and it was certainly no secret that the female body aroused me sexually. I had three kids, after all. There was only one answer for me: to wait until I had the surgery and see how I felt then. For the time being all that really mattered was getting myself through Life Test. Worrying about one problem at a time was just fine with me.

One thing I had to decide on was where I was going to have my surgery. I had thought a lot about going out to the small town of Trinidad, Colorado to have the famous Dr. Stanley Biber perform my surgery as he had for so many of my girlfriends in the support group. At the time he was the preeminent authority on doing male-to-female surgeries in the world. There was also the possibility of going somewhere else with a surgeon that was equally respected in the field. One of those places was Brussels, Belgium with Dr. Michel Seghers. Dr. Biber and Dr. Seghers had studied together and had both performed hundreds of successful surgeries. There were up-sides and down-sides to going to either place. Going to Colorado would keep me in the States where I basically knew and trusted how medical procedures were done. I knew several women who had been to Dr. Biber and had come back with nothing but good things to say about him. However, it was a bit difficult to get to and from Trinidad. The closest major airport was Colorado Springs and, once you got there, you had to take what was described as an hours-long bumpy bus ride to Trinidad. That wasn't so bad going but it was excruciatingly painful and long coming back after surgery. Going to Brussels was much simpler. I could fly directly there from Philadelphia and take modern transit into the city and anywhere afterwards I wanted to go. However, I didn't know anything about Belgian medical facilities, and I didn't speak French very well and knew no Flemish at all. I didn't even know if anyone would be able to speak English to me other than the doctor. I still remembered with dread my hospital stay in Djibouti while I was in the Navy.

Let's go back in time a bit here.

* * *

During one of my TAD trips out of Rota, the ship I was on had stopped in the port of Massawa, Ethiopia (now in Eritrea) for refueling. When we went out on liberty from the ship, we were warned not to drink the water or eat any fresh produce that had been rinsed in the local water. Not a problem – we all drank beer from bottles. Ok, there was a bit of a problem: the beer bottles had all been submerged in ice water to keep it cold. No one thought that just a little water on the bottles could make a person sick. After we got back on the ship and headed back out to sea, it didn't take long for a few people to start feeling ill. Of course, not to be outdone by anyone, I ended up being the sickest of all. The corpsmen on the ship had been giving me little bottles of powdered Kaopectate to mix with water and drink to get rid of the awful case of diarrhea I had contracted. I got so sick that I couldn't even get out of my bed to go the bathroom. The ship eventually had to make an emergency stop just for me in Djibouti, which was, at the time, a French colony with the only western-style hospital for thousands of miles. I was taken off the ship in a stretcher and put in an ambulance. The ship left me there to go back out on patrol. I don't remember much of what happened in the next few days except that I kept hearing the doctors saying a word in French that sounded suspiciously like "appendicitis". My intestines felt like someone had put a red-hot poker into my gut and was turning it slowly. The pain was so excruciating that I was screaming. They actually tied me to the bed to keep me from hurting myself. The doctors really thought I had an extreme case of appendicitis and had figured that I was going to have to have surgery right away. But they still weren't sure because my blood work hadn't come back. Because of the impending surgery, I couldn't have any water. Remember that I had horrible diarrhea, so I was losing body fluids rapidly. Keeping water from me was sheer hell.

Later that evening, the blood work came back saying that it wasn't appendicitis at all; I had intestinal typhoid! I learned this from the head doctor who could speak English; he was the only one who could, though. They immediately gave me my water bottle back and started me on the proper course of treatment. I slept with that bottle of water. No one could have taken it from me if they'd wanted to.

An interesting thing happened while I was recuperating, though. One day a chaplain came into the room, which was spacious and full of beds filled with other sick men, and started talking to each person individually. He would sit down on the bed and do some light chit-chat with the soldier lying there and then move on to the next bed. All of this conversation was in French. The only French I'd had was one year of it as a senior in high school. I wracked my brain for something to say to the chaplain before he got to my bed. When he sat down and asked me how I was, I told him in what I thought was pretty good French but most probably wasn't that good and was badly accented that I was an American from an American ship, and I couldn't really speak French very well. He sat there and looked at me for a moment and, without another word, simply got up and moved to the next bed. I knew my French wasn't great, but I hadn't thought it was *that* bad.

Another thing that happened during that time was that a rough-looking man dressed in drab green fatigues and sporting a red beret came and sat down on my bed, saying in a very British accent, "I hear you're a Yank!"

Surprised to hear another voice speaking English, I said that I was.

He then went into a long story about how he had left Great Britain and joined the French Foreign Legion where he was still serving. All during this time, he had his hand on my leg, squeezing it every once in a while, which I found very disconcerting. He then asked me with a suggestive smile if I'd like to go to the canteen with him where he could buy me a drink. I didn't even know they had a canteen in the hospital, but I wasn't about to go to one with *this* guy. I told him I couldn't get out of bed (I didn't know if that was true or not, but it seemed a good excuse). He frowned and said that maybe we could get together when I felt better. My thoughts returned with a shudder to the guy I had met on the beach in Monterey while I was in Chinese language class. He turned and left after giving my leg one more squeeze. What the hell about me was giving these guys the impression that I might be interested in them? I could only wonder.

Please realize that I was not then nor am I now in any way homophobic. As a man, it just wasn't my thing, and I *was* a child of my time and didn't know any better than to recoil from the thought of two men being intimate. I was still coming to terms with who I really was. I guess I was effeminate even back then, although I certainly wasn't trying to be.

And now back to the present.

* * *

The thing that finally decided for me where I was going to have my surgery was the cost. I could go to Colorado in the good old U.S. of A. and have the surgery done for about $12,000 in all, including transportation and lodging before and after surgery. I could go to Brussels and spend half that amount for the very same thing and get a wonderful vacation in a beautiful, historic European city to boot. I thought I could put up with the language differences just fine. Besides, I had plenty of time to study up on my French to prepare. My friends thought I was nuts. They couldn't imagine going to a foreign country alone, and it was inconceivable that I would go out of the country for major surgery. None of them had spent years of their adult lives living in other countries and experiencing other cultures as I had in the Navy, though. Different cultures fascinated me.

Once I had assured myself of Dr. Seghers' credentials, it was pretty much a no-brainer on where I would go. Dr. Seghers spoke excellent English (as well as French and Flemish and who knows what else) and he assured me that people at the hospital where he performed the surgeries did as well. I'm not one of those Americans who thinks that everyone should speak English but, in this case, I was glad that I wouldn't have to struggle so much with my poor French. We really should put more emphasis in this country in teaching our children at least one foreign language from an early age in school. In other countries it's mandatory. We're way behind in this country and it's really a shame.

Since insurance wasn't going to pay one cent of the costs of any of this regardless of where I was going to have the surgery, it would take me years of severe scrimping to save the money to go to Colorado and then all I'd see there was a small town mostly from the confines of my hospital bed. Brussels was full of history and museums and wonders I'd always read about. In the end, the decision was pretty easy for me.

There was only more hitch that I had to contend with. If I was going to go to Europe, I had to have a valid passport. That meant going through the whole ordeal of changing my legal documents one more time. I had no choice. My current passport wouldn't do me any good at all unless I traveled in drag as a man (that is SO ironic!). So, I went to the local county clerk's office and, armed with extra pictures from my work security badge, my new social security card and my name change papers, I filled out the paperwork to have my passport changed. I put my new name on the form and wrote my gender down as Female. The Clerk never batted an eyelid. A month later I had a new passport giving my new identity yet one more level of legality.

I started working on my high school level French to prepare myself for the biggest and most exciting adventure of my life.

Chapter 20
Brussels

Work during the coming year was good. I made many new friends and the women with whom I worked seemed to accept me more each day. The only real problem I had was when one of my female co-workers left a present on my desk one day. It was a Bible with the name "R. Thompson" embossed on it in gold along with pamphlets about the Christian concept of Heaven and Hell and how I was probably only going to be able to wave at the former on my way to the special place made for me in the latter. This little gift pretty much pissed me off more than anything else that I'd already suffered through at work – even the bathroom sign. How dare this woman pass judgment on me when her very religion dictated that she should not? How dare she push her faith on me in the hopes that it would somehow cure me of something that she obviously felt was all in my mind, or the result of Satan tapping me on the shoulder? How dare she say anything at all to me about what I was going through without ever having talked to me to learn what it was about? Seeing a very nice, deep color of red, I took the book and pamphlets back to her office and laid them down in front of her on her desk.

"I appreciate your concern for my well-being", I told her, controlling myself better than I had imagined was possible. "But I do not want, nor do I need your religious intervention in my life to try to change me. I can't accept these books and I want you to take them back and give them to someone who will appreciate them. If you want to learn something about what I'm going through, then I'll be happy to sit down and talk to you. But this isn't going to help me."

Part of me felt bad about confronting her like this because I have always kept a strict personal rule not to discuss religion with people. I understand that religion is an integral part of some people's lives and I have never felt that it was my place to interfere in any way with their beliefs. However, I make an exception when it comes to someone trying to force their religion on me no matter how much good they think they're doing me. This was an obvious attempt at coercion, and I wasn't going to stand for it, even if it did hurt her feelings. She certainly didn't have any such compunction about hurting mine.

I stood in front of her and waited for a response. After a few seconds of shock, she finally found her voice. Surprisingly, she apologized to me and tried to assure me that she meant no offense; she was only trying to help. We discussed the matter further in the following weeks and eventually became friends. Either I actually got through to her or she just wrote me off as a lost cause. There was a male friend of mine at work who also had tried for years to "save" me. He finally gave up. For that I was truly grateful. Amen.

The rest of the year went by surprisingly quickly. Work was challenging, and I was even given a technical lead position on a project that was behind schedule. I managed to get the programs delivered on time and in perfect working order. I hadn't lost my touch during all those years as a manager or as a technical leader.

* * *

Almost a year to the day after I walked into my new office in my new life, I arrived in Brussels, Belgium to begin my new life in earnest. It was early July 1992, and I had taken a long flight that wound its way from Philadelphia through Dulles in

Washington D.C. and finally to Brussels. At the customs desk in Brussels, I proudly presented my new passport, hoping desperately that the customs agent wouldn't wonder if this person in front of him was really female or not. When he asked me why I was in Belgium, I decided that answering, "I'm on vacation" was better than "I'm going to have a sex change operation". It seemed to be a good enough answer because I was permitted to enter the country with no trouble – not even a baggage check. Gathering my bags, I stepped out of the airport into the bright sunlight of the country where I was about to be reborn – the right way this time.

My first challenge was hailing a cab to get to the hotel that I had reserved in the northeast section of the city. I had tried to get into the Hotel Derby, a small hotel that was used widely by people like me because of its proximity to the Doctor's office and the hospital (not to mention very inexpensive), but they had no openings at the time. Instead, I was staying at a more expensive place a few more blocks away. The taxi driver had no real problem getting me to the hotel. My French was working pretty well so far. I had a nice room, but I quickly found that the proprietors spoke little English. On top of that, the bathroom was so small that I had to wedge myself between the bathroom door and the sink to use the toilet. I didn't think this was going to be very comfortable after I returned from my surgery. With this in mind, I managed to get a room at the Derby for when I left the hospital. That was a relief.

The day after my arrival I had an appointment to meet with Dr. Seghers at his home for an initial consultation. Up to this time I'd only really corresponded with the doctor through the mail and didn't really know what to expect. I was met at the door by his lovely wife who led me upstairs to the doctor's office to wait. The house was, by all American standards, a row home. But it didn't resemble most row homes in the U.S. at all. The

281

tree-lined streets and sidewalks were immaculately clean. The houses were all tastefully decorated with shutters and flowers, and each had a small but neatly trimmed lawn. Inside, the doctor's home was airy and bright and gave me an instant feeling of welcome. I certainly didn't feel like I was in Kansas anymore (not that I've actually ever *been* to Kansas, mind you).

When Dr. Seghers entered the room, I rose and shook his hand. Not a tall man, he had a slight build and bright, smiling eyes. His excellent English was tinged with a lilting French accent. He warmly welcomed me to Belgium, and we made small talk for a few minutes. Then we got down to business.

The first thing that he wanted was to see all of my paperwork. I had a letter from my doctor back home with all of my medical information on it (hormone treatments, negative AIDS test, blood type, other medications, etc.). I also gave him letters from two psychologists and a psychiatrist indicating that I had been through extensive therapy and that they all agreed that I suffered from Gender Dysphoria and should have the surgery. Then I signed $5,000 in Travelers' Checks in hundred-dollar denominations over to him, one at a time. I'd never paid anyone that much money in one shot in my life. Then again, I'd never paid for such an important thing in my life. It was almost surreal.

Once the paperwork was out of the way, it was time for the fun and games. Before admitting me to the hospital, Dr. Seghers needed to take a look at my genitals to see if he was going to have any problem with the surgery. If my scrotum and penis were too small, then he would have to take a skin graft from somewhere on my body to help to construct my new vagina and vulvae. I didn't have to worry about that, though. I had always been fairly large in that area, which was a constant source of embarrassment to me. For the first time in my life, I was thankful

282

to have the extra size that had embarrassed me so much. Recovering from a skin graft would just be one more discomfort to endure after the surgery.

With the examination complete and the promise that I would need no extra skin grafts, Dr. Seghers gave me directions to the hospital – it was only a few blocks away – and a date and time to be there. I had purposely arrived a few days early, so I could do some sightseeing before having to enter the hospital. It was time to play tourist. I thanked the Doctor and told him I'd see him in a few days. Then I headed for the city.

* * *

Brussels is one of the most beautiful cities in Europe. The plush, green parks that were scattered everywhere throughout the city made its beauty breathtaking. Just outside the Hotel Derby was a large park called the Parc du Cinquantenaire, or the 50th Anniversary Park, with a huge statue at its entrance. Inside the park were two museums, the Museum of Egyptian History and a Museum of Transportation containing old aircraft and cars. Between the two museums was a large, paved area that was used to show movies in the evening. For a few Belgian francs you could sit outside on a warm summer night and watch a film projected onto a large screen hung in a corner of the pavilion. The movies were almost always French, but it was still quite a nice thing to do under the stars.

Transportation wasn't a problem in the city. There is an extensive system of public transportation woven together to make it easy to get from place to place. There was a high-speed Metro station entrance right in front of the Hotel Derby that took passengers into the heart of the city. If the Metro didn't take you exactly where you wanted to go, you could take a trolley car. The pass you used on the Metro was good for the trolleys as well. And it was an honor system at that. You could buy a ticket ahead of time for multiple rides, each ride consisting of about 30 minutes on the vehicle. When you entered the car, you simply put your ticket into a reader by the door and a portion of the ticket would be snipped off with the date and time stamped next to it. The longer the ticket, the more rides you had. Then you simply sat down and got off wherever you needed to. No one ever came by to check your ticket. You were on your honor that you had paid for your ride. However, every once in a while, a Transit Policeman would board the vehicle and ask to see everyone's ticket. If you didn't have one, or yours was expired or not stamped (you were cheating), then you'd be slapped with a fine that amounted to around $50.00. Since the price of a transit ticket was only a few dollars at the most, it was just silly to take the chance of riding without paying. I never saw anyone kicked off or fined for not paying. Honor systems seem to work quite well in Belgium. I can just see trying that in an American city.

My first visit to the center of the city had two purposes. The first was to see the famous Grand Place (pronounced "plahss" in French). This was an incredibly beautiful place in the very heart of the city that consisted of an enormous cobblestone square lined with some of the most ornate buildings I'd ever seen. Most of them were Merchant Guild buildings that had stood for hundreds of years. Destroyed more than once by the numerous wars that continually seemed to pass through Belgium, they had all been rebuilt at one time or another in the past and were currently getting yet another face lift during my visit. The fasciae of the buildings were being embossed with gleaming gold leaf. It was a remarkable face lift.

Surrounding the square on three sides of the ground level were numerous cafés and restaurants. On the remaining side of the square was a very old and very imposing church with statues of saints perched everywhere. There was a large crane gently removing some of them for cleaning and restoring and even more gently putting others back.

The open area in the center of the Grand Place was filled every morning with street vendors selling flowers. The myriad of bright colors nestled within the august beauty of these old, ornate buildings was almost overwhelming. It took my breath away.

Around noon, as the vendors slowly packed up to leave, the little cafés and restaurants would bring out their outdoor tables. These were quickly filled with tourists from all over the world. It was amazing sitting there and listening to the different languages, catching phrases here and there, and wondering from what far off places these people had come to visit this gorgeous place. The sights and sounds of the square were almost too much for the senses. I felt like I was a citizen of the world, no longer isolated on the shores of America, much more so than I had ever felt while I was in the Navy. I've gone back several times to reminisce and never once failed to feel the same thing.

My second reason for coming into the city that day was to make dinner reservations. I had promised myself that the night before I had to go to the hospital, I would treat myself to dinner at the very best restaurant in all of Brussels. Top of most lists was Le Cygne D'Or – The Golden Swan – and it was nestled right there in a corner of the Grand Place. I felt a little funny being a single woman making reservations for one for dinner at such a posh place, but I really didn't care. No one gave my reservation request the slightest concern.

When I left the restaurant, I began my sightseeing in earnest. I spent that day and the next visiting as many museums as I could. Just outside the Grand Place were several, including the National Art Gallery and even a Museum of Ancient Musical

Instruments. As a musician I just *had* to go in there. You wouldn't believe what the first trombone looked like. You wouldn't recognize it.

I'd always loved going to museums, but I'd never seen anything like these before. The nearby National Art Gallery was filled with works from the old Flemish masters as well as others from all over the world. One giant room was devoted entirely to a single painting that literally covered an entire wall. I'd never seen anything like it.

While I was in the area, I also visited one of the biggest tourist attractions in all of Brussels – the Manneken Pis. Designed in 1619 and tucked away down a small street off the Grand Place that's more than a little hard to find, the Manneken Pis is the incredibly popular statue of a small boy urinating into a fountain. Does that sound like a popular tourist site or what? There are several legends surrounding this statue, the most famous of which is the tale of a little boy that wouldn't stop peeing in an old woman's flower beds, so she turned him to stone (I guess she was a bit of witch). It has become a custom on Belgian national holidays to dress the little boy up in various costumes appropriate for the particular celebration. You can't go anywhere in Brussels without seeing postcards with the brightly clad little boy happily peeing away for eternity in some festive outfit.

Overall, I visited as many places as I could inside and outside the city those first two days, including a place called the Atomium, a left-over exhibit from the 1958 World's Fair that was built to represent an iron molecule, only enlarged 165 billion times and reaching 335 feet tall. I kid you not. Inside on the different levels are ever-changing dioramas teaching about health concerns and other similar things. At the top is a restaurant with a beautiful view of the city and beyond. It was quite amazing.

My second day in Belgium was the day before I had to check into the hospital for my surgery. That evening I put on a very dressy outfit I'd brought just for the occasion consisting of a flowery and flowing multi-colored skirt, a blue silk blouse and a brightly colored jacket that matched everything perfectly. I did my hair and face nicely, slid on my matching pumps and headed off to catch the trolley to the Grand Place and Le Cygne D'Or. Night was just beginning to fall, and the air was warm and comfortable. At the restaurant I was escorted to a lovely little table overlooking the square. The restaurant, with its marble columns, gold filigree and stunning paintings, looked like it could have been a museum itself. I ordered a very nice bottle of wine while I did my best to figure out exactly what was on the menu. I could get by in French, but it wasn't *that* good. This was the first time I'd ever been to a restaurant like this, and I was not used to such attention as I was receiving. My wine glass was never empty; there was always someone there to refill it. As soon as I would finish one exquisite course a waiter would whisk my plate away and prepare the table for the next one. I really don't remember what I had for dinner that night, but I do remember being sublimely happy sitting in such an elegant place looking out over the beautifully lit Grand Place, all the while being treated like royalty. All was absolutely perfect with the world. I finally understood what it meant to do something for myself. I was doing it. And it felt good. I was at a point that only a few years ago I would have never dreamed would have been possible to reach. This was the defining moment of my life. I wasn't nervous at all about anything. I had made my peace with the world and with myself and I knew beyond a shadow of a doubt that I was where I was supposed to be. This was as close to heaven as I thought was humanly possible.

I finished my dinner and paid the tab. It was over $100 American which, for me, was the most I'd ever paid for a meal in my life. Before if I spent $40 at a restaurant, I thought I had overdone it a bit. But this was well worth it. I had treated myself to this fantastic restaurant for one simple reason: I was having surgery in the morning and whether or not I made it through alive, I was going to go out in style. I knew that what I was doing was right for me no matter what the outcome and I deserved a very special night on the eve of my rebirth.

I walked around the Grand Place for a while taking in the exotic sights, sounds and smells and enjoying the pleasant evening air. It was getting late, so I finally headed back to the hotel. I packed my bags to be ready in the morning and went to bed. Tomorrow was going to be a VERY BIG day. I slept very well that night.

Chapter 21
Surgery

On the morning of the 9th of July 1992, I checked into the hospital in Brussels that would help to usher in my new life. An unassuming place and, for the most part, a maternity hospital, it was nevertheless a fairly modern building with a very helpful staff that was quite used to people in my condition staying there. I introduced myself at the main desk in lousy French and a nurse was summoned to show me to my room.

Hospitals in Europe are not like those in the U.S. – well, at least not this one. We are so spoiled by everything in this country that we expect all kinds of amenities – motorized beds, TVs, telephones, private bathrooms – and yet we complain about the cost of it all. My room was plain. There was no television. Even if there was it really wouldn't have done much good with my limited language skills in this country. The beds were not motorized. If there were any adjustments to be made, a nurse would come and do it for you. To help in sitting up, there was a small trapeze-shaped bar dangling over the bed that you simply grabbed and used to pull yourself up. If you couldn't, you probably weren't supposed to be sitting up anyway.

I wasn't alone in my room. Across from me was a second bed with another woman who had just had some surgery. She was sleeping. I was later to find out that she was from Belgium and that she had had surgery to correct her original gender reassignment surgery that had been botched by a less-than-reputable doctor somewhere else in Belgium. Her second surgery was a complete success.

I had checked out of my hotel, leaving most of my bags at the Hotel Derby in anticipation of my release from the hospital in six days. I carried only a small bag with me that contained a few articles of clothing, books, music, toiletries, a towel and washcloth and some needlepoint I had been working on, a hobby that I had recently adopted and found quite enjoyable.

When I finished unpacking what little I had brought with me, a nurse came in and handed me a razor and a can of shaving cream. In broken English she said, "Go to bathroom and shave here." She pointed to my crotch. I can honestly say that I don't ever remember anyone ever asking me to do that before or since. It's certainly not something one hears every day.

I took my towel (you had to bring your own – the hospital didn't supply them) into the bathroom with the razor and shaving cream and got down to business. I don't know what was stranger - shaving my genitals or how they felt after they were shaved. It was quite unusual. I was really glad to be in a European hospital at this point. In America, a nurse would have come in to do it while I was lying in bed. It would have been horribly embarrassing to have someone lift up my nightgown to shave my testicles and groin. *I* didn't even want to look at them let alone let someone *else* look at them. It was much better to do it myself.

With this delicate mission completed, I returned to my bed and waited for more instructions. It didn't take long for a nurse to come back in, this time armed with two bottles of clear liquid. She handed them to me and pointed back to the bathroom. "Enema," she said. "Put in both and must wait fifteen minutes. Then go to bathroom again."

Being asked to do weird things was beginning to become a habit. At first, I was a bit taken aback by this, but I finally figured it wasn't any worse than having to shave myself. And, again, I didn't have to have some nurse do it for me. The idea of taking these enemas was to thoroughly flush out my system prior to surgery. Maybe this was a precautionary measure in case of an accidental puncture of the colon or something during the operation; I don't know. I later found out that another reason for it was to keep you from having to have a bowel movement for a while after surgery. Any straining could cause delicately place stitches to break. Not good. All I know is that although giving myself an enema ranked right up there in strangeness with the razor and shaving cream, it was a whole lot more uncomfortable.

I went into the bathroom and clumsily administered the enemas the best that I could. Then I went back to bed to wait for what turned out to be the longest fifteen minutes of my life. For the first few minutes nothing happened, and I wondered if I'd done everything properly. Then the gurgling began deep in my belly. I started to get uncomfortable. My bowels began talking to me. When the talking turned to yelling, I started to sweat. By the time the fifteen minutes were over I was in a full-blown panic, running as fast as my crossed legs would let me to the bathroom to finish the job. Afterwards I was much better. I didn't know I had all that in me. There are some, though, who call themselves my friends who say they knew it all along. I need new friends.

For the rest of the afternoon a steady stream of nurses came in to poke and prod me and give me all manner of pills to take. Late in the afternoon my roommate woke up and we were able to talk for the first time. She said her name was Michelle and she lived in a nearby town with her boyfriend, Roger. "Roger" didn't exactly seem like a Flemish or French name to me but what did I know? Michelle had an abnormally high voice – almost a forced falsetto – which was very hard to understand at times. Her broken English didn't help, either. She told me that she had never had any English lessons in school; she had learned it all from watching American and British television. I had heard of people being able to do this, but I still think that it's an extraordinary accomplishment. I can't imagine an American

291

non-Hispanic kid constantly watching Telemundo for the sole purpose of learning how to speak Spanish with no other help – or even wanting to try. I was very impressed with Michelle's ability to do this. Between the two of us with her broken English and my broken French we were able to converse fairly well after a short while. We discussed her botched surgery and how she had come to hear of Dr. Seghers and seek his help. She lovingly talked about her boyfriend whom she hoped to marry someday. He showed up once during the entire six days she was in the hospital. He said he'd been too busy to come for a visit. I even had to give Michelle cab money when Roger didn't show up to pick her up from the hospital several days later. He was a real catch, that one.

In the evening, the nurses came in and put a sign over my bed which, when loosely translated from the original French, read:

"DO NOT FEED OR WATER THE TRANSSEXUAL"

Ok, maybe it didn't *quite* say that but that was the gist of it. I discovered the withholding of food and water to be an internationally recognized medical practice used on all patients who are going to have surgery the next day. The purpose of it, I think, is to make the patient suffer a bit through the night and the next morning so that, upon awakening from surgery, the amount of misery from pain is magnified by thirst and hunger. You go to bed hungry and thirsty and wake up in the morning convinced that you would kill and rob the first person who walked by with a cup of coffee. Then, when you come out of the anesthesia, not only does everything hurt, it feels like someone put an entire roll of paper towels in your mouth to suck up every bit of moisture your body needs for itself. Doctors learn this practice in special medical school "Marquis de Sade Bedside Manner" classes.

Everyone I knew from before who had had surgery said that the night before their operation they had fretted and worried and paced around the room wondering if they were doing the right thing. After all, once the deed is done, there is no going back. It's not like they leave anything in a jar to sew back on in case you change your mind. A person had better be pretty darned sure of what she's doing before that bed gets wheeled into the operating room in the morning. I sat in my bed that evening with my needlepoint just enjoying myself. I wasn't nervous; I didn't have any doubts at all. I knew I was doing the right thing. I had even decided that if something went wrong during surgery and I didn't make it out alive, that was ok. I was doing what needed to be done. One way or another, my suffering was going to end. There was just no need to be scared.

* * *

After a good night's rest, I was ready for my transformation. I could have slept a bit longer, but I didn't know how to change my sign to say, *"Do Not Awaken the Sleeping Transsexual"*. The nurses came in bright and early, gave me a small pill to relax me and prepped me for surgery. When I finally had a few moments alone, I lifted my covers and nightgown and said goodbye to "the boys". I told them I had no hard feelings. And neither would they, ever again, in a few hours.

The nurses wheeled me out of my room as Michelle called out *"bon chance"*. I don't remember much after we entered the elevator, but the doctor said I was talking to him for a few moments in the operating room. I have to take his word for it. That little pill they gave me in my room must have been a lot stronger than it looked. The next thing I knew, I was back in my room, and everything was *fait accompli.*

* * *

Those same friends of mine who had told me how worried they had been on the eve of their surgeries also told me that the first thing that went through their minds when they woke up afterwards was *"I WANT MORPHINE!!!"*

They were in so much pain that the nurses would give them enough medication to put them out for another full day. Dreading the return to consciousness with this thought in mind, I slowly opened my eyes expecting to be hit by a blinding flash of excruciating pain at any moment. It didn't come. My first impression upon awakening was…that someone was sitting on my lap. There seemed to be a great weight on my groin but surprisingly no pain. When I had reassured myself that there was, in fact, no one perched on top of me, I groggily pulled my nightgown up to take a look. My vision was still a bit hazy so all I could make out was a mass of bandages with a single tube sticking out of them. Since the bandages didn't look all bloody and I didn't feel bad, I wondered if they'd done anything at all. A nurse came in and saw me staring at myself. She asked me how I felt, and I told her I actually felt fine. She said that everything had gone very well during surgery and then gave me a pain pill to take which I wasn't at all sure I was going to need. I did take them at times, though, but only when I started to feel uncomfortable. I can honestly say that I was never really in any bad pain at all. That was just amazing to me.

* * *

A few years later I returned to Belgium to have some secondary surgery done by Dr. Seghers. It was only then that it really hit me just how amazing it was that I'd had almost a total absence of pain after my first surgery. Upon my arrival at the hospital for my second stay, I met another woman who was about to have her first surgery. Her name was Michelle (déjà vu!) and she was from Texas and spoke with a slight Texas drawl. I discovered right away that we were going to be good friends; her sense of humor was almost as warped as mine. I like that in a transsexual (and other people). When she started joking about being in the hospital, I knew I had found a friend. We grew to know each other quite well within that first day and had lots of fun making each other laugh. When I told her that I was thinking of writing a book about my experiences, she asked me something very unusual. She wanted me to be in the operating room with her when she had her surgery and then describe what I had seen in my book. At first, I thought she was kidding but she quickly convinced me that she was not. I'd always been interested in watching a real operation, but this seemed a bit much at first. However, the more I thought about it, the more fascinating the prospect of seeing this amazing operation first-hand became. She put the question to Dr. Seghers, who was very hesitant at first. He'd previously had other doctors watch this type of surgery before and the results weren't always good. Most of the male doctors would turn very pale and leave the operating room after the first cut. One had even fainted dead away right on the instrument tray, stopping the operation until they could get more clean instruments. For some reason, Dr. Seghers decided to let me watch as long as I promised that I would leave at the first sign of queasiness.

Michelle's surgery was scheduled for the next morning. Mine wasn't scheduled until the afternoon. The nurses had me scrub up and put on a mask and gown, just like everyone else in the operating room. I was positioned directly behind the Doctor just a bit to his right during the entire procedure. There were a couple of extra nurses close to me, presumably to catch me just in case I started to do a nose dive anywhere near the instrument tray. Dr. Seghers talked to me the entire time during the operation, explaining what it was he was doing at each step. One time during the surgery, he turned to me and asked, "Ms. Thompson, how are you feeling?"

"Fine", I responded. "But could you move a little to your left? I could see better then." I think I really surprised him. This was one of the most fascinating things I'd ever seen in my life. But, as I said before, after watching what actually happened during the surgery, the lack of pain that I felt after my own surgery was nothing short of miraculous. In keeping my promise to my friend Michelle, and only speaking in laywoman's terms, here is what happened during her (and my) surgery:

WARNING!
WHAT FOLLOWS IS A GRAPHIC DESCRIPTION OF MALE TO FEMALE GENDER REASSIGNMENT SURGERY. IT MAY NOT BE SUITABLE FOR PEOPLE OF THE MALE PERSUASION WHO ARE NOT SUFFERING FROM GENDER DYSPHORIA AND CAN'T IMAGINE IN THEIR WORST NIGHTMARE EVER HAVING ANYONE COME NEAR THEIR GOD-GIVEN SACRED PLUMBING WITH A SHARP KNIFE. FOR THOSE INDIVIDUALS, IT IS HIGHLY RECOMMENDED THAT YOU EITHER SIT DOWN ON SOMETHING COMFORTABLE AND CLOSE TO THE FLOOR, KEEPING A WASTE RECEPTACLE READY IN CASE OF UNEXPECTED, SPONTANEOUS AND POSSIBLY VIOLENT REGURGITATION, OR SKIP ALL OF THIS AND GO DIRECTLY TO THE BOLD NOTE FOUND LATER IN THIS CHAPTER AFTER ALL THE GRUESOME STUFF IS OVER AND IT'S SAFE TO COME OUT.

When the patient is wheeled into the operating room and moved from the gurney onto the table, she is given a shot that finishes what the pill the nurses gave her in her room had started. She is in La-La-Land (in French that's *"Le Pays de La-La"*) almost before the nurse has finished administering the shot.

After it has been ascertained that she is indeed quite asleep (it wouldn't do to start cutting otherwise), she is placed into the most ignominious position that any human being can be placed (and all women can attest to this) – flat on her back on a table with her legs spread high and wide, held in place by stirrups. I can't imagine a more indelicate or less dignified position to be in. Everything is just laying out there for everyone to see and ready for whatever is to come. In this case, "the boys" are resting nicely, totally oblivious to the fate that awaits them.

The doctor first slathers the entire genital area liberally with dark orange Betadine solution, used to sterilize the area to reduce the risk of infection during surgery and also, as a side benefit, to make the patient look even more ridiculous than she already looks with her legs in the air. Once everything is nice color of orange, the cutting begins.

(ANY BRAVE GUYS STILL READING, TAKE A DEEP BREATH NOW!)

In this case, to paraphrase a popular song, the first cut is not the deepest. It is, however, fairly disturbing. The doctor makes an incision down the middle of the scrotal sac, exposing the little round testicles nestled snugly inside. He then takes one of the little guys in his hand, looks at it for a moment to make sure it's not a gall bladder or something, and then, with a quick snip, cuts it loose from its mooring. With barely a glance, he drops the freed testicle into a small receptacle[21] at his feet where it makes

297

an unnerving little "plop" sound. This may have been the point at which the previous doctor had fainted dead away. The surgeon quickly dispatches junior's brother in the same manner, leaving only the empty scrotal skin in two pieces just hanging in the breeze. This comes in handy later.

Once the scrotal sac is emptied *(STILL WITH ME, GUYS?)* and the various remaining tubes and veins are closed up, the doctor turns his attention to the main event – the penis. If it is lucky, the penis is still lying there blissfully unaware that two of its closest neighbors have been evicted and that changes are a'comin' for it as well. This is also one of those paradoxes that plague male-to-female transsexuals. As I'd said before, if the penis is large, then there is plenty of material for the doctor to work with to create a nice, deep vagina. Of course, if that's true then the pre-operative patient has most likely suffered as I did great pain from trying to hide the thing during Life Test.[22]

On the other hand, if the penis is small, then there probably wasn't as much embarrassment factor to begin with and it was easier to hide in tight pants for those brave enough to wear them. But the downside to this is that there may not be enough tissue to use in the surgery. In that case, the doctor has to take some surrounding area skin – usually from the insides of the thighs – to augment the penile skin needed to create the vagina. Now the patient has to recover from having peeled off patches of skin between her legs as well as the original surgery. One way or another, you win but you also lose. It's always something. Michelle and I both were among the former lucky/unlucky group – plenty of skin to use but not very happy to have it during all those years.

---

[21] Some call it a "bucket".

[22] I've heard that some female impersonators have actually learned how to push everything up inside their body cavities so it's all nice and hidden. I still don't believe it.

Now the penis is lifted, and the doctor examines it all around, presumably to make sure it's a real penis. (I have no idea why the doctor was always looking at these things so intently. Maybe he was steeling himself for what comes next or was giving a signal to others in the room to leave while they could.) He takes his scalpel and makes a careful incision underneath and along the entire length of the penis, all the way to the crown. Saving a bit of the underside of the crown where it is the most sensitive, he proceeds to cut all the way around the base of it and then splays the penile skin open, separating it from the spongy material that causes the penis to become hard by filling with blood. He closes off the blood vessels that had supplied the spongy material and removes the crown of the penis. By this time, all that is left is a flat flap of skin that used to hold the penis, still attached at the top of the groin, along with the urethra (the tube that you pee through) and the nerves that supplied the crown of the penis with feeling. A small hole is punched through the groin above what's left of the penile skin and the urethra is pulled through it. The nerve bundle is saved for a little later.

Next the doctor does a surprising thing – he sews the penile skin back together, closing up the tip end and basically creating a long empty tube closed at the top and still attached to the body at the bottom. Now the doctor makes the BIG cut (and you thought it couldn't get any worse). He places his scalpel just under the newly created tube and makes a long, deep cut in the area between where the penis used to be and the rectum. Then he literally puts his hand inside the cut and pushes back the muscles and fat, creating a cavity. Turning the penile skin tube inside out, he tucks it deftly into the cavity. With a few quick stitches, he anchors the skin all around the base of the inverted tube to the bottom and sides of the cavity. Voila! Where once was a penis, there is now a vagina! Just like that. The doctor now packs the new vagina with gauze so that it stays distended and

299

shaped inside the patient. A few stitches close up the opening temporarily to keep the packing in. Remember the lonely scrotal sac skin still hanging there? That is now folded inward and placed on the sides of the new vagina where it becomes labia. Pretty neat trick, eh?

Now comes the part of the operation that Doctor Seghers told me was the most difficult of all; he has to attach the urethra very carefully to the rest of the new genitalia. If this isn't done just right, the post-operative patient can have problems urinating from a urethra that has partially closed up or, even worse, urine can seep in between the stitches and get inside the body cavity, causing a horrible and possibly deadly infection. The doctor actually spends more time with this one detail during the surgery than almost all the other steps combined.

Once he is certain that the urethra is firmly connected, the doctor carefully inserts a catheter into it that goes up into the bladder. This catheter keeps the new urethral opening from closing and allows the patient to urinate while everything is healing. This also raises an interesting and ironic paradox. During Life Test and for quite a few years before, I never felt comfortable standing up to urinate, so I usually sat down on a toilet like any other woman would do. After my surgery and before the catheter was removed, there was no way to sit down and pee with the catheter hanging there. Here I was, after all those years and all that suffering, finally with the genitals that I knew that I should have had all along, and now I HAD to stand up to pee. The gods must have been rolling on the floor laughing.

With all the hardware-turned-software and plumbing in place, there is only one thing left to do – install the electricity. This is done by the careful positioning of the nerve bundle that had been saved from the erstwhile penis crown. The doctor actually rolls this bundle up and places it just under a little flap of skin beneath the labia pretty much where the clitoris would normally be found. After the healing process is done, the patient can have sex like a genetic woman, pee like a genetic woman, and have an orgasm like a genetic woman. Ok, she can't bear children, but overall, isn't science wonderful?

After a final check to make sure everything is right where it should be, and a quick check of all the instruments to make sure none of them have gone mysteriously missing, the patient is bandaged up tightly to compress everything and keep swelling down. The operation is over and it's off to the recovery room.

NOTE TO MALE NON-GENDER DYSPHORIC READERS: YOU MAY START READING AGAIN FROM THIS POINT ON. THE GRUESOME STUFF IS OVER.

SISSIES.

Now you understand why I was so amazed that I didn't feel much pain. After all that cutting and tugging and hollowing and sewing (sorry guys, maybe I shouldn't have had you start reading quite yet), it's a real wonder that I didn't want someone to just shoot me when I woke up from surgery. I just lifted up my blankets to take a quick look. All I knew was that all those little bits that I had detested for so long were now nothing but a memory. I smiled and went back to sleep.

Chapter 22
Recovery and Tourism

I was to stay in the hospital for six days recuperating. On the first day after surgery, Dr. Seghers came in to see me and told me to get out of bed and take a few steps. I wouldn't have thought that it was possible to do so this early after all my poor groin had just gone through. It was a little hard to move with all of those bandages down there but there simply wasn't any pain. There was, however, a bit of a problem with the room spinning, but the doctor said that my equilibrium would return to normal in a few days. I sat back down fairly quickly but eventually was able to actually walk tentatively around my room. Amazing.

Dr. Seghers was a real cut up in more than one sense of the word. During my convalescence in the hospital, I always looked forward to his daily visits with a mixture of anticipation and dread. The former was because he was funny. The latter was because he was *very* funny. He would come in, remove my bandages and have a look. Then he would crack some sort of joke that would have me in stitches (sorry, I couldn't resist that). But because I already WAS in stitches, laughing hurt like hell. Now I *needed* a pain pill. There were many times I told him to go away because he was hurting me and that just *had* to be a violation of the Hippocratic oath in some way. He would leave the room, promising to have more material when he came back. And if he wasn't making jokes to or about me, he was waking my roommate so he could make *her* miserable with them. He would tell her jokes in French, so I didn't get much of what he was saying but they must have been good because he had her doubled over in laughter and pain as much as he did me. I think Dr. Seghers had a real sadistic streak in him.

302

As the days progressed, I was able to move around the hospital more and more easily. With each passing day, more bandages and stitches were removed, making it progressively easier to walk. I can't say that it wasn't a bit painful as well, but it was an awful lot less than I expected so I didn't complain. On the third day of my recovery, I actually got a phone call from Lisa, my post-op TS friend back home. Because the phone was out in the hallway (nope – no phones in the rooms at each bed, either), a nurse answered it and then came to get me. When I got to the phone, Lisa was amazed to hear that I had walked to it under my own power so soon after surgery. She said it was six days before she had even been allowed to get out of bed when she'd had her surgery in Colorado. When I told her I'd be out of the hospital in only three more days, she was astounded.

And that's just what happened. Six days after my surgery, my bags were packed, and I was dressed and ready to go back to my hotel room. I had a few extra things to pack as well. I had received cards from people back in the States and a beautiful bouquet of flowers from my friends Herb and Marianne in Florida. (Herb and Marianne send me a birthday card every July 10th, too.) They all really lifted my spirits while I was there. There were a few catches with leaving the hospital after only six days, though. For one, I had to remain in the area for the next five days and visit Dr. Seghers in his home office each day so he could monitor the healing process. I walked to his office from my hotel room each day – not very fast but I got there just fine. I'm sure it helped me heal faster, too. I also had to put up with the inconvenience of having left the hospital with a catheter still inserted in my urethra. It had to stay there until my last day in Belgium. Walking was already hard enough without that thing sticking out of me, but it was for the best.

During my last few days of recuperation in the hospital, I had a visit from a lovely young woman from Dublin, Ireland. Her

303

name was Aine (pronounced AHN-ya) and she was in Brussels with her girlfriend, Deirdre, getting ready to check into the hospital for her own surgery. Aine and I became instant friends and remain so today. The first night we met, I was still in the hospital. We sat and talked about anything and everything, laughing through the night. My roommate Michelle finally yelled at us in broken English to please shut up so she could get some sleep.

My instructions while recuperating out of the hospital were to "take it easy". To me, that translated as "only play tourist for eight hours a day instead of ten". That's exactly what I did. Never to be kept down, especially in such a beautiful place as Brussels, I was on the Metro the very next day after leaving the hospital, heading for the heart of the city to visit museums that I had missed before my surgical adventure. Each day saw a different museum and each day I grew just a bit stronger. I do have to admit that the first day's excursion left me very weak and slightly afraid that I might not be able to make it back to the hotel without help. But I made it and, stubborn as always, I was out the next day finding something else to keep me busy. I really had a great time, especially now that I felt like a whole person for the first time in my life.

Aine, Deirdre and I spent those first few days together until it was Aine's turn to check into the hospital. After that, I spent every evening sitting with Aine in the hospital and having dinner with Deirdre. The last night of my stay in Brussels, Deirdre and I went to the Grand Place for dinner and sat outside in the beautiful summer evening enjoying classical music and as a light show played out on the buildings surrounding us, choreographed to stirring classical music. It was a perfect sendoff from my new birthplace.

It's hard to describe the feeling of elation that I got (and still get) when I put my hands between my legs and felt nothing but smoothness instead of what I'd been forced to live with for forty years. There was no bulge (except for the catheter) and nothing reminding me of how "wrong" I was. Nothing was wrong any more. It was an exhilarating feeling.

On the fifth day of my post-hospital recuperation, I saw the good Doctor for the last time. During my entire five days outside the hospital, I had been walking around Brussels with a catheter plugged into my urethra to keep it open and a vagina packed full of gauze to keep *it* open. Today all of that was to be removed.

Dr. Seghers was his usual pleasant self as he greeted me at the door of his home with a warm smile. He led me to the examining room and had me undress and lay on the table. For the first time in my life, someone asked me to put my feet in the stirrups at the end of the table (at least while I was conscious). In one way it was terribly exciting (*"Every woman goes through this and I'm no different anymore!!!"*) but in another way it was very embarrassing (*"Jesus, this MAN is staring at my naked crotch!!!"*), even if he was the one who put everything there in the first place. I still have never been able to get used to being in that position during my gynecological exams.

As he sat down on the small chair at the foot of the examination table, Dr. Seghers rubbed his hands together and, with a glimmer in his eye, said, "Ok. Let's see how everything is." With that, he removed the few stitches that were still holding my labia together, helping to keep all the packing in. It was very odd feeling tugging on a part of my body that just two short weeks before wasn't even there. After studying his handiwork for a few moments, he said, "Quite nice. I think we're ready to have everything come out."

He reached into my vagina (*"my* vagina" - what an unbelievable thing to say!) and, with a whimsical "Abracadabra!" started to pull on a piece of packing that he had

305

placed there just a few days earlier. The packing material was nothing more than a length of one-inch-wide gauze that he had literally wadded inside me to keep the walls of my vagina (MY VAGINA!!!! – pardon my outbursts of joy) separate while all the tissues healed. If he hadn't put the gauze there, the walls would have started to grow together and all of his work would have been in vain. I wouldn't have had the old plumbing, but the new plumbing wouldn't have worked at all.

I couldn't really feel a whole lot as he was tugging on the gauze, but I watched him in fascination as he pulled hand over hand on it, whistling while he worked and holding the gauze high between my legs. He pulled and pulled, and it seemed like it would never end. I couldn't believe all of that had actually been inside of me. Then the end of the gauze finally popped out. He stopped and looked at the end of it for a moment like something was wrong. Then he leaned back down, spread me apart a little more and, crying, "Aha!", reached in and started pulling on yet another length of gauze. "Good thing I didn't miss this," he said with a smile. It was like watching a magician working in a circus. He had me laughing again. He told me to stop. He was trying to work.

After the end of this piece came out, he took one more intense look, examining the tissues, and proudly exclaimed that his work was very good. That was good to hear. There was only one more thing to do – remove the catheter. By now the catheter had gone from being a nuisance to actually causing me physical discomfort when I moved. I was glad to be getting rid of it but more than a little concerned about how badly it would hurt to have it removed. Dr. Seghers checked the stitches around my urethral opening to make sure everything was in place and before I even knew what he was doing, he pulled the entire length of catheter out of me in one smooth movement. Now *that* was an odd feeling. It didn't hurt, exactly, but it felt oddly like he was pulling on my internal organs. Very strange. He checked my urethral opening once again to make sure it was staying open on its own and then moved back from the table. "We're all done here," he proclaimed. "You're free to go home now, young lady. Everything's fine!"

With more than a little relief, I put my legs down, got off the table and got dressed, very cognizant of the airy feeling now between my legs. No more stitches, no more packing, no catheter, NO PENIS, NO TESTICLES! I HAD A VAGINA! (Ok, I'll stop with the vagina thing now). I was finally anatomically correct, no different than any other woman in the world (who had had a full hysterectomy). It was nothing short of amazing. I'd never felt so free in my life. DID I MENTION I HAD A VAGINA? (Sorry, couldn't help myself.)

Dr. Seghers gave me a few more instructions on the Care and Feeding of my new vagina as I continued my recuperation and then handed me a long metallic "tissue expander", basically a cold metal dildo, with one half slightly larger around than the other. I was to lubricate the smaller end of the expander with K-Y Jelly (my new vagina was not made from mucous membranes so it would not lubricate on its own) and insert it into my vagina twice a day, leaving it there for about fifteen minutes each time. This was to help the tissues to "remember" that they were supposed to stay open. When it was comfortable for me, I was to start using the larger end to help it expand even further. I could then move on to a bigger one of my own choosing as I saw fit. I could hardly believe I was standing there with a large dildo in my hand that I was going to be using on myself. It was just too surreal. I also had to buy some sanitary napkins to use because I was still going to have some seepage and drainage for a few weeks to come. In the space of two weeks, I had gone from being able to wear a jock strap (not that I *would have*) to wearing sanitary napkins. It was just incredible – and it felt 100% natural.

It was like all those other years of being someone else had just never happened. This was me; it always had been me; and now it *always* would be me. I was whole.

I left Dr. Seghers with a hug and kiss on the cheek. As I walked away, he stood at the doorway of his beautiful little home, and I turned to take one last picture. In some ways I consider him my father, just as people who have gone to Dr. Biber in Colorado refer to themselves as "Biber Babies". I'm sure he considers all of us that he has helped as his daughters. He is a very sweet man and a very skilled doctor. I was to see him only a few more times, once at a Harry Benjamin Society meeting in New York City and then again for some secondary surgery a few years later. I was sad to hear that his beautiful wife of many years passed away not long afterwards.

Chapter 23
The DMV and Dating

My return home from Belgium was anything but uneventful. The plane ride itself across the Atlantic went without a hitch and I was in no discomfort from my surgery at all. It was trying to land that ended up being difficult.

My plane was scheduled to land at Dulles International Airport in Washington, D.C. but as it approached the East Coast of the U.S., a severe thunderstorm moved into the D.C. area, closing Dulles and prompting the captain to begin a wide circular pattern waiting for the storm to clear. It didn't. After circling for an hour, we were diverted to Harrisburg, Pennsylvania. After about thirty minutes of heading inland, the captain came on the intercom to announce that we had been diverted once again – this time to Philadelphia. Philadelphia was my final destination, and it was an international airport as well! I was going to actually get home early! We landed in Philly a few hours prior to when I was scheduled to arrive. The only problem with this was that a small crowd of my friends in the area were going to be waiting for me at the gate to welcome me home – hours from now. I started to think of ways to get in touch with them to tell them not to come. We didn't have cell phones then.

We taxied up to Gate 8 of the U.S. Airways terminal. The captain turned off the engines and the seat belt sign and…we waited. I had told the flight attendants that my baggage and I were booked through Dulles to Philly, and I could just get off here. They told me they would see what they could do. They didn't come back for some time.

We were parked at the gate for over an hour. During that time, I begged and pleaded with the flight attendants to let me off the plane. My computer programmer's brain could not see the logic in making me stay on board. Philly was my final destination, and it was an international airport so I could go through the rigors of customs there. Even though we weren't parked at the international terminal, I could be escorted to customs, couldn't I? Logic had nothing to do with this. I was not allowed to get off the plane. No passengers could disembark from the plane at any other place than our original flight destination. Those were the rules. I sat in frustration as the engines were started and we backed away from the gate to leave, knowing that once we got to Dulles, I was just going to get on another plane and come right back. How ridiculous was that?

The storm finally subsided over Washington, and we landed at Dulles…just as my flight to Philadelphia was taking off. We were so late coming in that my flight had left without me. Now I had to go through customs and get booked on another flight back to Philly. I was barely asked to stop as I breezed through customs with no delay at all (inside I was screaming) and found my way to the U.S. Airways ticket counter to exchange my plane ticket. They apologized for the problems and booked me on the next flight out – *four hours later* (inside I was not only screaming but was now pounding my fists against the wall). To try to make some sort of restitution, the airlines gave me a ticket for a complimentary dinner at an airport cafeteria. I was underwhelmed.

Five hours later and unnaturally filled with airport cafeteria mystery meat, I landed once again at Philadelphia International Airport. We taxied right up to Gate 6 – one gate over from where I had sat looking at the Philadelphia skyline earlier in the day. I just love red tape.

I had managed to contact my friends while I was in Dulles to let them know that I was delayed so they weren't waiting all that time at the airport for me. But when I did walk of the plane – fully twenty-three hours after I left Brussels – I was carrying all of my bags and moving just fine. My friends, all of whom had

310

already had their surgery in the U.S., were stunned at my ability to walk upright after all that traveling so soon after my surgery. They were expecting me to come waddling off the plane, pale with pain and effort and were aghast to see that I was actually carrying my own bags. I reassured them that I was just fine; I was a little sore and a whole lot irritated, but other than that, I was fit as the proverbial fiddle. They couldn't believe it. Their trips back from Colorado after their surgeries were usually described as "grueling" and "extremely painful". I told them they should have gone to Belgium – no horrible pain at any time, half the price, and a gorgeous vacation to boot. They were all jealous.

Once I got back home, not everything went as well as I had hoped. Remember what I said earlier about problems with surgeries? After a few days I started to notice that it was becoming increasingly difficult to urinate. When I went to see my doctor, he discovered that my newly placed urethra was almost totally closed up. It was no wonder I was having trouble peeing. He contacted a local urologist that he regularly referred his patients to and got me an emergency appointment to see him right away. He had to explain to the urologist why I was having this problem and, much to the urologist's credit, he had no qualms about seeing me. I drove quickly to his office where he examined me. (Once again, my legs were up in stirrups – what fun!) He marveled at the work that Dr. Seghers had done but told me that I was going to have to have my urethra distended. The surrounding tissue had contracted as it healed, causing the opening to get very small. If I hadn't come in when I did, it would have closed up completely in another day. I had no idea what he had to do to distend my urethra, but I found out fast. The doctor took a small tapered rod, lubricated it, and quite literally pushed it up into my urethra slowly but repeatedly until it reopened to a normal dimension. I don't recommend this to anyone. It hurt like hell. I had to come back a few more times and have the procedure repeated until the doctor felt certain that it wouldn't close up again. I still don't urinate in a torrent, but the closure was, thankfully, a one-time event. The really ironic thing about this is that the first time anyone lubricated anything to slide in and out of my new genitals was to make my urethra larger. How sexy is that?

* * *

After two weeks' rest at home, and the small medical mishap behind me, I went back to work. There was no great fanfare, and I didn't expect any. Some of my good friends were glad to see I'd made it back safe and sound, but most people didn't pay any attention at all. The very first thing I did after I got resituated back at my office was to take my little *"Do Not Enter"* bathroom signs and rip them up, placing the tiny pieces over the sinks in each ladies' room in the building. It was my not-too-subtle way of saying,

"I'm back. I'm fully female. Deal with it!"

I never had any more problems with bathrooms in the building. I was almost hoping that someone would make a stink about it. I had been so humiliated for so long at the demand of so few that I was itching for a chance to put them in their places. It never happened, which was probably for the best. I didn't really need any more people pissed at me than I already had.

The next few things I had to do were all in the legal arena. My first stop was the New Jersey Division of Motor Vehicles – the infamous DMV. As you might remember from earlier, I had been denied changing the gender designation on my driver's license when I legally changed my name because I needed a letter from my doctor saying that I'd had the surgery. With said letter squarely in hand, I triumphantly marched into the DMV to right this terrible wrong.

When it was my turn, I explained to the clerk at the counter what had happened earlier and that I was there to get the gender on my license changed once and for all. Smiling in anticipation, I handed her the letter from Dr. Seghers. She looked at it curiously for a few moments and then excused herself to go back to talk with her supervisor for instructions. I waited patiently, knowing that this was finally going to happen.

When the clerk returned, she handed my letter back to me and said, "I'm sorry Ma'am, but we can't accept this. It has to be notarized."

I just stood gaping at her in disbelief. No one had told me before that the paper had to be notarized. They just said that I had to have it. I never even considered getting the paper notarized. I had quite a few things on my mind at the time and, believe me, that wasn't one of them. I found out later that to get anything notarized overseas so that it was valid in the U.S., you had to make an appointment at the nearest U.S. Embassy and then take the letter, along with the signer, to the Embassy to have it signed in a dignitary's presence and then notarized, if someone authorized to do that was actually on duty at the time. What a hassle! I was not pleased. With my temperature rising, I informed the clerk that no one had bothered to inform me that the letter had to be notarized and that the doctor who had written it **WAS IN FREAKING BELGIUM!!!!** I struggled to maintain my composure.

The clerk, turning a bit pale, said quietly that she was sorry, but she didn't know what else she could do. That's when the idea hit me. I gathered myself, lowered my voice to a whisper and motioned her closer. When I was sure I had her full attention, I looked directly into her eyes and calmly said, "I'll tell you what I'm going to do. There is no way that I can get this letter notarized and so there's only one way I can prove to you that I've really had the surgery. Let's you and I go to the Ladies' Room right now *and I'll just show you.*"

I didn't think it was possible, but the clerk turned even paler than she had been during my outburst. She backed slowly away from me, her mouth moving but no sound coming out of it. When she finally found her voice, she said softly, "Please, Miss Thompson, have a seat and I'll see what I can do." She walked back to her desk and slowly sat down. I had a seat in the waiting room.

No more than two minutes later, the loudspeakers blared, "Miss Rachael Thompson...Aisle Three, please." I went up to Aisle Three and the very same woman, still rather pale, handed me a brand-new New Jersey Driver's License with my corrected gender proudly display under my name in a large, triumphant 'F'. She managed a meek, "Have a nice day." I thanked her and walked jubilantly out the door.

Logic: 1, Inane Government Bureaucracy: 0.

* * *

It was time to get my life going again. I was now an ex-transsexual[23] woman whose whole life stretched out in front of her. It had been such a long time since I'd really had a social life, I hardly remembered what it was like to have one. During my transition period I had adhered to a strict self-imposed

[23]The American Heritage Dictionary defines the prefix "trans-" to mean *"going across"*. I had gone across and landed firmly on the other side. Therefore, I consider myself an "ex-transsexual". So there.

314

moratorium on dating. I didn't want anyone to think I was trying to be something I wasn't which, at the least, would have been dishonest and, at the most, potentially dangerous. Now I had no hurdles in my way and could finally start thinking about a social life. The only problem was – who do I date? Now that I was fully a woman with all the proper new equipment nicely in place, was I supposed to be dating guys? I had never been attracted to men before. Why should I be now? On the other hand, now that I didn't have the "old" equipment that I'd had before, how *could* I date other women? I had no idea how to make love to a woman as a woman. Although I'd done that all my life on a psychological level, there was always the physical thing necessary for my own release. Besides, if I started dating women, I'd now be called a lesbian. Just what I needed – another label.

After much thought, I decided to try the easy way first and start dating men. Of course, my first problem with this was how to meet men that didn't know anything about my past. I didn't want to date anyone who knew me from before. I would just be an oddity, or worse, a perverse turn-on. I didn't want to be either. Unknown to me, just that sort of thing was to crop up later.

* * *

One day a few months later at work I got a call from a man named Forrest with whom I had worked for several years. He had transferred some time ago to one of our company sites in Maine. Forrest was married with children, and I had known him as a friend for a long time. I hadn't seen him for years. In his phone call to me he told me that he was in town and had heard about my change. He was really interested in meeting and talking to me about it. I suggested that we meet for lunch

315

somewhere, but he said that he was too busy during the day. He asked if I could meet him in his hotel room near where I worked after work.

Now here's a good example of the difference in life as a man and life as a woman. A person raised as female would be very wary of an invitation like that, even from an old friend. I, on the other hand, having been raised as a male, was not. As a matter of fact, any hint of impropriety or danger had never crossed my mind. Yet.

When I went to meet Forrest at his hotel room, I had just gotten out of karate class where I was studying Tae Kwon Do. I was wearing denim shorts and a white lacy tank-top and was still flushed a bit from my hour-long workout. As I walked down the dimly lit corridor on the fourth floor of the hotel, some little warning bell started clanging in my mind. This didn't feel right. But I was just being silly. I'd known this man for years. This was all just a platonic meeting of two friends. Bolstered by my faulty and naïve logic, I continued down the hall to his room and knocked on the door. When it opened, Forrest stood there looking at me for a moment and then suddenly rushed forward, grabbed me and kissed me hard on the mouth. That little alarm bell started to get louder. When this guy last saw me, I was a man. His first reaction was not to shake my hand but to kiss me in a manner than even I knew was not platonic. That would have been a little buss on the cheek. This was tongue. *Ewwwwwwwwww!* I pushed away from him to put some distance between us. All I could think to say was, "It's good to see you, too," and laughed nervously.

When he motioned for me to have a seat, I had my first chance to look around the room. It was a typical hotel room with a small sofa and a chair next to it. The queen-sized bed was neatly made up – with a bottle of red wine lying on it with a label that read "Cheap Red Wine". Forrest had taken a seat on the end of the bed. The alarm bells were now just short of deafening. Instead of sitting at the place on the bed next to him that he was patting, I went over to the sofa and chair. I almost sat down on the sofa (it looked more comfortable) but thought better of it and had a seat on the chair just next to it where I could have my own personal space. Forrest immediately moved from the bed to the sofa and sat down at the end as close to me as he could. Without a moment's hesitation he put his hand uncomfortably high on my left thigh and leaned in close enough that I could feel his breath on my face. I noticed that he was started to sweat. In a hushed and excited tone, he asked, "So, did they *really* cut off your penis?"

The alarm bells were now hitting me in the head with large mallets. I finally decided to start listening to them. In one movement that would have made my karate instructor proud, I grabbed his hand, which had steadily begun moving even higher up on my thigh, removed it and pushed him away from me. I stood up and, pointing my finger at him, said, "Look. I came here to see you as a friend *AND NOTHING ELSE!* If you want to talk to me to catch up on old times, that's fine but if you have anything else in mind, get it out of there right now." I was so angry I was starting to shake. And I was so disgusted that I thought I was going to throw up.

Forrest put up both of his hands in mock defense and said, "No, no. You've got the wrong idea. I just wanted to talk."

"What about the wine on the bed", I asked.

"Oh", he said, grinning, "I just thought we might have a little wine later after we…", he hesitated, "…talked."

I headed toward the door, exclaiming loudly that there wouldn't BE a "later". Before I was able to open the door, Forrest grabbed me and tried to kiss me again, pleading for me not to leave. This time I pushed him away so forcefully I thought he was going to fall down. I didn't care. I opened the door and hurried out of the room, saying nothing more and only wanting to get as far away from him as possible. As I stormed down the hall, he stood in the doorway of his room and yelled after me, "Would you like to see some magazines?" I wasn't exactly sure what he meant by that, but I certainly didn't want to know in any case. I quickened my pace down the hallway and flew down the stairs, not wanting to wait for the elevator. When I got to my car I sat down, locked all my doors and started to cry. How could I have been so stupid? How could this man that I had thought was my friend turn out to be such a pervert? He was married! He had kids! There is a dictionary somewhere in the world that just has to have a large picture of me next to the definition of *"naïve"*. In that same dictionary, the words *"stupid"* and *"gullible"* have as their definitions – *"see naïve"*. When I got home, I took off all my clothes and scrubbed myself in the shower for a very long time. If I'd had any Brillo pads I might have thought to use them. I'd never felt so dirty in my whole life.

That's why I decided not to date people that I'd known before my "change". Forrest transferred back to our facility a few years later and tried constantly to be friendly with me. If I answered him at all, it was in one-word responses trying hard to get fire to come out of my eyes to incinerate him on the spot. By the time he had returned to New Jersey, I held a second-degree Black Belt in the martial arts and a small undisciplined corner of my mind was just begging for him to grab me – just once. He never did; and I never told a soul about our little meeting. It was just my word against his and I felt stupid for going to see him in that hotel room in the first place. He was actually fired some years later for inappropriate behavior at work. Sometimes people *do* get what they deserve.

* * *

Since I clearly couldn't date people at work and I wasn't the sort of person to go to bars to pick someone up (or go to bars, *period*), I felt that the only recourse I had was to go to a dating service. There was one conveniently placed just across the road from where I worked. One day I worked up the courage to go in and take a look at what they offered. After giving them $1,000 I couldn't afford and filling out a bunch of questions about my likes and dislikes, they promised me that I'd hear from them soon. And I did. I got my first notice from them within a week about a man who lived nearby and was little older than me. It seemed on the surface that we shared a lot of the same interests, so I said yes. He called me after a few days, and we set a date to meet for the weekend.

He picked me up at my house and we drove to a nice park in the area for a walk. He was a tall man, fairly thin with a small moustache and thinning hair. There was something about him that made me a bit uneasy. He seemed nice enough, but I couldn't put my finger on what it was about him that was bothering me.

As we talked, I found out that he was an avid hunter, a fairly religious person and felt that a man's duty in life was to be the family breadwinner. It was a perfect match for my first date. I detest hunting and killing animals for sport, I'm not religious at all, and I feel a husband's duty in life is to treat his wife as an equal and partner in all things, not as an owned object to be sheltered and protected. This was going to be a really fun date.

When we went for our walk, I had to slow down so he could keep up with me. It turned out he wasn't much into outdoor activities at all unless they involved sitting in a tree blind with a beer waiting to blast an unsuspecting deer below into oblivion.

319

In other words, either he had lied about nearly everything on his form with the dating service, or they weren't paying much attention. I learned later that it was probably some of the former but a whole lot of the latter.

When he dropped me off at home, I gave him a friendly little kiss on the cheek and told that I didn't think we were going to work out very well. I think he was relieved. Sometime later it dawned on me what it was that made me so uneasy about him. He bore an uncanny resemblance to my stepfather. I love my stepfather, but I sure didn't want to date him.

I called the dating service and gave them a piece of my mind about the success of my first "match". They sent me a few others, but they all lived much farther away than I had requested, were a lot older than I was and seemed to share little in common with me. I didn't accept any of them and lodged a complaint with the service. I tried to get my money back from them, even threatening them with a lawsuit for fraud. They refused and showed me in the fine print of my contract that they didn't have to refund my money. I gave up. They went out of business. I guess I wasn't the only one who didn't like them. Now I not only wasn't dating anyone, I was out $1,000.

I pretty much gave up on the idea of dating men. I realize that I had only one date with that one guy, but at some subconscious level a romantic relationship with a man just didn't feel right. I did not then, nor have I ever felt any sexual attraction toward a man. The thought of a sweaty man lying on top of me pumping away and finally filling me with sticky goo went WAY beyond my idea of fun (I guess that description pretty much proves no sexual attraction there, doesn't it?). So, I only had one other choice – try dating women. What's one more label? If it didn't work out, I'd be an old maid for the rest of my life. I'd been successful on my own before and figured I could do it again. I had thought before of moving out to Montana and living in the mountains away from people in general, anyway.

Since bars were still out of the question, gay or straight, I had to figure out how to meet women as a woman. Hanging out at the Home Depot seemed to be a bit of a stereotyped dead end (that was awful, wasn't it?) so I had to think of something else. Before I could really come up with a workable idea, fate stepped in and hit me in the face.

For years, I had been playing the Sousaphone with the Golden Eagle Band. I transitioned from Ricky to Rachael while in the band and did so, as I'd said before, with the blessings and support of my fellow musicians. I eventually changed over from the Sousaphone to the Baritone Horn, which had been my first instrument in school. A young man named John who had just gotten out of the Navy had just joined the band and played Baritone in the seat right next to me. We hit it off as friends right away, and, so he wouldn't hear it from someone else first, I told him about my transition. I was now post-operative and fully into my new life. He had no problems with it at all. We talked about our times in the Navy and joked around quite a lot. I really liked John.

One evening John invited me to his house to meet his wife, Jan, who was a neonatal nurse at an area hospital. The moment that Jan and I touched hands and looked at each other, a very unexpected thing happened – we were both immediately and deeply attracted to each other. I had never been so enamored with a person at first glance in my whole life. And I could tell by her reaction to me that I wasn't alone. That attraction made us both a bit nervous but somehow, we managed to play it down. We all quickly became very close friends and all three of us started spending a lot of time together. John and Jan even took a backpacking course that I was teaching with the Outdoor Club of South Jersey. Our friendship grew stronger by the day.

One night, Jan called me to say that John had been ordered away for a week's worth of training in the Naval Reserves. There was an event going on the next evening at a local watering hole for the Outdoor Club that she had been planning to attend with her husband. She wanted to know if I would be there, so she wouldn't have to go alone. I told her I had been planning to go and we met at the bar the next night. We talked through the evening. We also drank a bit more than we should have. As the hour grew later, we decided it was time to go. My condo was just down the street, but her house was several miles away. We had drunk a bit too much and she didn't feel comfortable driving. She asked if she could stay at my place. We were good friends, so I didn't see why not. Of course, I said yes. I had a very comfortable and roomy couch for her to sleep on.

We went back to my place and sat and talked into the wee hours of the morning. The more we talked, the more I was impressed with her knowledge, her charm, her intellect and her beauty. She was quite simply one of the most fascinating women I'd ever known. Finally, we were getting just too tired to talk more so I got her some bed linens and made up the couch for her. I gave her one of my t-shirts to wear and she snuggled into the makeshift bed. I sat on the floor beside the couch, and we talked for a bit more. This time the talk started to turn much more personal in nature, and we found ourselves talking about turn-ons and fantasies. That's when she told me that she found me very attractive and had always wondered what it was like to kiss another woman.

I have always held to a very strict code in my adult life – no relationships with anyone who was married (and no relationships when *I* was married). I knew first-hand how horrible it felt to have my spouse cheat on me and vowed that I would *never, ever* do that to someone else. For some reason, whether it was the alcohol or the late hour or both, I forgot about that code. All I wanted to do was to drink in those eyes, taste those lips and feel the heat of that body next to mine. Without speaking further, I leaned down and softly kissed Jan on the mouth. When I looked at her again, her eyes had turned liquid and her face turned upward, seeking more. This time we kissed with a passion that grew almost unbearable. I thought that I would be lost at any moment in her arms. Her hands found the edge of my t-shirt and pulled it up as she smothered her face between my breasts. Her mouth covered my nipples, pulling and sucking with wild abandon. I had never known such a feeling. My whole body felt like it was on fire. A low, husky moan emanated from her and her whole body literally began to shake as she smothered herself against me. I had never seen such unbridled passion in another person before – and it was all directed at me.

When she came up for air and gazed into my eyes, I took her hand and led her into the bedroom. For the first time in my life, I made love as a woman, complete in body and mind. It was wonderful. We made love all through the night. I never actually had an orgasm, but I can't imagine how it was possible to get closer to one. I thought I would die from the sheer pleasure of the feelings coursing through my body. Ironically, we were making love on the same bed where I had sat a little more than a year ago, staring at a small heap of pills that would put me out of my horrible misery. I was never so glad to have failed at something in my entire life.

From that time on, Jan and I had a steamy relationship behind her husband's back. I gave her a key to my condo and, when she was working the night shift, she would get off work in the early hours of the morning, drive directly to my place and slip into bed with me where we would make love until dawn. Then she would go home to John, very often making love to him. What we were doing was wrong and we both knew it, but we were so intoxicated with each other that the idea of not being with each other was unthinkable.

Eventually, we started thinking about having a life together. John had courted Jan for a long time, asking her to marry him almost constantly even though she continued to say no. She finally said yes when she saw how much her continually saying no was hurting him and she realized how much he loved and needed her. Even now, she still didn't want to hurt him, but she was in love with me and wanted us to be together. She even started thinking about splitting up with John. That's when everything started to fall apart.

Jan felt sure that she could never tell her family in Indiana about us because they wouldn't be able to accept her as a lesbian. She was terrified that she might lose her family and the possibility started to weigh heavily on her. She knew what I had gone through with my own family and was constantly amazed that I was able to deal with it so well. She didn't even think she could tell her co-workers about us. I, on the other hand, wasn't comfortable about having to live a secret life with her. I'd had far too much of that sort of thing to last me for a lifetime. The more she thought about it, the more it scared her. She started falling apart at the seams. The guilt of leaving and hurting John, along with the fear of losing her family, overwhelmed her to the point where she couldn't take it anymore. She broke down and told John about the two of us. I don't know exactly how much she told him, but he now knew that we had been together for quite some time behind his back.

Much to his credit and to my amazement, John didn't react angrily. He sat down with me before band practice one evening and told me very matter-of-factly that I had to stop seeing Jan.

He was worried for her health, and he was her husband, after all. I told him that I was very sorry for everything that was happening but that I found myself deeply in love with her myself and that I understood why he loved her so much. We finally agreed that I wouldn't see her anymore and I kept my promise for as long as I could. It was hell being without her and, before long, we were seeing each other again. At first everything was just as it had been, but the stress started to come back, and she was soon miserable again.

I tried to tell Jan, rightly or wrongly, that her stress was simply because she was afraid to admit what she was and step into unknown social territory as a lesbian. I tried to show her how obvious it was that we were madly in love with each other and that if she decided to stay with John, she would be denying her true nature and be miserable for the rest of her life. I truly believed that, based on how passionate our love making was and how sadly she talked of her relationship with John. I was also desperate to keep her. I underestimated how deep her fear really was. It all fell apart the day that she told me she was pregnant.

Jan had decided that she and John could be happy together if they had a baby. She also thought it would help to make her feelings about me go away. I was crushed. I was convinced that she was doing the very worst thing she could do and tried everything I could think of to get her to understand that. I knew about this sort of thing first-hand. It was no use. She was determined to stay with John and her safe little un-scary life. There was nothing I could do but cry – for a long time.

John quit his job and they moved back to Indiana. I never saw them again, but I've never forgotten her and my first torrid love affair as a woman.

* * *

During this time, I found another medical problem that no one could have anticipated. Jan had introduced me to her gynecologist, who agreed to see me regularly. Even though I was still more than a little embarrassed to find myself flat on my back in stirrups with someone peering into me again, it was different this time. This doctor was a woman and was constantly telling me how amazed she was at what a good job that Dr. Seghers had done on me. She made me feel very comfortable in her office, as did all of her staff.

During one of my appointments with her, she found something disturbing. Curiously, during the examination, she asked me if I had been experiencing any pain during bowel movements. I had been but didn't know how she knew that. It turned out that I had an errant stitch inside me. After my surgery, all of the stitches that Dr. Seghers had used to create my new vagina had, in time, worked their way through the healing tissue and simply fell out as they were designed to do, usually during one of my dilation sessions. One of them, however, hadn't. This particular stitch had been put in a bit too deep and had been caught in a muscle. Because the stitch couldn't work its way out through muscle, it had stayed in place, causing so much irritation in the surrounding tissue that it had caused an abscess to form in the wall between my vagina and my rectum. It had to be removed at once before it caused life-threatening damage. I ended up having day surgery performed by a tag team of my gynecologist and a proctologist working in tandem to fix what was wrong in their individual area of expertise. Jan drove me home from the medical clinic when it was over.

* * *

With Jan gone from my life, I was alone again. Months went by before I could even think about socializing with anyone. I felt like someone had sucked the life out of me. I didn't want to do anything or go anywhere. I was horribly depressed. However, I slowly came to realize that even though I was depressed and knew this feeling intimately; my thoughts hadn't once turned to suicide. Before my surgery those two things went hand in hand. I really was a whole, healthy person! Lots of people get depressed all the time but don't think about suicide. In a perverse way, this was great! It was very strange realizing that I was happy because I was sad. I was still sad that I wasn't happy, though. Does that make sense?

One day while reading the local newspaper, I happened across the Personal Ads. There were hundreds of listings there for "Men Seeking Women", "Women Seeking Men", and even "Men Seeking Men" and "Women Seeking Women". I'd never paid much attention to this before but for some reason I found myself intrigued. After scanning through the "Women Seeking Women" column, I got the idea that this might just be something to check out. It couldn't hurt, right? These women were looking for companionship, just like I was. This might actually work. I put together an ad of my own seeking a woman who enjoyed outdoor activities and called the newspaper to have it run. I didn't say anything about being an ex-TS, though. Honesty is usually the best policy but too much honesty can be a bad thing sometimes.

Within a few days I got my first call. The way it worked was that the newspaper had a voice mail system that the caller would dial into, punch in the number for your ad, and then leave a message for you. The woman who had left a message for me seemed very nice and left a phone number for me to call her. When I did, we talked for a little while and finally decided to meet at the Philadelphia Art Museum. I said yes and braced myself for my first foray into the "real" Lesbian world.

I met the woman a few nights later at our pre-determined spot outside the museum. She was a very pleasant looking and well-dressed young black woman who said she had a small daughter. We talked for a little while and she finally said she'd like to continue our conversation at a small restaurant in the area, but she had to take her daughter to her mother's house first. She said she'd meet me there. I went to the restaurant and waited for her for two hours. She never did show up. *(NOTE: See dictionary entry for the word – Naïve.)* I guess there was something about me that she didn't like, and she didn't have the courage or the maturity to tell me to my face.

Wow. That was fun. I couldn't wait for my next date. I didn't have to wait long.

A few days later I got a call from a woman who lived in Southern New Jersey, not far from where I lived. We met at a local shopping mall. This one was quite different from the last one. She was a young white woman who talked very loudly and looked and dressed like a teenage boy. We actually did enjoy doing the same types of things outdoors and at ended up spending little time together. A few days after she met me, she was already grilling me about why I hadn't been home when she had called. This was just not going to be good at all. It was very difficult to extricate myself from her but somehow, I finally managed.

I let my week-long contract with the newspaper Personal Ads expire when I decided that I'd had just about enough of *that*. I thought it might be better if *I* did the calling and sort them out for myself, so I found myself looking through the columns with a different eye. One ad that I found intrigued me. It was from a

328

woman who liked outdoors activities and was looking for a companion. At the end of the listing, it read *"Must like men"*. Now, I read this to mean no raving lunatic "all men are scum" types. Ok. I didn't actually *hate* men – I just didn't find them sexually attractive. I called and left my message and phone number. My call was returned the next day – by a man. A married man.

It turned out that this man's wife was having a birthday and one of the things that she had always fantasized about was making love with another woman – while her husband watched and later…are you ready for this?…joined in if he so desired. He wanted to give his wife (and himself) a special little present. Me. Can I pick 'em or what?

After I gave him a resounding and very heartfelt "OH, HELL, NO!" and had gone through yet another box of Brillo pads in the shower, I didn't go back to the Personal Ads for another couple of weeks. I figured there would be a whole different set of people looking for a mate. I was right. I tried again.

This time I answered an ad from a woman who sounded like someone more my type. She volunteered her time working at an animal shelter and sounded pretty down to earth. I called. Her name was Marlene. When we first met, I was immediately struck by her personality. She was very outgoing and enormously assertive. And she was almost as big as me. She kind of reminded me of a weight lifter. I took a liking to her almost at once.

We got to know each other pretty well in a short time. She really liked my guitar playing and singing and threw a party so that I could meet her friends and play for them. This was going pretty well. Then, that night, everything changed and I didn't even know it. As I left her house, we had our first kiss. It was great. She wrapped her arms around me in a great bear hug and kissed me so hard I thought she was going to take the breath away from me. When we parted, she stood back and looked at me like she wanted to say something. All I could say was "Wow! You made my knees weak!" It was not an exaggeration. She looked at me and smiled. We promised to see each other again soon and I left to go home. We didn't actually see each other for a few weeks. Marlene was busy at work in her construction business, and we never really got a good chance to get together. When I did hear from her next, she invited me to yet another party at her house and asked that I bring my guitar. I was happy to oblige and eager to see her again.

When I arrived at the party, she introduced me to a few new friends she had invited, including one woman named Sue who she seemed to be showering with attention - attention that I didn't seem to be getting at all. As a matter of fact, when we all sat down at the table to eat, she made a great show of standing behind Sue and rubbing her shoulders while Sue reached up and held one of her hands. This was not good. Something was terribly wrong (you think?). The entire evening continued in this vein to the point where I finally just left, dragging my unused guitar behind me. I had no idea what was happening, but I was smart enough to know that I was being snubbed. I didn't know why, and I didn't know why I had been invited if I wasn't wanted. What was I, just the traveling minstrel to entertain the troops? I was devastated.

I didn't talk to Marlene for another few weeks. I couldn't; I hadn't felt so used in my entire life. I wanted to know why I had been treated this way but was so hurt that I didn't want to talk to her. Finally, I wrote her a letter telling her how I felt and how unfairly I thought she had treated me. She called me at work a few days later and asked to meet me in a local park for lunch.

We met with a surprising amount of cordiality. I was happy to see her again, never having been one to hold a grudge. Still, I was skeptical about what she was going to say. As we walked along the pathway in the park, I asked her point blank what I had done to deserve such treatment from her. She looked at me and said, "You know what it is."

I stared at her and said, "No, I honestly don't. You're going to have to tell me what's wrong."

"You lied to me."

My worst fear was now taking shape in my mind. Somehow, she had "read" me. But maybe I was wrong. "I have never lied to you", I replied. "Why would you think I did?"

"You know what I'm talking about", she continued, accusingly.

I was adamant that she was going to have to say it out loud before I offered anything myself. "No, Marlene, I don't. Tell me what you think I lied to you about."

It came out flatly and accusingly. "You're a transsexual."

Now I knew. Somehow, she had figured it out the night of that kiss. How in the world did that happen? Is there such a thing as kissing "like a man"? But I was angry. I had not lied to her. She had never asked me about it and if she had I would have admitted it freely. She was just angry that I had never told her in the first place. "I used to be a transsexual", I told her. "I'm a woman now in every way. I never told you anything different and I never misrepresented myself to you."

"You should have told me at first", she said. "It wasn't right for you not to tell me at first." That was when I talked to her about my reasoning for not offering that kind of information on a first date. Would she have gone out with me then? I explained that I wanted her to get to know me before she came to any judgments about what I "used to be". I again asserted that I had never lied to her.

331

We sat on a bench and talked more about what had happened. She seemed to understand my reasoning for not offering more information than was necessary, but she still seemed hurt that I hadn't told her in the first place. When I asked how she figured out about my past, she said when we kissed that night, she felt beard stubble. I had been continuing electrolysis treatments but was far from done at the time. It had never dawned on me that I had a bit of facial hair growing at that late hour. I had conveniently forgotten about the "5 o'clock shadow" syndrome. My facial hair was all gray, so it didn't show but someone who wasn't expecting any would notice it fairly quickly, especially from so close up. I never made that mistake again. I continued to go through electrolysis on the occasion when I forget how much it hurts. I started having laser treatments to finish the job. They were more expensive but vastly less painful. I just couldn't stand electrolysis any more. As it turned out, laser electrolysis doesn't work on gray hair. I spent a lot of money for nothing. Now it's back to electrolysis when I can afford it. I still have to shave my face almost every morning.

Marlene agreed that she had not handled her "revelation" as well as she could have and apologized for treating me so callously. I, however, could not apologize for not telling her of my previous condition earlier. Some may feel differently, but I don't believe that I had been untruthful in any way. Would it have mattered what religion I might have been before, or what State I was from, or what my political affiliation was? Ok, so this was previous gender, and some people would say that it's a whole lot different from those other things. But why is that? I've always known that I was female; I'd just been born, through some cosmic error, with a male body. After my operation, the only thing different from a genetically born woman and myself was that I didn't have a uterus. There is a female medical condition called *Vaginal Agenesis* in which a female is born without a uterus. Even then, I am an older woman without a womb; millions of women my age have had hysterectomies. I've never had a period. Some women are also born that way, a condition called *Primary Amenorrhoea*. I had to take female hormones to supplement my body's lack of estrogen production; so do millions of post-menopausal women. My build is different than a lot of women's - I don't have an "hourglass" figure with wide hips. I have large hands and large feet. I know lots of genetically born women who are in the same boat. So, the only real difference between me and other women is *perception*. Somehow, the fact that I was born with that little extra bit of skin between my legs that caused me to be raised as a male makes all the difference. This is one of the major reasons I never tell people about my past right away. That perception changes the way they interact with me from that point on. An older man at work who didn't know about my earlier life always treated me with the utmost gentlemanly respect. If he uttered a curse word, he would apologize. After I told him about myself, everything changed. He then started telling me dirty jokes. The apologies had stopped. He didn't mean anything bad by it - his inner perception was now that, 'Hey, she used to be a man; she's heard this stuff all before so it's ok.' Again, I am the victim of *perception*. It still hurts to be regarded like this to this day. Is it any wonder that I don't let more people know about my past?

Despite our disagreements, Marlene and I have remained friends. We both understand how the other feels and have moved on with our lives, putting this behind us like mature adults.

In the meantime, I was stuck back in the same boat I had been in before I met Marlene - I was alone again. So, it was back to the newspaper ads.

This time I hit the jackpot.

Chapter 24
Love, Fear and Finally, Happiness

The Personal Ad listing caught my eye right away. This particular woman was looking for a friend with whom to share her love of outdoor activities. That was pretty much what I was looking for as well. I'd never had a partner who enjoyed the same activities as me. It's always more fun to share experiences with someone rather than do things all by yourself. In this case, who knows where "friendship" might ultimately lead, right?

I screwed up my courage for one last time and called the number. I heard this very nice, down-to-earth voice saying, "Hi! If you're an outgoing, fun person interested in sharing your love of the outdoors with me, leave your name and a number where I can reach you and I'll get back to you soon. Bye!"

Ok, that was nice. However, I still didn't know to whom I was talking. She didn't leave her name - not even her first name. How do I handle this? I took a chance that this unknown woman had a sense of humor and, shifting mine into high gear, I left my reply. "Ok, that's not fair!" I said to the answering machine. "You want me to leave my name, but you didn't leave yours! I'll give you a second chance if you call me back. My name is Rachael and I love the outdoors. I've been camping and canoeing since I was little. Whoever you are, you sound like a very interesting person. I'm looking forward to your call...and your name. It's better than calling you 'Hey, you!'" I left my phone number and hung up.

Was that too much? Would she think I was some kind of nutcase? Maybe I should call back and leave a little less flippant message. I thought about it for a while and then decided that I might as well wait. Either she'd call me back or she wouldn't.

The next day she did. I found out her name was Marilyn and that she lived about thirty minutes to the south of me in a small house in the woods with her dog, cat and a twenty-three-year-old horse. She said she thought my response to her message was funny. She was intrigued enough to return my call and find out more about me. (BINGO!!!!!) We agreed to meet at a nearby restaurant a few nights later for dinner, traded phone numbers and said goodbye.

It turned out that it was a good thing I got her phone number. The next day I was told at work that I had to go to a meeting all the way down in Washington, D.C. on the very day I was to meet Marilyn for the first time. I was going to be carpooling as part of a team, but they assured me that we would be back early in the evening. Our date was for 7:00 pm. I called Marilyn and told her that there was a chance that I might be late because of where I was going to be during the day. I hate being late for things, particularly first dates. I'm very punctual, almost to the point of being anal retentive about it. She said she understood and that she'd be waiting at the bar of the restaurant for me. I reassured her that I'd be very easy to pick out in the restaurant. "Just look for the very tall blonde in the gray business suit," I told her. "You can't miss me." She said she'd be in jeans and a blouse and that she was medium height with short dark hair.

The scene was set. All I had to do was get there on time.

Our meeting in D.C. was uneventful except for the bad case of butterflies I had in my stomach all day. Everything wrapped up when we expected, and we headed back for southern New Jersey, about three hours to the north. Since I was riding with others, my car was parked at work - about twenty miles north of the restaurant where I was to meet Marilyn; the very restaurant that we drove right by on the way back to the office. I had to pick up my car and then drive back the way we'd come. It turned out I wasn't terribly late - only about fifteen minutes or so - but it felt like hours. Was she really going to be there? Would she think I was going to stand her up and just leave? Would she like me? Would she read me right away? I parked my car and sat in the darkness for a few moments trying to collect myself and calm my nerves. I checked my hair and makeup in the mirror, smoothed my suit and walked into the unknown.

* * *

The restaurant was fairly crowded. The dinner crowd was in full swing, and the bar was crowded with people waiting for seats. At the far end of the bar sat a lone woman with short dark hair, jeans and a modest blouse. It had to be Marilyn. She looked up from her beer and, spotting me instantly, waved me over. I couldn't remember a time that I had been so nervous. What would she think of me? Would she look at me and see a man in drag? Oh, my God, I was actually going to do this!!!!! I smiled, introduced myself to her and sat down. I apologized for being so overdressed, but she shushed me and complimented me on how nice I looked. This was already going much better than I had expected. We made small talk for a few minutes until we were called to the table that she'd already reserved for us.

Dinner was a blur. This woman was amazing. It turned out that she was a biologist working for the local electric company – not a combination most people would usually think of. Her eyes were large and mesmerizing, and she made me laugh easily. We talked about everything that we liked to do and were stunned by our similarities. It turns out that she had taken the very same backpacking course that I taught – a year before I started teaching, it but the same course, nevertheless. She enjoyed hiking and canoeing. She had a black belt in karate and was an avid scuba diver. She played tennis in an evening league with friends and enjoyed being out in the woods away from people and noise. She wasn't a religious person, and her political ideals were progressive and very caring for the underprivileged. She didn't smoke and didn't drink much at all. I think by this time that we were both wondering how it was possible that we were meeting another person so much like ourselves. It was simply astounding.

We must have talked for hours. As we finished our dinner and conversation, we left the restaurant and got another surprise. I had unknowingly parked my car next to hers. It turned out that we both owned Mazdas. Hey, it's a stretch but the similarities were just uncanny. This was just one more. She gave me a little kiss goodnight and promised to call me later to set something up to do together. I drove home in a daze. I couldn't believe that I found someone like her. She was everything I had been looking for. I wasn't even thinking about how or when I was going to tell her about myself. All I could think of was her.

Much to my surprise and delight, she called me the very next day and asked me if I'd be interested in going canoeing that weekend in the New Jersey Pine Barrens with her and some friends. She actually called me back! I couldn't believe it! Of course, I said yes. Now all I had to do was wonder what to wear.

We had a good time canoeing and worked together in the canoe as a team without even thinking about it. Her friends, also avid outdoors people, were also a lot of fun. We ended the day by setting up our next "date" to go camping on Chincoteague Island in Virginia. I'd never been there and had always wanted to see the herds of wild ponies that roamed the area. I had a tent that was big enough for the both of us and even went out and bought sand stakes for it because we would be camping on sand dunes. She gave me directions to get to her house and, when the weekend came, I went to pick her up for our first camping trip together. It would also be the first time we would be sleeping together – albeit with friends all around.

Marilyn's home was very quaint. Tucked back into the woods off a little dead-end street that didn't even show up on area maps, it was a small house that had actually at one time been a lake-side bungalow. Decades earlier, a private dam that had created the lake had burst in a bad storm and had never been repaired. The lake was gone but the ambiance was still there. The house sat back off the road about 200 feet down a dirt driveway. A large pasture on the left surrounded by a split rail fence was the home of a beautiful thoroughbred horse that stood there munching lazily on the grass, barely giving me a glance as I drove up. A small white barn stood at the end of the driveway to the left of the house completing the idyllic setting of this quiet little home in the woods. Moving down the driveway I had one of the oddest feelings that I've ever had. I had never been here before; had never seen this house or even really been in this area. But I had the strangest feeling that I was home. I dismissed the feeling as a bit of déjà vu.

As I pulled the car up to the house, Marilyn came out to greet me. She was followed closely by a gorgeous old golden retriever named Coty. What a beautiful place this was. The house itself was tiny, barely a thousand square feet. It had electric baseboard heat augmented by a small wood stove in the living room that easily warmed the entire house. I loved this house and everything about it at first sight.

Marilyn and I drove off for our camping trip, leaving the horse, the dog and her cat to be taken care of by a pet baby sitter. We shared life stories during the entire four-hour trip down to Chincoteague Island, me being careful not to share *too* much. I

338

wasn't ready to divulge my past in anything other than generalities. When we arrived, we set up our tent behind the sand dunes and, after a nice dinner by the camp fire with our friends, settled down for our first night together.

I had one real problem, though, that had kept me worried from the time that I agreed to go overnight camping. I still hadn't finished electrolysis. Although I had suffered through almost a hundred hours of electrolysis by that time, it hadn't seemed to work very well, and I still had an embarrassing growth on my face every morning. There was no way I could let Marilyn see me like that, so I was going to have to get up in the morning to go the bathroom and shave my face before she awoke. And I couldn't shave in front of a mirror in the ladies' room for fear of another woman walking in and seeing me with shaving cream all over my face. That would have been very difficult to explain. So, I ended up sitting on the toilet in a closed stall just after sunrise, with a wet face cloth, a small hand mirror and my shaving kit that I had in a small flowered make-up bag, doing the best I could. Much to my relief, no one discovered me, and Marilyn turned out to be a perennial late sleeper. This was a problem that would haunt me for a very long time, both with Marilyn and eventually spending time camping with friends.

Electrolysis was never easy to bear. It's extremely painful. For some reason it has become so increasingly painful that it is almost unbearable to me now. I would like nothing better than to get rid of the rest of my facial hair, but after one hour of treatment, I'm usually in tears and ready to scream. There is no doubt that the hormones that I've been taking for so many years have made my skin much softer and smoother, but it seems that they've also made it incredibly more sensitive. I had all but resigned myself to a life of having to shave my face every morning. Fortunately, I eventually found a cream called "Emla" that numbs the skin before electrolysis. It was a bit embarrassing to use, though, because I had to spread the cream over the area that was going to be worked on, cover the area with plastic wrap to keep air away from it, and leave it that way for an hour. I must have looked pretty funny driving to the electrologist's office with the lower part of my face covered with Saran Wrap. I learned to go early in the morning on the weekends.

Marilyn and I saw each other for months, both with the same thoughts and reservations: "she's too good to be true but this is too early after a bad breakup". Just before we met, Marilyn had had a relationship of her own that quite literally mirrored mine. The woman was married, very interested in a relationship with another woman, but afraid to commit and leave her husband. As these things almost always do, her relationship ended badly, just as mine did. It was uncanny. I think we were destined to be together.

One weekend during our first summer together, we went canoeing and camping with friends in what is called the "Grand Canyon of Pennsylvania" just north of Williamsport, PA. The water level in the river flowing through the gorge was low but the canoeing was still fun. That night at the campground, we went for a walk after dinner and found ourselves standing under the stars and full moon at a viewing platform overlooking the spectacular canyon vista. We stood there in the moonlight, gazing into each other's eyes. Each of us wanted to say the same thing but neither had the courage to say it. Finally, Marilyn broke the silence.

"I think I'm falling in love with you."

"You're too late", I replied softly. "I fell in love with you the first time I saw you."

We kissed passionately in the moonlight and then sat talking into the night, discovering that we both had felt the same way from the beginning. Neither of us wanted a "rebound" relationship but, in spite of ourselves, we had fallen hopelessly in love with each other almost from the start. We just figured that there just had to be something wrong with something that seemed so good.

We made love for the first time at my place the next night. We had both wanted to do this before but were afraid to take the relationship this far. Now that we knew how we both felt, it was time. But this time making love was different. Jan had known who and what I was from the outset but had never thought of me as anything other than a woman. Marilyn didn't know about my past at all. I kept the lights off as we undressed, afraid that by just seeing my naked body shape would set off alarms in her. I may have been female in most respects, but I couldn't change my skeletal structure. I just don't have a feminine figure with a narrow waist and wide hips.

I made love to her eagerly and passionately, bringing her to a shuddering climax, being careful not to give her the opportunity to explore my body with her hands to any great detail. But when she had regained her composure, she turned her attention to me. As I said before, my body was female in almost every respect now. My hips were larger and my breasts had formed, although they were still small. My waist was not as defined as most genetic females', so I still had more or less a male body shape. The main difference, though, was that although my genitals looked for the most part the same as a normal female's, my vagina did not consist of mucous membranes. I cannot self-lubricate. And my vaginal opening is small and tight. On top of that, my clitoris was not in the same position, nor did it resemble a normal clitoris. It's actually sub-dermal. These differences might not have been noticed by a man during lovemaking, but they would be hard to miss for another woman. Almost as soon as Marilyn reached down to begin stimulating me, I felt her

341

hesitate. I immediately explained to her that I didn't lubricate well and that seemed to mollify her for the moment. But her ministrations to me were short lived and our lovemaking ended soon after.

We didn't make love much after that first night and I feared the worst. Marilyn didn't treat me any differently and I was sure that she still loved me, but I felt that she was becoming suspicious. In our conversations, she began to talk about how much she valued honesty in a relationship. At first, I didn't think anything of her comments other than sharing her feelings about what was important to her. But as the subject came up more and more often, I began to feel that she knew something was different about me and that she wanted me to tell her what it was.

I couldn't. I was scared to death to tell her. After all these years and all the pain of getting to where I was, I had found my soul mate. I was sure of that. If I told her, I risked losing her. I was horribly afraid that she would be angry that I had somehow lied to her all this time, or that she would be disgusted by what I was. No matter what I said or how I said it, I was convinced that the outcome would not and could not be good. But I knew that I had to tell her; and soon.

One night we went into Philadelphia to see a movie. I don't recall what the movie was, but I do remember that the main theme of the movie had something to do with a relationship that had broken up because of dishonesty. Great. As if I wasn't feeling the pressure enough already, I paid for movie tickets, bridge tolls and parking to be slapped in the face with guilt. As she drove me back to my place, there was a dead silence in the car. We were both afraid to say anything. I knew it was time for me to tell her, but I didn't know if I could find the courage. This was worse than telling Kate and the people at work what I had to do those few years earlier. But I had no choice.

We pulled up to my front door and she turned the car off. Sitting in silence for a few moments, I reached out for her hand, trying hard not to look too deeply into her eyes, afraid of what I might see.

"I know how you've been hinting about honesty these last few weeks," I began. "And you know that I agree that honesty is important to make a relationship work. There's something that I need to tell you about myself but it's very difficult for me." I swallowed hard. "But I don't know how to tell you."

I stopped talking and stared at my hands, blinking back tears. Marilyn looked at me, holding my hand in hers, and softly said, "Just tell me."

So, I did. I told her the entire story about how I'd grown up, about my summers in that small field and about my struggle to be whole. I tried to explain to her why it was important for me to let her get to know me first before letting her know *about* me and that I hoped that she could find it in her heart not to hate me for not being honest up front.

"I love you", I said, barely able to hold back the tears now. "I can't imagine my life any more without you. But I won't blame you if this is too much for you to take."

She looked at me and said, "I had thought that there was something." She paused for a moment. "I can't say that I know how I feel right now. I'm going to need some time to think about this. I'll call you in a couple of weeks, ok?"

I gave her a kiss, apologizing once more as I got out of the car, and watched her drive away into the night with my life in her hands.

That night was one of the worst in my life. I just knew that this was not going to turn out well for me; that she was going to call back at the end of those two weeks, if not earlier, and tell me that she was disgusted and that we were through. I didn't know what to do. I didn't know how I was going to survive those two weeks not knowing what she was thinking; not being able to be there to explain things to her better than my feeble attempts in the car. But I knew I had to give her space to think this over. I can't honestly say what I would have done had I been in her place.

Two excruciatingly long days later, I got a call from Marilyn. My heart leapt into my throat upon hearing her voice and then crashed to my feet in anticipation of what I was certain I was about to hear.

"Why don't you bring your clothes down to the house tonight and stay over?" she asked. "You can go to work from here in the morning."

I wasn't sure I had gotten that right. This wasn't what I was supposed to be hearing. Something was wrong. I asked her to repeat what she had just said.

"Look", she scolded playfully. "Would you rather sleep alone tonight in your empty little place or come over here and cuddle with the person who loves you?"

I could barely stand. She loved me, and my past life meant nothing to her. She loved me for who I was. This was truly the person that I had been waiting for - my life mate.

We moved in together by the end of that year and have been inseparable ever since. I did end up living in that little house in the woods after all. One year later, we had a Commitment Ceremony on the lawn outside of our house with over seventy neighbors, friends and family members in attendance. Our rings have never come off.

And they never will.

Epilogue

The summer evening was peaceful and warm. The sun had dropped below the old city a short while ago bathing the weathered cobblestones of the large square with the mysterious and soothing lights of the night. Ancient towering buildings loomed over the crowd for all to see; their huge spires carved from history, their massive columns holding up the night sky as they had for hundreds of years past.

A soft expectant breeze whispered gently around the tables that lined the square, ruffling each colorful parasol just enough to make its presence known. The air was filled with the voices of people who had come from all corners of the world to be there this night, creating a cacophony of languages, laughter, and love. Aproned waiters and waitresses gliding among the tables added to the wonderful commotion with the clink of coins and glasses.

At one table along the edge of the square sat two women, one Irish and one American, enjoying a small pitcher of sangria together. The Irishwoman had never tasted the Spanish wine concoction before and was delighted at the experience. To the American the sangria brought back warm memories of nights in southern Spain in a different life and a different time. The two women had met just days before in a local hospital and had become immediate and long-lasting friends. The dark-haired Irish girl had come to be with her lover who was recuperating from surgery at the hospital. The tall blonde American had recently been released from that same hospital and was looking forward to returning home in a few short days. They had both come to this square, as had hundreds of others, in expectation of a summer spectacle that was to begin after nightfall. For one of them, the night would hold a deeper meaning than any other person in attendance could ever hope to fathom.

A clock somewhere in the city pealed nine o'clock and a hush fell over the crowd. From a darkened alcove in one of the massive buildings that lined the square arose the soft sounds of the music of Gioacchino Rossini slowly drifting with the night breeze. It was the anniversary of the birth of the great Italian composer and the Grand Place of Brussels had been chosen as a setting for his tribute.

As a deep and resonant orchestral chord sounded, a colorful light grew from the darkness, illuminating one spire of the old great church building. As that light faded another answered in a different color on a different spire, keeping time with the powerful music. Suddenly the face of another nearby building erupted in light followed by another and then another until the ancient buildings seemed to dance around the square with the sweet music, whirling to the refrains and dazzling lights. One minute the music would soften, and the colors would dim in respect. In the next, the sounds of the orchestra would swell, and the colors would overpower the senses, dazzling eyes and ears with a perfect choreography of radiant brilliance. The crowd watched the spectacle in awe.

As the final few notes of the piece drifted along with the bright colors into the night, the American woman brushed at the tears in her eyes. This beautiful night seemed to her to have been the fulfillment of a longtime dream. Her journey to this place had taken a lifetime. She had traveled far to get to this moment - from a small, lonely field of dreams in the rural America of her childhood to the crowded, festive city streets of Europe in which she found herself now. But this person was different from the one that started out on that solitary road so many years before. This person was finally at peace with herself. For the first time in her life, she knew what it felt like to be complete. She no longer had to awaken every morning knowing that the ache of a terrible inner struggle would be with her again for yet another dreary and painful day. She no longer had to pretend to be someone she was not. She no longer had to be afraid to **BE**. *A new life beckoned now with the beginning of each new day. She realized that for the first time in her life she was truly glad to be alive.*

As the last chords of the music faded and the bright colors slipped back into the night, the tall American woman's gaze was transfixed by a final ray of bright, hopeful color that had arisen to the heavens along the highest spire of the old church in the square. As her eyes followed the solitary ray of light, she noticed for the first time how cloudless the night sky was, framed by the majestic buildings surrounding her. More importantly, she noticed a single light that shone like a beacon in the very center of that dark patch of sky; a single shimmering point that she alone saw clearly for the first time since she started looking those lonely summer nights so very, very long ago. The star and her were alone in this crowded place and for the first time they spoke together in silence that only the two of them could understand.

Brushing away the gleaming tears from her eyes, the young woman looked at the first star she had seen that night and, smiling, simply said,

"Thank you"

The Beginning

Afterword

It is now over 25 years since I started this book. It's a bit of an understatement, but I must say that, after looking back at all I've gone through to find myself, it has been an interesting journey. To my surprise, I discovered that reliving some of these memories as I wrote them down, especially my first divorce, was almost as painful as experiencing them for the first time. In fact, after retelling the story of my divorce from Helen, I put the book down and couldn't get myself to start writing again for nearly two years.

But I can honestly say that if I had to do this all over again and re-experience the pain to get to where I am now, I'd do it again in a heartbeat. I've had my ups and downs during these years since my surgery, but never in any of the "downs" have my thoughts turned to suicide. I no longer have the horrible weight on my shoulders of knowing that I'm not who I'm supposed to be. The hopelessness I felt about never being able to become a complete person is gone forever.

* * *

A year after Marilyn and I met, I returned to Belgium to have a second set of basically cosmetic surgeries, one to make my labia look more realistic and the other to remove what little "Adams's Apple" I had.

In my original surgery, my labia were positioned parallel to each other and not joined at the top as normal labia would appear. This was done on purpose at the time because it was thought that enough surgery had been done for one outing. To do both surgeries to complete the effect of "normalcy", it was considered too traumatic to both the tissue and the patient to go any further during the first surgery. (A way has been developed since then to do both surgeries at once.) The "Z-Plasty", as Dr. Seghers called this minor labial surgery, was designed to bring the tops of the two vertical labia together to create a more natural look. It got its name from the Z-shaped incision that the doctor makes across the top of the labia to put the tissue back together in order to minimize any unusual distention or puckering of the surrounding skin. The removal of the Adam's Apple, or *tracheal shave* as it is medically called, was a simple shaving of the thick cartilage that forms over men's thicker vocal chords to protect them from injury. The Z-Plasty wasn't nearly as important to me as the tracheal shave, but I couldn't find anyone in the Philadelphia area who did it. Dr. Seghers, on the other hand, did both and charged me less for both than it would have cost me for either to be done in the U.S. It also gave me a chance to go back to Belgium and, on the way, stop in Ireland and visit my friends Aine and Dierdre. (It seems like we visited every pub in Dublin's downtown area that night.) Also, it was during this trip that I was to meet my friend Michelle from Texas and watch her surgery. Both of my surgeries went without any trouble, and I had a fun vacation as well. So, all in all, it was a wonderful trip. Except for one thing. Remember that little thing about having bad luck with surgeries?

While I was recuperating in Brussels from the Z-Plasty, I had noticed a swelling and bruising of my pubic area. At the time it didn't really strike me as very odd, given all the work that had been done down there but it did seem like it was getting worse with each passing day. When Dr. Seghers removed my final stitches in his office before I left Belgium, he, too, noticed that it seemed to have gotten worse. A few alarms went off in my head when he asked if I minded him taking a few pictures. He assured me that this was just a little subcutaneous bleeding that would subside by itself. I believed him, even though the swelling was becoming more and more uncomfortable.

On the second day after I returned home, I was sitting on the toilet, looking in growing concern at my now hideously distended pubic area. By this time the skin was tight as a drum and dark purple, with seepage coming from somewhere that I could not see. As I pushed gingerly around the swollen tissue to find the leaking area, I was horrified to watch the stitches suddenly pop open at the top of my labia and release a flood of dark, jellied blood that spilled over my lap and down to the bathroom floor. It was all I could do to keep from screaming. "My God!" I thought. "What's happening to me? I'm bleeding to death!" When the torrent finally subsided a few moments later (it seemed like hours), I pressed my hand over the gaping wound and staggered to the phone. I didn't want to call an ambulance because then I'd have to explain to them how I got like this. I was in enough terror without having to add embarrassment to it as well. I called my doctor in Philadelphia. He told me to put a bandage over the wound, cover it with a few sanitary napkins that I had for seepage, and come see him at once.

I was able to drive but I was so traumatized that the only thing I remember is walking into the Doctor's office in a panic. He led me immediately onto an examination table and, when he pushed lightly on the area, even more of the coagulated blood came gushing out. The dam finally burst, and I began to sob uncontrollably. The nurse held my hand and tried to calm me while the doctor studied the wound. After cleaning everything and getting a better look, he assured me that what I was seeing was just old blood that had been amassing behind the skin from what was probably just a small seeping blood vessel that had since stopped, most likely because of the pressure of the old blood against it. He finished cleaning the wound, put butterfly bandages on it and, when I regained control of myself, sent me home with explicit instructions not to overexert myself physically for at least a week. The wound healed fine, and I never had any more problems with it.

However, it did leave me with a problem from which I never did recover. Either by nicking nerves with the scalpel during the Z-Plasty surgery or by some damage caused by the excessive swelling of the aftermath, I found that I now had almost no feeling at all in my clitoris. Because of that, my sex drive has dropped to almost nil. I would have welcomed such an occurrence as a man (I don't know of any man who would say that!) but as a woman in a wonderful physical and spiritual relationship with my soul mate, it was devastating. I've tried hard over the years to convince myself that I should feel fortunate that this was the only thing that had really gone wrong considering everything that had been done, but it has caused the only real problem between Marilyn and me that we've ever really had. With no sex drive and no sexual feeling, our lovemaking has diminished to nothing. That doesn't keep us from being close, but I constantly yearn for the normal relationship with her that I fear we're never going to be able to have. She doesn't say anything about it, but I know that, deep down, it bothers her, too.

Another problem that I still had was in my job. I continued to work at the same company that helped me make my transition so long ago and many of people I'd known from "before" still worked with me. From time to time I'd still be referred to by some of my old friends as "he". I usually gave them one or two chances to correct themselves before I took them aside and said something. There were some people, mostly very religious, who still looked at me like I'm the Anti-Christ and would go out of their way not to be in the same room with me, especially the ladies' room. But the hardest thing to bear was being referred to as "he" by people that *never* knew Ricky.

352

Sometimes they would be people I didn't even *know*. Everyone knew my name, and everyone seemed to know about what I'd done and who I was. It was maddening to have someone who I didn't know say, "Hi, Rachael", to me when we would pass in the hallways. It made me feel that I wasn't so much a person at work as I was a curiosity, even after all of those years. And when I was referred to with male pronouns by people who didn't know me before just made that feeling all that much harder to endure. Sometimes it made me just want to yell at them, "Look at me! Do I look like a *HE*"? But I didn't because I was never sure that I wanted to hear their answer. Even though it's now hard for me to remember Ricky at all, I can still see him sometimes when I look in the mirror.

If I could have, I would have quit my job in an instant and moved to somewhere else where no one knew me for anything except for who I am. And that's actually what happened since I first published this book in 2007.

As far as my life in general is concerned, it has been a wonderful time since Marilyn and I met. We've traveled all over the world scuba diving together, we've survived wilderness canoe camping during a tornado after our Commitment Ceremony (a whole 'nuther story), we got legally married (civilly unioned?) in Vermont in 2002 after which I legally changed my last name to hers, and we had planned to retire early and move to a house we'd built in another state in the mountains.[24] I have overcome adversity in the male-oriented world of the martial arts and, despite the misogynistic attitudes of my first instructor, I earned a

---

[24] SPECIAL NOTE: In June of 2015, on the 20th anniversary of our commitment ceremony in New Jersey, Marilyn and I got legally, fully married at our house in New Hampshire in front of a roomful of friends. For our second honeymoon we rode our motorcycles all the way up to Cape Breton in Nova Scotia – 800 miles each way. We had a blast but our butts were sore for weeks.

second-degree black belt in the Martial Arts and Weaponry. This is quite possibly the one thing in my life of which I am proudest. Overall, I couldn't be happier with the way my life has turned out.

Okay, maybe I could. I have only just recently found my youngest children, Julie and Michael. They're all grown up and are living with their mother and stepfather in the south. Julie is 37 and has two children and Michael, now 36, is just living at home. I tracked them down using a social security number search on the internet and finally got to speak to them. I just had a wonderful family reunion with my daughter. Michael, however, isn't so responsive. It's going to take him some more time, if he ever comes to accept me. He is actually planning on taking his stepfather's last name and has told me that he really can't handle having a relationship with me. I can't really blame him. He's never really known me as a father and now he has to learn to relate to me as something else entirely. It's still hard to think that I've lost him, but at least (I tell myself) I have two other children who love me anyway. He did actually call me once, but I've had to make it ok with myself to let him go. It seems that his earlier heart problem did exactly what we had feared would happen; the limitation of oxygen getting to his brain in his first year of life caused by his failing heart had caused irreparable damage to his brain. Even though he's a full-grown man now, he has the IQ of an early teenager and still lives with his mother and stepfather. His mother, Lynne, had told both of our kids things about me that were just not true and, while my daughter could sort out the truths from the lies, my son could not. In addition, he is convinced that I had done "something" to him during our brief time together as a family that he can never forgive me for. I have no idea what it is, and he won't explain it to anyone. I just have to not let it bother me and let him move on with his life. It's hard but I know it's for the best for him. I wish him the very best in life, but I told him that I'm here if he ever needed me. He is my son, after all.

My oldest son, Cal, who stood up for me at our Commitment Ceremony, is 43 now, married and has two children. For some time when the kids were very young, he would not allow me to see my grandchildren, saying they were "too young to understand". When he did let me see them, I had to agree to let them call me "Aunt" Rachael instead of "Grandma" Rachael. Again, he figured they were too young to understand anything else. Of course, the flaw in that logic is that they don't really need to fully understand everything as young children. When small children meet someone, that person is to them, exactly as they are presented with full acceptance and no questions asked, especially when the presenter is one or both of their parents. In my case, when they're finally deemed old enough to "understand", then I'll just be in the same predicament with my own flesh and blood as I am with people who didn't know me at work but just knew me for "what" I was. At least this is a step in a right direction, even though it hurts deeply to be relegated to "Aunt" status when I am really so much more to them. I want them to know they're my grandchildren. It is very difficult to get them birthday cards for a niece and a nephew. But for now, I'll take what I can get. It is better to have them in my life as their aunt than not to have them in my life at all. I just hope that when they're older and they find out the truth, that they won't be as angry with their parents and with me as I was at my parents when I found out that they had lied to me all those years about my father.[25]

---

[25] SPECIAL NOTE: In the winter of 2013 my son and his wife finally told my grandchildren who I really am in their lives. They took it very well so my fear of them being angry so far haven't come true. However, according to my son they feel uncomfortable even now calling me "Grandma" so they want to stick with calling me "Aunt". Rachael" for the time being. I've recently spoken to them in person

I also hadn't been home to Ohio for a very long time. My parents, who had sold their house years ago to become retired RV nomads, decided to finally move back. Ever since that time, my brothers and sister, with whom I had visited a few times after my surgery before our parents moved back, had cut off all communications with me. The passing of years had not softened my parents' demands that they still didn't want me to come home and their presence in Ohio cooled the acceptance I had previously received from my brothers and sister. I had written to my parents many times in the fifteen years since I'd seen them last, sometimes going overboard trying to be nice, loving and conciliatory, other times being hurt, angry and demanding. Nothing changed their minds about me for years. They refused to use my name in any correspondence to me, preferring instead to just use 'R' in place of Rachael. Their letters to me, whenever I did get any, never ended with "Love, Mom and Dad" as they always had before. Now they just ended with no signature at all.

My greatest fear for the longest time was that my next visit to see my parents would be at one of their funerals. The thought of that was almost too much to bear. However, something amazing happened to turn all of that around. In the summer of 2005, I suddenly got very sick and almost died, hospitalized in a coma with an extremely serious and deadly tick-borne disease called Rocky Mountain Spotted Fever. The illness caused diffuse damage on the left side of my brain, leaving me with right side weakness (I had to learn to walk again and still walk with a cane), memory loss and difficulty concentrating. The doctors think I may have had a stroke while I was in the coma. Prior to my illness, I had arranged for my daughter Julie to come up to

---

and asked for a compromise that they call me "Nana Rachael". I'm' not their "Aunt". I'm so much more than that. Whether they call me that or not I will continue to refer to myself that way in correspondences to them.

visit us at Cal's home. After I had been released from the
hospital and had somewhat recuperated from the disease's
debilitating effects, we went to my son's home for the
reunion that had already been planned. I can't describe how
fantastic it was to see my daughter for the first time since
she was eight, standing outside of her brother's house now
as a full-grown woman. We hugged like we were never
going to let go of each other. My son let us have our
moment together and then took me by the hand and led me
into the house with a big grin on his face to meet someone.
Inside, I saw an older woman sitting on Cal's couch in the
living room. My eyes recognized her, but my mind refused
to believe it. There on the couch sat my mother! When she
smiled and walked over to me with her arms open, there
was no doubt left. I dropped my walking cane and wept for
joy. It took more than 15 years and a near-death experience,
but I was finally back in my family's lives. It's been like a
dream come true. Two in one lifetime ain't bad.

I did actually get to come home barely a month later, but it
was a terrible homecoming: my little brother, Tim, had
unexpectedly died. It was a bittersweet reunion with my
whole family, to say the least. After the funeral, though, my
father's oldest brother was brought to me and asked if he
recognized me. At first, he said no, so I took off my glasses
and asked that he look again. This time, his eyes widened,
and he said, "You must be Rachael". I said yes. Then he
did something totally unexpected. He came closer to me
and, in a low voice, said, "I have one question for you. Are
you happy?" I assured him that I was happier with my life
now than ever before. He responded by saying, "Good.
That's all that matters." Even under these awful
circumstances, I realized that I was ok with my family after
all these years. I was finally home.

* * *

My married family was another hurdle. For years Marilyn and I agreed that there was no reason to tell her family about my past. It had no bearing on most things in my life now and really didn't seem to be important to us that they know. I had already felt the loss of one family, had just gotten it back and was in no hurry to lose another. All this time I've just been Aunt Rachael to Marilyn's three nieces, Sister-in-Law to her sister, and, best of all, Daughter to her mother, Marion. I will never forget at our Commitment Ceremony when Marion (or Mom, as I called her) came up to me, gave me a long, tearful hug and told me that she loved me as her own daughter. Afterwards she always introduced me to all of her friends as her daughter. Unfortunately, Marion died in 2002 from complications following emergency surgery to repair an aortic aneurysm in her stomach. But I will always love her as much as my own mother and, because of that, I felt her loss almost as much as Marilyn did. Her passing was a terrible blow to all of us.

Through the years (and lots of expensive therapy sessions) I have come to realize that by not telling those that are closest to me about my past, I was using an awful lot of energy trying to either steer conversations away from talking about the past or coming up with some way to discuss it without actually lying. For example, every time one of our nieces was pregnant, I lived in fear of finding myself in the middle of a conversation with them about pregnancy and labor. They all knew I had three children and it would have only been natural for them to ask about my experiences in childbirth. I had actually come up with an emergency plan on how to respond if that situation happened. My answer would have been to use one of my wives' experiences and never really attribute it to me. It would have been something like, "Oh, labor for the first one was about eighteen hours and was pretty hard."

Sneaky, huh? I was being totally truthful in the details, so I wasn't lying; just not offering any more information than was needed. It was that kind of situation that made me very uncomfortable and hesitant to really be part of the family like I wanted to be. I usually walked away when conversation took a turn to these kinds of difficult subjects. One day, Marilyn got a call from one of her nieces who said she had spoken with a mutual friend of ours that we hadn't seen for a long time. The conversation somehow had come around to Marilyn and me and our friend mentioned that he had known me "from before when I was a man". He just wanted to know how I was doing. Our niece, knowing that I had three children and assuming, as did everyone in the family, that I was their mother, figured that the friend wasn't talking about the same person she knew. She basically just wrote off the conversation as odd but thought it humorous enough to mention to Marilyn. I was terrified when I heard about it. I want to back up just a bit for a moment here.

* * *

For quite a few years earlier after speaking in the nurses' class about transgender issues for my therapist, I took up speaking to classes on my own. I spoke with students at the University of Pennsylvania, Beaver College (now called Acadia University), SUNY in Albany, and New Jersey/Philadelphia area community colleges and other schools (including hospitals). I never charged anything for these lectures because I didn't want anyone to think that I had any other reason for doing this other than to help the general populace understand about the condition. I didn't want anyone to think I was only "in it for the money".

The way I would teach these classes was always fun. I tried several different ways including reading the Prologue

359

from this book (too dry and didn't work), starting off joking by saying my name and stating that I was an alcoholic, looking perplexed when everyone else looked at me funny and then correcting myself by saying, "Oh, this isn't one of those meetings" (no one ever got the humor in that one), and then finally settling on spending the first half of the class talking about my story and then opening the floor for any and all questions. I would stress that there was no question I hadn't heard and no question I wouldn't answer openly and honestly. My favorite part of this was always the first question. I'd pick someone from the class and, no matter what the question was, I'd look shocked and act speechless for a few seconds, mumbling that no one had ever asked me that before. Then I'd laugh and say I was just kidding. The effect of this broke the ice in the class and put everyone at ease so they felt free to ask me anything.

Some of my favorite questions were, "Do you have periods?", "Did they give you a uterus", and "Aren't you afraid of going to Hell for going against God and how He made you?". (As an atheist I just LOVED that last question.) It was also fun to answer the question that was ALWAYS asked, and ALWAYS by a woman, to describe my surgery. Every guy in the class would immediately sit up, shift in his seat, and cross his legs. Guys are really attached to that little thing and even the THOUGHT of anyone touching it with a knife is unthinkable.

One of my most interesting classes, though, was when I did a sociology class at a university. The woman who ran the class let me go on about my life and then, after everyone had asked their questions, she asked me how it made me feel using my "male privilege" to get so far in business just so I could make enough money to have my "change". I took great exception to this question, telling her that I had NEVER asked for any of my positions or salaries and that, when I did get into a position in management where I had enough clout to hire and promote people, I set a lot of things right that my predecessor never did – I promoted and hired as many women as possible in my department. Since the Navy when women were trained to do the same job as me yet weren't allowed to actually go DO that job, I hated that women still got second class citizen status in life simply because they didn't have a penis. I was determined to change that as much as I could. I didn't go back to talk in that class again.

In one other earlier and fantastic class I talked in, the class was being held in a small room where I sat with the professor waiting for the students to come in. I had just come from work, so I was wearing a nice blouse, jacket, skirt and pumps. The class started to trickle in and finally the door was shut so we could start. After the class was over every woman there came over to talk to me saying that they knew that a transgendered person was coming in to talk with them and were confused when the door shut and this person still hadn't come in. Then they were amazed to find out this "person" was me. How great a compliment was that? They, like many people, expected to see an obvious guy dressed in a K-Mart blue-light special bad dress. That made my day and many more to come.

One time when I was lecturing in a class at the University of Pennsylvania, a young woman came up to me and asked if my partner's name was Marilyn. When I said that it was, she told me she was the sister of the husband of one of our nieces. There are millions of people in the Philadelphia area and more universities and colleges than you can shake a stick at, and I managed to pick the one class in the one school that has a family member in it. What are the odds of that? I gave her a homework assignment for the rest of her life not to say anything to her brother or the rest of the family until she heard *them* talk about it. And she actually didn't ever say a word. Some people *can* actually keep secrets.

361

And now, back to our regularly scheduled afterword chapter.

After these episodes with things coming out about me from friends, and the gut-wrenching work of constantly trying not to lie to everyone about my previous life without being seen as secretive, and with the advent of finally getting around to finishing this book, I decided that the time had come to open up. During a family get-together in late 2003, I called an impromptu meeting of all the adults and, with my heart trying hard to claw its way out of my throat, finally ended my years of secrecy with the family that has taken me in as one of their own. I didn't know exactly how it would be taken but I knew that I couldn't keep it hidden any longer. I told them the story of my life and watched as they sat dumbfounded in front of me not knowing what to say. When they did respond, it was in the form of a kiss, a hug, and a heartfelt declaration from each of them that they were happy to have me as part of their family and that my past didn't matter to them. After all, they didn't know this male person I was talking about. I'm still the aunt and the sister-in-law to them that I always was. I found out much later from Marilyn that they'd actually known for some time before I told them. But they never showed any less acceptance or love for me.

In the months surrounding that time, I had also told Marilyn's and my closest and dearest friends about my past, tired of spinning tales to them as well. They all said that it didn't matter to them (they always thought I was weird anyway) and we remain as close of friends as always, if not closer for my sharing. There are really no words that I can say to let them know how much I appreciate and love all of them. But I think they already know.

After my illness, I had to retire from my job as a computer scientist because I could no longer concentrate well enough to do my job. I had problems walking and doing ordinary tasks as well. Marilyn was able to retire early at 55 with full retirement benefits so she sold our small house in New Jersey and moved north to the mountains in New England to our newly built log home where we've lived ever since. I continue to get disability payments from my insurance company at work, plus Social Security disability and am on Medicare. As of this date in 2016, I still am unable to work, even though I have tried to do small things like being a substitute teacher in a local high school and even teaching a beginning course in Chinese at a community college – but none of them are very successful because of my inability now to concentrate for long periods of time. I had planned upon retirement to open my own Women's Martial Arts and Self Defense school but still couldn't throw a front snap kick if my life depended on it. My balance is still compromised, and any heavy concentration tires me severely. I don't know if this will ever repair itself but, as I tell people, I'm still looking at the daisies from the top down. Good outlook on life, don't you think?

So now I fill my days volunteering to do things for others. I have volunteered at our little one-room school house in our town to keep the computers running or help the kids with their studies. In the winter I help other disabled people learn to ski with the New England Disabled Sports (NEDS) program at Bretton Woods in northern New Hampshire. They got me back on skis after I was strong enough to try but I have to ski with outriggers[26] to help my balance, coordination and stamina. When I found out the instructors were all volunteers, I thought it only right that I

[26] Outriggers looks like MS-type crutches with little skis on the bottoms of them.

go back and volunteer to help others. I also volunteer at a local hospital playing the guitar and singing to patients. These things help me feel I can still make a difference in the world – or at least in my community.

* * *

So, this has been my life, at least up until now. I have learned a lot in what I consider to have been both of my lifetimes. I've come to appreciate the unique gift - sometimes curse - of having lived in both the male and the female worlds. There aren't a lot of people who can, with any authority, say that they truly understand the opposite sex. I'm still not really sure I can say it myself, but I know now without a doubt where I belong. This knowledge gives me great insight in my dealings with people socially and at work.

I have seen fair-weather friends come and go, and true friends stay. In 2003, after almost thirty years of searching, I was finally able to track down Larry and Cathy from the Philippines. We had a tearful and joyous reunion at their home in Nevada, where we caught up on all that had happened in the long years since we had last said goodbye. I learned that they had also been trying to find me but had finally given up, assuming that I had managed to somehow find the courage to go through with my operation, changing my name and making it nearly impossible for them to find me. I am grateful that they have a very unusual last name and that I came across a site on the internet that allowed me to finally find them. Their daughter Lisa, now probably forty-five years old, told me that she still remembers me from when I took care of her so long ago. She now calls me Aunt Rachael. They remain three of the dearest people in my life.

I've also learned that love is not always unconditional, even when it is expected to be. I never thought for a moment that my own flesh and blood family would turn their backs on me when I needed them most. The fact that they did was a heart-piercing pain that I carried with me for years. It took my almost fatal illness and the death of my little brother to bring my family back together again. We still don't talk about what I've "done" but it's not really necessary. It's best to just let the water flow under the bridge without disturbing it. It is so wonderful having them back in my life that what came before hardly matters any more. I just want them to know that none of what has happened to me was ever their fault. I was always their daughter; they just never knew it. I know it's still hard for them to accept but they're now really trying, and I know that they love me as much as I love them. My mother introduces me to her friends as her daughter now and her and my father's use of male pronouns continues to get less and less frequent.

Most importantly, I've learned that there are a lot of people in the world who see and love others for *who* they are and not *what* they are or what they want them to be. It gives me hope for the human race. And if you're going through this awful transition in your life, or you know someone who is, it should give you hope as well. What I've gone through has undeniably been a very rocky journey. I have experienced indescribable joy with the birth of my children and other memorable events in my life; I have also seen times of horrible despair that I sometimes believed (and often hoped) I would not live through. Every person I have ever come into contact with who has experienced the same problem has had the same story as me; gone through the same gamut of feelings, fighting for their very lives just as I've done. There is no doubt that the despair of this condition is the most dangerous thing to overcome. It can

365

easily overwhelm a person and become so all-encompassing in that person's life that suicide seems to be the only rational solution to a mind that has become totally irrational from the fear, guilt and anguish that accompanies this condition.

An interesting aside from all of this is something a trans-friend of mine said once about going in and out of closets. She said that trans-people are closeted for much of their lives, afraid to let anyone know how they feel inside. Once they find the courage or conviction to go ahead and make their life change, the come out of that closet only to go right back in because NOW they don't want anyone to know who they once were. I had never thought of this before, but I know now that I had been back into that closet for a long time. As I said before it was extremely difficult to talk around my past. That was a self-inflicted problem that I didn't need. I'm not that person anymore. I'm proud of who I am, what kind of person I am, and of how I managed to survive my journey across the gender divide all on my own. Now that I'm older and have spent almost 25 years as the person I've always known I should have been all along, I'm no longer afraid to reveal my past. I'm comfortable with myself and proud that I've come through so much with my head held high. I am who I am and if people don't like it, that's not my problem. I'm always eager to teach people about what being transgender means and am always happy when a light turns on in their eyes that says, 'I never knew that before!'. I know I've helped one person understand and, with any luck, that person will help others, and perhaps some other unfortunate person going through this will have a bit of an easier time with his or her life.

I never professed to having been a particularly strong person. Perhaps my experience has made me stronger. All I know is that if I could live through this, could find the courage and conviction to get help and find happiness that in the brightest of my earlier days I never would have dared hope could happen, you or your loved one can, too. There is no doubt that there is horrible darkness to be found along the road on this journey but there is also no doubt that there can be an incredible reward of finally feeling whole at the journey's end. You just have to be strong enough to make the trip.

It's worth it. Wishes do sometimes come true. I know.

Rachael Evelyn Booth
March, 2016

Marilyn and Rachael
Now and Forever

Rachael & Marilyn Booth at home in 2010 with their two
golden retrievers Casey Puppins and Barney Bear.

Special Addendum

It is 2022 and a lot has happened since I originally published this book in 2007. I am 70 years old now and no longer consider myself "transgender". The prefix "trans" means "going across" and I consider myself as having gone across thirty-one years ago. Been there, done that. I am no different physically than any other woman who has had a complete hysterectomy.

I don't get "read" anymore in any situation and never feel uncomfortable in public at all. I have continued to participate with other members of the transgender community where I live in public discussions about what it means to be transgender to better educate the public.

Even though I'm retired now since 2005, I work occasionally doing everything from giving piano and guitar lessons in my home, to working at a local ski resort where I get to speak with visiting Chinese and Arabic speaking visitors from time to time. I have also been a substitute teacher at local high schools, mostly for foreign language classes, where I am also able to work with transgender students that I meet – you'd be surprised how many there are - to help them in their own personal journeys. When I tell them that I am just like them, their jaws drop open at first because they had never suspected a thing (very gratifying to me) and then they grin from ear to ear and give me enormous hugs. It's good to be able to show them living proof that they can be who they were always supposed to have been.

I've worked for years with a local hospital singing with my guitar for their Music Therapy program, helping recovering patients break the doldrums of lying in a hospital bed recuperating from whatever illness or surgeries they've had. I've also performed monthly for a local assisted living home, even doing my performances online on Skype from my living room during the COVID-19 pandemic as well as doing live performances on Facebook to entertain people who can't get out because of the pandemic.

This year, I got the chance to fulfill yet one more life-long dream: being a school music teacher. I was asked to be the long-term substitute for a local middle/high school instrumental music teacher who was out on maternity leave for 6 weeks. If you recall, my goal when I left home after high school was to join the Navy, put in my four years so I could get the GI Bill benefits I needed to go to college to become a music teacher. Life took its turns and that never happened, but I never gave up the dream. I finally got to teach instrumental music to the entire school's music program for 6 full weeks. It was a glorious experience. Standing in front of those bands and directing them, I felt something I had never felt before. When I was a linguist, I knew I was very good at it. When I was a computer scientist, I knew that I excelled at that. But I *belonged* in front of those students, directing them, and helping them to grow musically.

How many people can say that they've achieved any of their lifetime dreams, let alone three of them? I've become my true self even though it took 40 years to get there, I met and married the person who is my true life-mate, together now for almost 28 years, and I was able to become a real music teacher, however limited that time was. How could anyone ask for more?

But life does go on.

On Memorial Day, 2018, I got a call from my father to come home immediately. My mother, now 85, was in the hospital and had taken a turn for the worse. He didn't say it, but I knew from just his call that my mother was dying. I dropped everything and broke land speed records driving the 800 miles there, hoping beyond hope that I could get there in time. She was on a respirator and plugged into all kinds of machines. Her kidneys had failed, she had a terrible infection in her blood, and her heart was barely able to continue on its own. She looked like a corpse being artificially kept alive. It was one of the most awful things I've ever had to see but I needed to be there. Although she never knew I was by her side, I stayed with her for the three days it took for my sister and my father to agree with me that it was time to make the decision to let her go. They unhooked her from everything, and she continued to breathe for the next ten minutes, then peacefully slipped away from us forever.

She had been in my life for her last thirteen years, years I thought I would never spend with her after I told her what I was going to do back in 1989. Her response, if you remember, was to tell me never to come home "like that". But I got that time with her, even though I had to nearly die for her to come back to me. It was wonderful during those years to finally hear her call me daughter (even though she continually mis-gendered me) and it was a horrible blow to lose her, but I was grateful to have been able to be there with her holding her hand and speaking with her softly as she took her last breath. My 94-year-old legally blind stepfather still lives in rural Ohio, and I see him as regularly as I can, given the 800-mile distance between us.

* * *

371

My children are a different matter. My son, Cal, finally told his two children who I really was in their lives. They took the news remarkably well and, when I went to see them years ago in Arizona, I talked to them about it, asking them not to call me their aunt anymore because I was so much more than that to them. When they were infants, my son had made me agree that they should call me "Aunt Rachael" even though I pleaded with him to call me "Grandma Rachael". I wasn't their aunt and if they called me Grandma from the start, that's all I'd ever be to them. My greatest fear was that if they continued to call me Aunt Rachael, the lie would boomerang on both of us when they learned my true place in their lives. He countered that they already had two grandmas and having a third would only confuse them. I reminded him that they were only small children and that I had had three grandmas when I was growing up - my birth-father Ernie's mother, my mom's mother, and my stepfather's mother - and that didn't confuse me at all. It just *was* and I never questioned it. But they were his children and I had to acquiesce to his demands whether I liked it or not. When I talked to my nearly grown grandchildren about what to call me, they said they weren't comfortable with calling me Grandma, so I suggested a diminutive of the word, such as Nanna. If that wasn't good enough, we could discuss it further. I had suggested they might still call me aunt but the more I thought about that, the more I hated the idea. I did *not* want them to continue to call me Aunt Rachael. I was taught as a child to respect my elder's wishes and I would have thought they'd have respected mine. If they'd been raised to know me as my true self, they would have.

The last time I saw them a year or so later at my grandson's high school graduation was one of the best visits I'd

372

ever had with them. My granddaughter was going to college and my grandson was getting ready to join the Navy. We had a great time, but something bothered me after I left. They had never called me anything at all – not Nana Rachael, not Aunt Rachael. They didn't refer to me by name at all - not once. When I got home, I asked my son about it, and he said the kids decided they just couldn't refer to me as any form of "Grandma" because that's not what I ever was to them.

The lie had come home to roost just as I'd feared.

When I insisted that I didn't want to be called "aunt" any more, getting incredibly angry at my son for causing all of this, the entire family severed all communications with me. I have not heard from any of them for years now.

It was crushing blow at first, but I've come to the conclusion that it's not my problem. My grandchildren will either contact me again in their adult lives or they won't. I can no longer let that pain control me.

My daughter has her own problems from her childhood living with her vituperative mother and abusive grandparents and has turned inside herself, becoming a virtual hermit. One of her daughters lives with her father in another state and the other lives with my former wife's mother. I never hear from any of them, even though we had a great relationship before. Again, there is just nothing I can do about it but sit and wait.

* * *

None of this matters, though. My life couldn't possibly be any better. At 70, I'm starting to have all the aches and pains that come with age, but that's just a normal part of getting old. I don't have to worry about this on top of not feeling like I'm in the right body. I'm just getting to be an old lady.

I don't give up, though. I stay as active as I can and, still living by my motto of "if you haven't learned something new today, you've wasted that entire day", I've been teaching myself German and learning how to play even more musical instruments just for the joy of it. I've written and published a book about the history of my home town in Ohio called "The Little Port in the Cornfields – A History of Evansport, Ohio" and just finished a third book, a science fiction novel entitled "Time Slip" about a trip into the past in a time machine that goes horribly wrong. I have a fourth already formed in my mind and ready to start next.

Life is good. Life is very good. If I was a religious person, I'd say I was truly blessed. But I'm not. I describe myself as an "Evangelical Atheist". I don't have any problem sharing the "Good News" with people that organized religions are all a scam and that no god or gods have ever had any hand at all in my existence. I made my life what it is today all by myself through my own grit and determination, never ever giving up on myself. I don't know how much more time I have left in this life, but it doesn't matter.

I'm the real me and I can't ask for anything more.

Rachael Evelyn Booth - 2022

Made in the USA
Middletown, DE
06 March 2023